The Real Estate Investment Decision

Lexington Books Special Series in
Real Estate and Urban Land Economics

William B. Kinnard, Jr., Editor

The Real Estate Investment Decision

Gaylon E. Greer
DePaul University

LexingtonBooks
D.C. Heath and Company
Lexington, Massachusetts
Toronto

Library of Congress Cataloging in Publication Data

Greer, Gaylon E.
  The real estate investment decision.

  Includes index.
  1. Real estate investment.   I.   Title.
HD1375.G693   658.1'5242   77–81792
ISBN 0–669–01951–8

Second printing, July 1980

Published simultaneously in Canada.

Printed in the United States of America.

International Standard Book Number: 0–669–01951–8

Library of Congress Catalog Card Number: 77–81792

To Dee Dee, and to the Ellis and Jones clans

Contents

Contents

List of Figures

List of Tables

Preface

Why another book on real estate investment? With bookstore shelves already overburdened, one might question whether anything is left to be said. Existing titles range from flashy and quick-to-read manuals on how to go from rags to riches in one year, through reasoned but dull restatement of time-honored platitudes about real estate fundamentals, to exotic tomes on real estate economics and law.

More to the point, why should the reader, weary of books that promise more than they deliver, bother to read further? Certainly, adding another voice to the cacophony needs justification.

A prominent real estate authority recently observed that "the development of the real estate literature appears to lag behind other disciplines by about five to ten years . . . (and) often by as much as twenty years."[1] Real estate theorists appear to be rediscovering many concepts developed in the mainstream of economics almost half a century ago.

Many real estate texts give mere lip service to contemporary investment theory and often treat well-established concepts as if they were beyond the current state of the art. This book attempts to remedy this shortcoming by introducing into a basic text some of those concepts which are fundamental to economics and corporate finance. It sets forth, at a fairly basic level, a framework for real estate investment analysis which utilizes work done in other branches of investments and finance, but which has not heretofore been well developed in the mainstream of real estate literature. I have borrowed liberally from subjects taught at the sophomore level in corporate finance, and I have introduced a sprinkling of information from related disciplines.

Readers seeking a get-rich-overnight formula should look elsewhere. No such secret will be found here. Neither will scholars alert for new theoretical breakthroughs find the book rewarding. No concepts are employed that have not previously found general acceptance in some other subfield of economics or finance. If the book is to be characterized at all, it should be as an attempt to accelerate intellectual cross-fertilization between real estate and related fields.

The book is intended for readers already familiar with real estate fundamentals. Accordingly, introductory principles which often comprise a goodly segment of investments texts have been omitted entirely. But while not intended as an introductory work, neither does the book require advanced knowledge. Anyone who has taken a high-school or college-level course in real estate principles, or who has been actively engaged in some branch of the industry, should be adequately equipped to handle the contents.

Readers not familiar with corporate finance as taught in recent years may find information to which they have not been previously exposed. Elementary present-value and probability concepts employed in the text are explained fully, and readers will not find the application of these concepts to real estate investment situations particularly taxing.

The book is intended, however, to be studied. No accommodation is made to casual browsers. Information is developed sequentially, with each section containing concepts and information vital to an understanding of subsequent presentations. It is important to start from the beginning and follow the illustrations straight through, skimming where the content is a part of a previous store of knowledge and studying where the terrain is less familiar.

There are three parts to this book. Part I presents an overview of the investment decision model and introduces the perspective from which investment opportunities are to be viewed. It treats fundamental issues of cash-flow projection, including market analysis, income tax factors, third-party financing, and pro-forma financial statements.

Part II provides an analytical framework for measuring the worth of an investment opportunity. Both traditional and contemporary approaches are discussed. Relative strengths and weaknesses of each technique are considered, and a case is made for using a contemporary approach which rationally discriminates between opportunities that differ in the timing of anticipated cash inflows.

The final section of the book (Part III) addresses an issue which is all too frequently ignored or considered only in passing: the problem of risk associated with investment projects. It provides a working definition, permitting quantification, of the risk element and incorporates a risk measure into comparative analysis of investment alternatives. The section concludes with a discussion of how a group of investments held in a single portfolio may interrelate to yield an aggregate risk exposure that is quite different from the sum of the risks associated with each individual investment in isolation.

Examples and illustrations are employed liberally throughout the book. I firmly believe that it is difficult to overdo the use of examples. Part I includes an extended example of an apartment house project, which is continued intermittently throughout the balance of the book. The example is extended and elaborated in each section to demonstrate the continuity of topics treated in the different sections.

Note

1. Austin J. Jaffe, "Is There a 'New' Internal Rate of Return Literature?" *AREUEA Journal* 4 (Winter 1977): 483.

Acknowledgments

I am grateful to Mr. Michael Farrel (DePaul University) for verbal interchanges in which many of the ideas for this book were conceived, and to students in my real estate investment classes who provided the crucible in which the concepts were finally forged. I wish also to thank Mrs. Peach Henry (DePaul University) for her diligence and persistence in preparing the manuscript, and DePaul University for financial support.

Part I
Investment Decisions
and Profit Planning

The first six chapters of this book represent a traditional approach to generating and presenting cash-flow forecasts. Essentially, the procedure involves extending the most recently available income and expense data into the future, employing the trend suggested by the data. Trend data are not projected blindly, however, but are adjusted to reflect considered opinion of the effect of likely changes in the economic and social environment during the forecast period.

The bottom line of the forecast is expected cash flow to the equity position, on an after-tax basis. Toward that end, chapter 6 covers basic federal income tax factors affecting cash flows.

In the first six chapters, cash-flow forecasts are treated as point estimates. The questions of uncertainty and risk are reserved for Part III, which introduces the possibility that forecasts may—indeed, almost certainly will—err.

1

The Investment Decision in Perspective

Decisions are a necessary concomitant to existence. We must decide whether to arise early or late, what to have for breakfast, what career to pursue, and what investments to make in order to ensure adequate return and an acceptable measure of financial security. Many decisions have become so automatic through constant repetition that we hardly consider them at all. Others require much soul-searching.

Investment decisions are of the latter type. Indeed, their complexity often requires more ability than investors can command without professional assistance. Alternative opportunities must be carefully considered, and comparative risks must be weighed against differential expected returns.

Systematic Analysis and Investment Success

From the close of World War II until the decade of the 1960s, careful analysis was a nicety without which many real estate investors found they could do very well. Profitability was virtually assured by remarkable growth and expansion in the shelter industry, which experienced few financial difficulties and an almost negligible failure rate throughout the period. Pent-up housing demand from the war years, combined with persistent inflationary increases in the value of real property, carried even the most ill-conceived projects to a modicum of success.

Fortunate economic policy in the early 1960s created a decade of almost uninterrupted national prosperity, of which real estate investors and entrepreneurs were once again principal beneficiaries. Economic disruptions during the last half of that decade did trouble many developers, and caused financial disaster to overtake a few. But most projects continued heirs to abundant capital and unbounded enthusiasm on the part of investors.

That the benign climate of the postwar economic environment had begun to turn ugly for some real estate businesses during the late 1960s was a mere portent of the financial devastation to come. In the early 1970s, a seemingly insatiable appetite for borrowed funds on the part of the federal government, coupled with increasing demand for capital from rapidly expanding foreign industries, created competition for funds which drove interest rates to record levels. Spectacular failures of real estate-related companies and financial institutions taught the industry an expensive and painful lesson in basic economics.

By 1974 escalating interest rates and scarcity of capital joined forces with general price inflation to spread chaos and ruin among real estate developers and lenders. Overbuilding in many market areas prevented values of completed projects from reflecting the increased interest rates and construction costs incurred by builders.

During this same period, existing properties also came under pressure from escalating operating costs not fully offset by increases in rental rates. Consequent reductions in net operating income rendered many investors unable to meet their mortgage debt obligations, and put pressure on them to restructure their portfolios. Owners under such pressure could not avoid sustaining substantial financial losses, and many were forced into foreclosure. Thus both new and recently constructed properties came back on the market at prices substantially below their cost of construction.

As the decade of the 1970s drew to a close, real estate investment decisions were being made in a drastically altered financial environment—one in which the old ways of doing things no longer sufficed. No longer could investors rely solely on rules of thumb, trusting constant economic expansion and general but orderly inflation to bail them out of bad decisions. The type of carefully considered planning and analysis which has characterized other fields of business endeavor for decades will now be increasingly practiced in real estate decision making.

The Decision Process

From personal experience everyone knows decision making to be a burdensome task. It is generally achieved only by overcoming, with great effort, a tendency to procrastinate and equivocate. Decisions, once made, are frequently and agonizingly reconsidered on the assumption that whatever the decision, it was probably wrong.

While the capacity to make decisions is generally somewhat limited, it can be expanded by experience and appropriate training. Attendant agony is greatly lessened if the decision–making process is reduced to a system. Such a system for making real estate investment decisions is the sole purpose of this book.

Investment decisions in real estate are not fundamentally different from those in other fields. Real estate is, in fact, simply one among many options available to investors. Alternatives include stocks, bonds, notes, antiques, art, and a variety of other assets. Whatever the vehicle, the investment decision process remains invariant. Abstracted from any particular context, the process might be described as follows:

1. Set goals based on value judgments. Goals are so basic that psychol-

ogists have a lexicon for irrational actions that includes non-goal-oriented behavior. Goals are unique to individual decision makers and need not correspond to any objectively defined criteria. Goal-setting must precede investment analysis, because analysis draws on the goals for decision criteria.

2. Develop a method for identifying opportunities consistent with goals. Investment opportunities are virtually limitless, and all of them cannot possibly be considered. Yet the more opportunities that pass through the investor's analytical model, the greater is the probability of achieving predetermined goals. A systematic process for identifying those opportunities deserving detailed analysis increases the number that can be considered and thus expedites goal achievement.

3. Construct a decision system for selecting opportunities. Such analytical systems are often called *decision models*, and they are very useful in facilitating systematic decision making.

Criteria for a Decision Model

Models—simplified representations of those aspects of a situation which are of primary importance to the problem being considered—vary from simplistic to exceedingly complex. At the absurdly simple extreme, one might merely flip a coin and take action based on whether "heads" or "tails" shows. The other extreme is open-ended. A relatively complex model is introduced in chapter 14, based on a simulation approach. Even this is dwarfed by many corporate capital-budgeting models.

Choice of decision models depends on the information available upon which to base a decision, the ability of the analyst to employ the model, and the importance of the decision to be generated. The model chosen should be appropriate to the situation and should satisfy three basic criteria: it should use all readily available information; it should generate data that are understandable to the decision maker; and it should be cost-effective.

An Efficient Model Does Not Waste Information

Information is valuable and frequently costly to obtain. As with other precious and scarce commodities, it should not be wasted. Therefore, the model chosen should utilize all readily available information relevant to the decision to be made. Such a model is said to be *efficient*.

If, for example, the only information available concerning a proposal is the initial cash outlay required and the expected net cash flow during the first year of the proposed holding period, then the so-called cash-on-cash, or broker's rate of return, model (discussed in chapter 7) might be appropriate for the evaluation. But if the decision maker is in possession of a forecast of net cash flows for the entire life of the project, reliance on this simple model would be inappropriate because it does not use data on expected cash flows beyond the first year and therefore wastes the additional information.

Simplicity Is a Virtue

Astute decision makers require advisors to explain and justify their recommendations. Even the best advice will be useless to such a client if it is not communicated in a comprehensible manner. Thus the model employed should be sufficiently simple for the ultimate user to understand. The appropriate model, therefore, will vary with the sophistication of the user.

Cost-Effectiveness Is Essential

There is virtually no end to the elaboration possible in modern decision models. Further information can almost always be generated, given enough time and a sufficiently large research budget. The value of each increment of information or elaboration must be weighed against its cost. When additional cost approaches the additional value expected to be derived therefrom, the model has reached its maximum level of cost-effectiveness.

Overview of the Decision Model

The analytical model employed in this book represents an elementary application of the capital-budgeting process long employed among corporate financial analysts. It contains explicit recognition of the probabilistic nature of expected future net cash flows and incorporates an adjustment for differences in timing of expected future cash inflows and outflows.

Single-Venture Orientation

Analysis is generally limited to establishing the risk and expected value of single-investment proposals in isolation and is not oriented to analyzing risk associated with combinations of ventures. A basic premise is that an individual venture can be separated from an individual's overall portfolio of assets. All pertinent revenues and expenditures and all associated liabilities are identified in isolation from cash flows and liabilities resulting from the investor's other undertakings.

Part III does introduce portfolio analysis, and an explanation is given of how aggregate risk might differ from the sum of that associated with individual ventures comprising the portfolio, but the issue is not pursued in depth.

Valuation Criterion

Investor's wealth maximization is the basic criterion for evaluating a proposal. This criterion is not exact because maximization of present wealth might result in less than maximum wealth at some other time. Nevertheless, it is an acceptable approximation of what we would like a measure of investment worth to accomplish. Moreover, no alternative criterion better accomplishes our goal.

Most proposals involve both benefits and expenditures spread differentially through time. The valuation problem created by timing differences is alleviated by discounting future cash flows to account for the time value of money. This is far superior to the straight maximization of expected net cash receipts, because the latter approach does not take into account the likely difference in timing of receipts and disbursements.

Cash-Flow Estimates

Cash receipts and disbursements for a specific time period are sometimes combined into a single estimate of net cash flow for that period. If, during a specified time period, cash receipts exceed disbursements, we speak of the net cash proceeds; if expenditures exceed the proceeds, we may speak of net cash outlays or net expenditures. As a convenience, we adopt the convention of expressing net cash inflows and outlays for a period by using positive or negative dollar amounts, respectively. We refer to the entire series of net proceeds and net outlays associated with a project as the *cash flow* of the project.

When incorporating risk analysis into the model, it becomes more convenient to discount cash receipts and cash disbursements separately. The present value of all future receipts and the present value of all future disbursements are then combined into a single estimate of present value of net cash flows. This variation in the presentation expedites risk analysis, but does not alter the estimate of present value of net cash flows.

That net cash flow is not the same as net income cannot be overstressed.

Income is a concept developed by the accounting profession. It has a definition which specifically distinguishes it from cash flow. The major difference is that when estimating cash proceeds, depreciation and amortization charges attributed by accountants to fixed assets are not subtracted from gross revenue, because no cash expenditures are required. Other differences are generally minor, but the distinction is essential to correct application of the cash-flow model.

The Impact of Taxation

Cash proceeds are measured on an after-tax basis. Income taxes are determined on the basis of accounting profits rather than cash flows. Therefore, there may often be a tax-deductible loss from operations combined with a large net cash flow. Less frequently, investors may incur an income tax liability for accounting profits from a venture, combined with negative net cash flows.

The Problem of Inflation

No special adjustment is required for changes in the purchasing power of the dollar. One merely forecasts actual dollar cash flows expected to occur in each time period, taking into account the inflationary trend. The discount rate employed to adjust for differences in timing of cash flows automatically adjusts for the inflationary trend, because it will have been considered in deciding on the appropriate rate to apply in the discounting process.

The appropriate discount rate is that attainable on alternative cash flows of similar risk, and expected attainable rates include the effects of inflation.

Risk Adjustments

Risk is introduced in Part III as a measurable factor in the investment equation. Risk is the variance between expectations and realization. Risk management aims to conserve capital and is concerned with the degree to which the forecast returns can be realized.

Certain risks can be avoided by judicious choice of investment opportunities. Others can be shifted by contract, such as by insurance or options. Remaining risks can be measured in terms of the probability of specified losses. Combining these techniques permits budgeting of risk as an operating expense of the enterprise, or creation of appropriate loss reserves.

Summary

Pent-up demand and steady inflation have caused persistant increases in property values, making real estate investment a relatively low-risk enterprise during the early post-World War II period. These phenomena masked many investment mistakes. Change in the investment climate during the decade of the 1970s, however, increased the failure rate among real estate ventures and placed a greater premium on careful and thorough analysis.

Systematic investment decision making follows a fairly uniform path, regardless of the nature of the investment. Goal-setting is essential because all decisions must be based on the contribution they make toward these goals. Opportunities are evaluated in terms of predetermined criteria. A systematic decision system facilitates evaluation of alternative opportunities. Such a system is often called a *decision model.*

Models are simplified representations of some aspect of reality. The appropriate decision model varies with the nature of the decision and with the amount of information available. The model employed should use all readily available information, should be understandable by the decision maker, and should be cost-effective.

The real estate investment analysis model employed in this book is a slightly modified corporate capital-budgeting model. It involves discounting all expected future cash flows and comparing their present value with the initial cash outlay associated with a proposal. Cash flows are expressed on an after-tax basis. No explicit adjustment is made for changes in purchasing power because this is accounted for in choosing a discount rate. *Risk*, in the decision model, is defined as the probability of variance from expected outcomes.

2

The Economic Foundation of Real Estate Value

Investors are not equally endowed with wisdom and foresight. Some are wise, while others are foolish; some are cautious, others impetuous; some employ elaborate financial analytical models to arrive at investment decisions, while others do their calculations on the backs of old envelopes. But all investors, the prudent and the imprudent, the learned and the naive, have in common one general approach: all are concerned with the ability of a property to generate a return on investment over and above the cost of acquisition.

In this respect, real estate investment is not analytically different from the problem facing corporations that contemplate capital-expenditure decisions. A corporation acquires capital equipment with which to produce goods and services to be made available, for a fee, to customers at a desired time and place. This also succinctly describes the activity of real estate investors. They acquire capital goods (real estate) with which to provide a product. Their product is the right to occupy a three-dimensional space on the urban landscape over a specified period of time.

The product provided by income-property investors has been aptly described as *space-time*.[1] The market value of space-time is determined in much the same way as the value of any other economic good. It is a function of the interaction of the want-satisfying power of the product to the consumer, the consumer's ability to afford the good, and the availability and prices of close substitutes.

The desirability of a particular property (expressed as its investment value) depends on its ability to command rents. Evaluating investment worth, therefore, involves estimating the market value of the space-time a property will produce over the projected holding period and the market value of the property itself at the end of the period. An investment is worthwhile only when the present value (discounted worth) of expected net proceeds from it exceeds acquisition cost by a sufficient margin to justify the perceived risk.

Understanding the economic nature of space-time and the basis of its ability to command rent is essential for an accurate cash-flow forecast. Failure to appreciate the nature of the market for space-time accounts for simple-minded extrapolation of past experience into the indefinite future. It is frequently disastrous for investors and lenders alike and often typifies real estate investment "analysis."

Observation of past operating results and rental and building trends forms a first step in assessing the investment worth of a proposal. These data must be tempered, however, with an appreciation of the economic and social forces in the immediate future which may drastically alter past trends. To instill an awareness of these forces, the present chapter is devoted to explaining the nature of real estate productivity, which is the basis of space-time's power to command rent.

Productivity analysis requires a firm grasp of the concepts of supply and demand, and of their role in determining market prices. The following section develops these concepts in a somewhat abstract form. They are then applied to analysis of space-time throughout the balance of the chapter.

Supply, Demand, and Market Value

Readers may grow impatient with a discussion of the abstract concepts of supply and demand, but mastery of these abstractions facilitates understanding of the power of space-time to command rent. This section explains the role of supply and demand phenomena in setting market-determined prices. The examples use price and quantity of space-time to illustrate the issue, but any other freely traded commodity could serve just as well.

Demand in a Free Market

Buying any one good or service means surrendering purchasing power, and thus ultimately foregoing the enjoyment of some other good or service. Because of the universal constraint of limited purchasing power, shoppers must weigh the merits of competing goods in terms of the relative satisfaction expected from their consumption. The common denominator for this comparison is the dollar price (or some other unit of money); rational consumers order their purchases to yield the maximum total satisfaction with their available budget.

It follows that, in general, the lower the price of a good relative to its ability to satisfy the needs and wants of potential buyers, the more that good will be purchased in the marketplace. This relationship between market price and total quantity purchased is called a *demand function*, or a *demand schedule*. Table 2-1 illustrates the idea with a series of potential prices for space-time in prime downtown office buildings and the corresponding quantities demanded. The example assumes that if prime space rents for $5 per square foot per annum, 2.5 million square feet are demanded per year in this particular market. At $5.25 per square foot, the amount demanded declines to 2.4 million feet, as would-be tenants opt

Table 2-1
Hypothetical Demand Schedule for Prime Office Space in a Downtown Area

Rental Rates (Price) per Square Foot per Annum	Millions of Square Feet Demanded
$6.00	2.1
5.75	2.2
5.50	2.3
5.25	2.4
5.00	2.5
4.75	2.6
4.50	2.7
4.25	2.8
4.00	2.9
3.75	3.0

instead for less-than-prime space or for space outside the downtown area. At lower prices, correspondingly greater quantities are demanded.

Utility and Individual Demand Profiles

Table 2-1 illustrates the relationship between price and quantity demanded in a specified market area. It suggests that the greater the aggregate demand for space-time, the greater will be the per-unit price of the space-time demanded. Of course, this is not the perception of the individual user of space-time. His perception of the price-quantity relationship is more likely to be that he can contract for all the space he desires at currently prevailing rates. He may, in fact, discover that because of quantity discounts, he can reduce his per unit costs somewhat when contracting for large quantities of floor space.

The apparent discrepancy between aggregate market phenomena and the perception of individual market participants is explained by the principle of decreasing marginal utility. *Utility* has been described as the "want-satisfying power" embodied in a good. A *good* is, of course, any desired entity or goal. For an individual, something is a good if he desires it.

Marginal utility refers to the additional satisfaction derived from consuming or owning an additional unit of a good. The relationship between marginal utility and market price determines whether an individual will purchase more of a product or service.

An individual faced with a market price that is less than the value to him of the marginal utility embodied in a good will continue purchasing additional units until the last one acquired adds just sufficient utility to compensate for the per unit cost. Cost, though measured nominally in monetary units, can be expressed in terms of the marginal utility foregone by using funds for this purpose rather than applying them to the purchase of some alternative good.

The *principle of diminishing marginal utility* says that as additional units of a good are possessed or consumed per unit of time, the additional (marginal) utility of each successive unit is less than that of the preceding unit. Translated into a tenant's decision about the amount of office space to lease, this means he will decide on an office size such that additional space will increase his costs more than it will enhance the benefits of tenancy.

The concept is not intuitively difficult. A firm with very little office space relative to its volume of business will be severely handicapped by cramped quarters. For such a firm, the benefit of a small expansion in available space might far exceed the modest increase in total office rental expense. However, as total office size increases, operations are less cramped and additional space, while enjoyable, might have a negligible influence on productivity. Further expansion beyond this point will increase rental expense more than it will add to the value of office productivity.

Market rental rates, and the marginal value of space to the user, therefore, determine the amount of office space for which a potential tenant will contract. So long as he can rent whatever amount he chooses, he will increase his office area to the point where he values the last unit rented at exactly its market price. To contract for more space would yield a lower increment in value than the increase in rental expense, so he would take additional space only if the incremental price were lower.

The Unstable Nature of Market Demand

Our discussion of the relation between price and quantity demanded so far has implicitly assumed that all other causal factors remain constant. Demand for space–time is affected, of course, by a number of factors other than rental rates. These include wealth, custom, productivity, and expectations about future space needs and availability. The relationship between price and quantity depicted on table 2–1 assumes that all these other factors remain unchanged as the rental rate moves along the scale of possible rates per square foot.

Things seldom remain unchanged for long, however. If, for example, there should be an increase in optimism about future business prospects, many businessmen would make simultaneous decisions to acquire more prime downtown office space. The results would include an increase in the quantity of space demanded at all possible rental rates. Illustrative of the

Table 2-2
Revised Demand Schedule for Prime Downtown Office
Space, Due to Improved Business Outlook

Rental Rates per Square Foot per Annum	Millions of Square Feet Demanded
$6.00	2.48
5.75	2.56
5.50	2.64
5.25	2.72
5.00	2.80
4.75	2.88
4.50	2.96
4.25	3.04
4.00	3.12
3.75	3.20

new demand schedule for prime downtown space is the hypothetical revised demand schedule in table 2-2.

These relationships are illustrated graphically in figure 2-1. Line D_1D_1 depicts the demand schedule from table 2-1. Revisions in quantity demanded incident to changes in rental rates are illustrated by moving up or down the column in table 2-1, or by sliding along the demand line D_1D_1 in figure 2-1. Changes in the quantity demanded consequent to shifts, in considerations other than price, reflect a shift in demand. For example, the change in business climate referred to earlier results in a shift from the schedule shown in table 2-1 to that depicted in table 2-2, or a shift from line D_1D_1 to line D_2D_2 in figure 2-1. The quantity demanded will have increased for every possible price. Table 2-2 and the new demand function D_2D_2 in figure 2-1 represent a new relationship between price and quantity of office space demanded, resulting from the altered business climate.

Understanding this distinction between variations in quantity demanded (movement along a given demand schedule as a result of price changes) and a shift in the whole demand schedule (caused by a change in some factor other than price) is crucial to accurate analysis of the most probable cash flow from real estate investment. It therefore merits elaboration.

The relationship depicted by table 2-1, or by the line D_1D_1 in figure 2-1, reflects the analyst's assessment of current market conditions. Since flux and change are constant conditions of nature, these "current conditions" are fleeting. The challenge to the analyst is to "guess" the nature of the economic and social environment in which a particular investment will mature. Changes in market-determining factors will be reflected by a shift

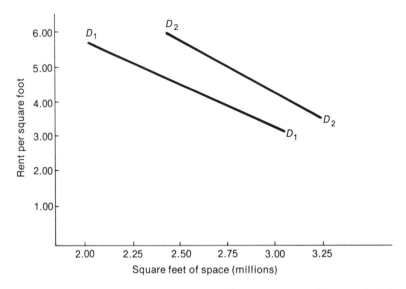

Figure 2-1. Demand for Downtown Office Space, Before and After Change in Business Outlook.

in the location and/or slope of the line D_1D_1 in figure 2-1. The analyst might predict, for example, that by the second year of the life of an investment in a prime office building, the demand function in figure 2-1 will have shifted, as depicted by the line D_2D_2. This has obvious implications for the ability of the space to command rent.

The Role of Supply

Relative scarcity is also a factor in the power of a product or service to command value in exchange. Many items from which we derive great satisfaction have little or no exchange value. The most common example of this seeming paradox is the relationship between water and diamonds. Water, as a basic requirement of life, certainly has as much want–satisfying power as can be imagined. Diamonds, on the other hand, bear little relationship to the survival needs of the species. Yet lives are sacrificed and revolutions fomented in search of precious stones, especially diamonds.

Of course, the missing element in the apparent paradox is the factor of relative scarcity. No matter how useful an item is, it will not command substantial value in exchange if it is relatively abundant. Water generally has very little exchange value, except in desert regions or during a period of drought. In those places and at those times, the additional element of scarcity makes water indeed more precious than diamonds.

To appreciate the role of supply in determining the market price of space–time, consider again the graph in figure 2-1. The demand schedule illustrated there indicates a whole series of possible market rental rates and a corresponding series of quantities of space demanded by renters. The schedule, taken alone, provides no clue to the market rental rate or the amount of office space that will actually be rented. This requires the addition of a supply schedule.

Suppose there are 2.5 million square feet of prime office space available in the market represented by table 2-1. At any rental rate below $5 per square foot, the quantity of space demanded will exceed the available supply. In such a situation, who determines how the available space will be allocated between would–be tenants? The answer is that no one need make such a decision. In the absence of arbitrary price controls, allocation will be accomplished by impersonal market forces.

As vacancy rates decline as a result of the manifest quantity demanded at prevailing rental rates, landlords will perceive that they are charging less than their office space is "worth" in the market. Self-interest will cause them to increase rents for new tenants or for lease renewals. As rates creep up, prospective tenants will begin to economize on space, to accept less than prime accommodations, or to search out alternatives to central-city locations. In this fashion, the "higgling and jiggling" of the marketplace results in allocation of available space to those users who value it the greatest.

Figure 2-2, which superimposes a supply curve on the demand schedule from table 2-1, illustrates this concept. At rental rate r_1 the quantity of space demanded by tenants is Q_1, while the space made available is indicated by the vertical supply curve SS. The distance on the horizontal axis from Q_1 to Q_2 represents excess capacity (vacancies) that will exist at this market rate of rent. As rates decline due to the efforts of landlords to fill their buildings, the gap between Q_1 and Q_2 narrows until, at a rental rate r_2, the available quantity of space will be just adequate to satisfy the desires of tenants at that price. At rental rate r_3, the quantity of space demanded (Q_3) will exceed available supply, as indicated by the distance between Q_2 and Q_3. The shortfall in available space will persist until competing users of prime space bid the price up to the level indicated by r_2, at which point equilibrium will once again exist between quantities demanded and supplied.

Careful readers will have noted two difficulties with this explanation. The first has to do with the concept of equilibrium between quantities supplied and demanded: How does one reconcile it with the observation that there are almost always some vacancies in every market, regardless of the level of rents? The other difficulty arises as a result of the static nature of the analysis: Why does figure 2-2 indicate that supply is constant at all levels of rent, when supply is actually in a constant state of flux due to new construction, renovation of aging facilities, and demolition or succession of uses?

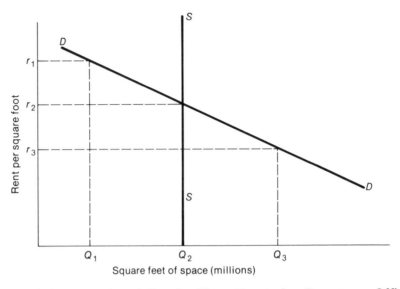

Figure 2-2. Demand and Supply (Short Term) for Downtown Office Space.

The concept of equilibration of quantities supplied and demanded through price fluctuations is most directly applicable in an auction market. There a product is brought to market and sold to the highest bidder, with all market participants fully aware of the available supply and of competitors' bids. In such a market, where the product is homogeneous and fully divisible, there will indeed be an equilibrium price which will result in no unsold product. No potential buyer is left without as much of the product as he desires at the then-prevailing price.

But dropping the unrealistic assumption of an extremely efficient market requires a slight modification of the model. Inefficiencies are introduced by lack of free-flowing information between market participants, by slight differences in product quality or character, and by reluctance of sellers to readily adjust prices in the face of weakened demand for their product. These are all characteristics which exist in the market for rental space. To compensate for these inefficiencies, dealers must maintain an inventory of their product. Thus there will nearly always be *some* vacancies in any real estate market, regardless of the level of demand.

The graph in figure 2-2 indicates that the supply of rentable space remains constant, regardless of the market price of space-time. This will hold true over a considerable range of rental rates, but only for a very short period of time. There is, of course, some very low rental rate which will make it more profitable to hold space off the market and so economize on expenditures for light, heat, maintenance, and management. Moreover, there are very high rates which might induce present users to sublet some of their space to others. Therefore, even over the relatively short run, there is some responsiveness of supply to radical swings in the market rate of rent.

Other than for these extremes, however, the quantity of space available for use by tenants is relatively fixed over the very short run. Some time will be required to bring additional space on–line by new construction, renovation, or succession-of-use techniques. It becomes necessary, therefore, to distinguish between the short–run supply schedule and the long–run supply schedule. The distinction between short–run, intermediate–run, and long–run supply is explored more fully in a later section of this chapter.

Purpose of Demand and Supply Concepts

Understanding how market prices are determined makes possible a more accurate forecast of future prices. Having isolated the primary determinants of both supply and demand, analysts concentrate on estimating what is most likely to happen to these key variables. In this way, they can more accurately estimate the direction and magnitude of changes in rental rates over the projection period.

The next two sections explore in more detail the determinants of demand for space–time in a specific segment of the apartment rental market. The final section of the chapter addresses the question of determinants of supply and how the short–run supply schedule is likely to shift over time.

The Demand for Space–Time

Having discussed the concept of demand in a somewhat abstract way, we are now ready to apply it to the concrete issue of determining the relative desirability of particular units of space–time. First, approach the problem by investigating the interrelationship between demand schedules for different categories of space–time. Then, zero in on the basis of all demand: the utility derived from possession or consumption. This issue in turn leads to the point of the whole discussion: those characteristics of space–time which affect its relative desirability and, thereby, its ability to command rents.

Defining the Market

Before considering the demand factors at work in a particular real estate market, the market itself must be delineated. This is no simple task. The unadorned concept of a market is not ambiguous, but its application to real estate is complicated both by the nature of the product and by the characteristics of market participants.

In general, a *market* is an institutional arrangement or mechanism whereby buyers and sellers are brought into contact with each other. It is not necessarily a physical entity or a geographical location. There is, for example, a world market for national currency, which is comprised of an informal network of dealers connected by telephone.

A market might be defined in terms of commonality of product. This leads to a description of a real estate market for industrial property, another for farm land, another for commercial sites, and so on. But, with notable exceptions for large industrial and commercial sites, the market in each of these segments is fragmented geographically, because of the tendency of participants to concentrate in the geographical area with which they are most familiar. For most real estate, therefore, there is no truly national market.

Illustrating the nature of the problem, the following categories of real estate "markets" are described by one author:[2]

The owner-occupant market

The renter-occupant market

Multifamily investment

Nonresidential market

This is a useful categorization of markets by type of product. Yet there obviously is no national market for owner-occupied property. Indeed, the owner-occupied segment may be the most fragmented of all real estate markets because of strong preferences of owner-occupants for specific locations.

Within each broad market category, therefore, it is necessary to define submarkets within which determinable market forces work more or less uniformly. Kinnard has described these submarkets as neighborhoods.[3] A *neighborhood*, as described by Kinnard, is a geographical area within which change has a "direct and immediate effect" on the property under analysis. Delineating neighborhoods in this manner permits direct investigation of the forces impinging upon the supply and demand equation. The problem of submarket delineation is addressed more extensively in chapter 4, in connection with forecasting revenues over the proposed holding period.

Interdependence of Demand Schedules

The amount of a good demanded at any specific price depends also on the price of substitute goods and on the price of goods to be consumed along with the item in question. Goods which are consumed *instead* of the one in question are called *substitutes* (hot dogs or hamburgers, movies or ball games, wine of beer, etc.). Goods to be consumed *along with* the one in question are called *complements* (peanut butter and crackers, automobile tires and gasoline, movie tickets and popcorn, etc.). The equilibrium price of a good will vary directly with the price of complements and inversely with the price of substitutes.

To explore the relationship between the price of particular units of space-time and their substitutes, consider the demand schedule in figure 2–3. Remember, such schedules assume all significant factors, except the price of the product illustrated, remain constant. Changes in price will cause a change in the quantity of space-time demanded, as indicated by a movement along the demand curve D_1D_1 from an old price to a new one.

Among those factors presumed to have remained unchanged in constructing the demand function D_1D_1 in figure 2–3 is the rental rate applicable to space considered a relatively close substitute for that included in this market segment. This includes space available in the same area, but considered somewhat less desirable because of age or condition, or the nature of other tenants. Space embodying the same amenities, but located elsewhere, must also be considered a substitute good.

If the market-clearing price for substitute space declines (perhaps because of an increase in the total supply of such space provided by developers, or because of a decrease in demand at all price levels resulting from

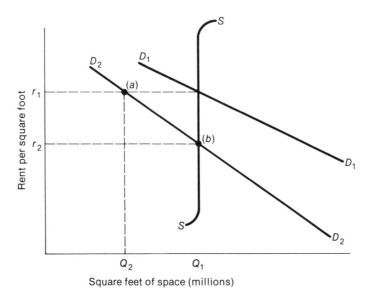

Figure 2–3. Demand for Downtown Office Space, Before and After Change in the Price of Substitute Space.

an out-migration of a major user of such space), many of the tenants who previously opted for this market area may now be lured away by the relatively lower-priced substitute space. As a consequence, less space in this market will be taken by tenants at each possible rental rate. This is illustrated in figure 2-3 as a shift from schedule D_1D_1 to schedule D_2D_2.

In order to keep available space in the market fully occupied in the face of increased competition from other locales, landlords will have to lower rental rates for new tenants and for lease renewals. At the previously prevailing market rate r_1, there will now be a vacancy rate, as indicated by the distance on the quantity axis from Q_2 to Q_1. Successive rent concessions will reduce the market price of space to r_2, at which approximate price tenants will demand all available space in the area once again. This phenomenon represents a movement along the new demand schedule in figure 2-3 from point a to point b.[4]

Of course, should space in other market areas become relatively *more* expensive as a result (for example) of an influx of new residents seeking to locate there, the shift in the demand schedule for substitute space will in turn cause a shift in the demand schedule for space in our area. Tenants who are "priced out" of the substitute space will seek to relocate in our now relatively less costly space. Thus, more space in our market area will be demanded at every possible market rental rate.

Finding vacancy rates declining below that level considered "normal," landlords will begin to increase rates for new tenants and for lease renewals to the point at which the available supply will once again approximately satisfy those seeking such space.

Supply: The Other Blade of the Shears

Alfred Marshall, an early authority on economic processes and the developer of much of modern economic theory of the firm, likened the relationship between supply and demand to the two blades of a pair of scissors—neither blade can be said to have done the cutting, yet both are essential to the process. The discussion of the impact of changes in demand on prices for rental space has taken supply as a given. This may be a realistic assumption over a very short time period, but high rental rates have the effect of inducing construction of additional rental units where possible or conversion of space from alternative uses, so that supply does not remain constant over an extended period of time.

Just as *demand* is defined as the relationship between price and the quantity taken off the market during a time period, for all possible alternative prices, so *supply* is defined as the relationship between price and the quantity of a product suppliers place on the market during a specified time period, for all possible prices. A key phrase in this definition is *during a specified time period*. The supply function differs rather drastically as the specified time period is lengthened or shortened.

For a very short period of time, the quantity of rental space placed on the market generally does not vary significantly with changes in market rates of rent. It is irrational to hold available space off the market so long as rental rates are sufficient to cover at least the variable costs of providing the space, unless the lower rates are a temporary market aberration. Therefore, a reduction in market rents will not cause space to be taken off the market under most circumstances. Even large increases in market rents will not make it possible to create additional space faster than the time required for construction.

The supply curve in figure 2-3 depicts this relationship. Over the mid-range of possible market prices for space, the available space cannot be expanded when prices increase and cannot be contracted when they decrease. Only at extreme ranges does market price affect the quantity supplied over the very short run. At some very high price, it becomes worthwhile to create additional space by construction of prefabricated structures or conversion. This happens, for example, when a boom town blossoms around a new mineral find.

At the other extreme there is a sufficiently low rate that space will be held vacant rather than be rented at the prevailing rate. This occurs when the market rate is so low that property owners suffer a lesser net loss from holding property vacant than by renting it. That is, the increase in costs of operation and maintenance when rented exceeds the rental income.[5] This is, of course, an unlikely event since the variable costs associated with most rental property are a very low percentage of total costs.[6]

Consider the impact of a decrease in the demand schedule for space-time over the short run, as depicted in figure 2-3. If, for some reason, there is a decrease in the demand for space-time at all possible rental rates, as depicted by the shift from demand curve D_1D_1 to curve D_2D_2, note that over the short run the only impact will be a decline in prevailing rental rates from r_1 to r_2. Price serves over the short run to allocate the available space among competing users, ascertaining that the space goes to the highest bidders (who presumably value the space more than do those who decline to place winning bids).

Over the longer term, however, the quantity of space-time will be more responsive to changes in price (rents). An increase in market rental rates will make it more profitable to construct additional space and thus to increase the total market supply of space-time.

The impact on the market-clearing price of a shift in the demand for

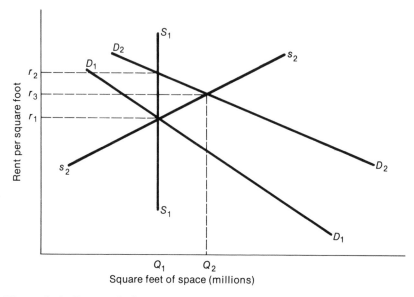

Figure 2-4. Demand for Downtown Office Space, Before and After Change in Business Outlook, Coupled with Short-Term and Long-Term Supply Functions.

space-time over the short term and the longer term is compared in figure 2-4. Start with the relationship depicted by the demand curve D_1D_1 and the short-run supply curve S_1S_1. An initial shift in demand, as indicated by the demand curve D_2D_2, has no short-term impact on the quantity of space-time available, but drives up prevailing rents from r_1 to r_2. The new, higher price of space-time induces developers to start new projects, however, and increases the total supply.

Over the longer term, the quantity supplied responds, as indicated by movement along the long-term supply curve s_2s_2, so that longer-term equilibrium is achieved with a market rental rate of r_3 and a total supply of space-time of Q_2.

This brings us to another basic supply and demand concept: the longer a price persists, the more responsive will be the supply function to that price, because the longer the period of adjustment, the more fully the market can accommodate a new set of supply and demand relationships. Over the very long term, not only can additional structures be built on available land, but additional land can be cleared or converted from alternative uses to more profitable use. This relationship between the length of the time period involved and the responsiveness of supply to price changes is depicted in figure 2-5.

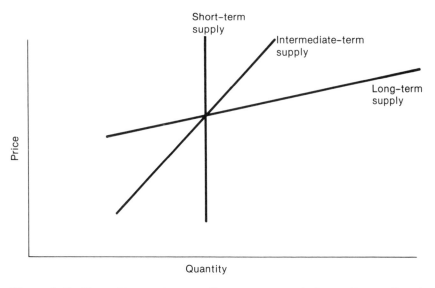

Figure 2–5. Short-Term, Intermediate-Term, and Long-Term Supply Functions.

Summary

Rental property owners are businessmen who produce and sell the right to occupy a three-dimensional space for specified time periods. The price at which space–time sells (rent) on a free market is determined by the interaction of supply and demand. For a given set of economic conditions, tastes, fashion, expectations, etc., the quantity of space–time demanded by tenants varies inversely with price. A change in any of the above-mentioned variables alters the relationship between price and quantity demanded, although the relationship remains inverse in nature.

Over a very short term, the supply of space–time is fixed and thus does not vary with market price. Changes in the demand relationship, therefore, are fully reflected in revised rental rates over the short run, with no variation in the total quantity of space–time made available.

Over a longer term, however, the quantity of space–time supplied varies directly with market price. Given sufficient time, new buildings are constructed when rental rates move up enough to make such construction profitable, so that consistently high rents call forth an increased supply of space–time. If rental rates are consistently below levels which make building profitable, the total supply of space–time declines as older buildings are abandoned with no new construction to replace the space thus taken off the market.

Notes

1. The space-time concept was employed in the writings of Richard U. Ratcliff (see, for example, *Real Estate Analysis*, New York: McGraw-Hill, 1961). It has been honed into a fine-edged analytical tool by James Graaskamp of the University of Wisconsin at Madison.

2. Thomas W. Shafer, *Real Estate and Economics* (Reston Va.: Reston, 1975).

3. William N. Kinnard, Jr., *Income Property Valuation* (Lexington, Mass.: Lexington Books, 1971), p. 302.

4. Remember that equilibrium between available space and quantity demanded will be achieved at some vacancy level in excess of zero. This "normal" or "frictional" vacancy rate is necessary to compensate for inefficiencies in the rental market which result from lack of information on the part of market participants, imperfect divisibility of space, and inability of users to readily command space for time periods other than provided by standard lease terms.

5. For analytical purposes it is often helpful to divide costs into variable and fixed components. Those costs effected by the level of operations (in our case, by the occupancy level) are designated as *variable*. Costs remaining invariant when the level of operations varies are, by definition, *fixed*. So long as the revenue from operations exceeds variable costs, it is better for management to operate at a loss than to simply cease operations. At least some of the fixed costs are met by operations. If operations were to cease, the fixed costs would continue with no offsetting revenue. This, of course, ignores the possibility of divesting oneself of the operation by sale or abandonment.

6. Because property is often under long-term lease arrangements, management might be induced to hold the property vacant (at a substantial loss in terms of current cash flow) in anticipation of signing a long-term tenant at a far higher rental rate in the future. Expectations are, therefore, a powerful and often volatile influence.

3 Developing the Operating Statement

Neophytes in real estate analysis are almost universally afflicted with a "sticks and bricks" fixation. That the physical structure is coincidental to the investment decision is a difficult concept for beginners to grasp. Soundness of construction, architectural elegance, and harmony with physical surroundings are significant only as they affect the stream of anticipated after-tax cash receipts, and the desirability of an investment proposal is strictly a function of the anticipated amount, timing, and certainty of these cash flows.

This is not to say that nonfinancial aspects of real estate are unimportant. Aesthetics, indeed, are often valued as an end in themselves, apart from the question of economic worth. Such issues transcend the investment equation, however, and are not amenable to economic analysis. Having received a dispassionate economic evaluation of a proposal, an investor may elect to factor noneconomic criteria into his decision-making process. He should do so, however, with full knowledge of the economic consequences.

Rational investment decisions require evaluation of all anticipated future cash flows. This involves a forecast of the flows over the investment period and an assessment of probable forecast error. The importance of understanding the process transcends being able to develop such forecasts. Analysts who understand the mechanics of forecasting are better equipped to appreciate associated elements of risk and uncertainty. Healthy skepticism is thus a valuable byproduct of technical competence.

This chapter and the next explain how cash-flow forecasts are developed. The present chapter first addresses the matter of format and makeup of financial statements. While not matching the uniformity achieved in corporate accounting, there have developed over the years certain conventions in statement presentation. Understanding these conventions enhances statement readability and contributes to economy of effort in their preparation and interpretation.

After addressing issues of format and conventional presentation, this chapter considers the problem of data generation. Both conventional and certain innovative approaches to estimating future cash flows are included.

Overview of the Operating Statement

The financial statement conventionally used in real estate investment analysis first presents cash inflows and outflows from operations and then extends the presentation to include certain nonoperating cash flows. There are important differences between this and the income statement typically prepared by accountants, who concentrate on the flow of income and expenses rather than cash receipts and disbursements. An appreciation of the distinction between accounting flows and cash flows is critical to the mastery of real estate investment analysis. Accountants' income statements are concerned with recording income "when earned," whether or not there has been a corresponding receipt of cash. Likewise, accountants record expenses "when incurred," without reference to when the resultant obligation for cash disbursement is fulfilled. Investment analysts, in contrast, are concerned with the timing of actual cash receipts and disbursements, without particular reference to when receipts are earned or when obligations to make expenditures are incurred. In the vernacular of the analyst, "only cash matters."

One consequence of this difference in perspective is that the accountant's income statement will vary rather drastically from the analyst's operating statement. The most significant difference relates to provision for the wasting away of capital assets. This provision, called *depreciation*, is recorded by accountants as a current expense on the income statement. Since depreciation is not an expense item requiring a corresponding cash outlay, it is not reflected on the analyst's statement as an expense item reducing net operating income.[1]

A second major departure from the typical accountant's format lies in the treatment of nonoperating items. After presenting net income from operations, investment analysts include other items of cash receipts and deduct other items of cash disbursements. These include, but are not necessarily limited to, debt service, capital improvements, and income tax payments (or income tax savings as a consequence of the investment).

Figure 3-1 illustrates a typical income-property operating statement. The various headings on the statement are explained in the following sections.

Potential Gross Income

The amount of annual gross rental income a property will generate with 100 percent occupancy is termed *potential gross income.* Since a vacancy factor is associated with almost all rental property, the potential gross is not expected to be actually realized. Occasional losses are also experienced from inability to collect rent, although this can be minimized by judicious choice

XYZ Apartment Building Reconstructed Operating Statement		
Potential gross income		$XXX,XXX
Less: Allowance for vacancy		
and rent loss		XXX
		$XXX,XXX
Plus: Other income:		
Parking fees	$ X,XXX	
Concession income	X,XXX	$ XX,XXX
Effective gross income		$XXX,XXX
Less: Operating expenses:		
Property tax	$ X,XXX	
Insurance	X,XXX	
Maintenance	X,XXX	
Etc.	X,XXX	XXX,XXX
Net operating income		$XXX,XXX
Less: Debt service:		
Interest	$XX,XXX	
Principal	X,XXX	XX,XXX
Cash flow before income taxes		$ XX,XXX
Less: Income tax obligation		XXX
Net cash flow		$ XX,XXX

Figure 3–1. Income Property Operating Statement

of tenants and appropriate security deposits, coupled with timely and vigorous collection efforts. Nevertheless, provision for rent losses increases the gap between potential gross income and actual collections.

Potential gross is predicated upon the prevailing market rental rates for the type occupancy involved, unless current tenants hold long-term leases. In this latter case, the proper basis for estimating potential gross income is the actual, or contract, rate of rent for the period that existing leases are in effect.

Income from other sources is added to potential gross income to determine effective gross. This includes all income generated from sources other than space rental. Examples include rental of equipment and income from coin–operated washers and other vending machines. It generally does *not* include interest earned on tenants' security deposits, because in most jurisdictions, any such interest income belongs to the tenants themselves.

Effective Gross Income

Adjusting potential gross income for vacancy and collection losses, and for receipt of other income, yields *effective gross income.* In a historical statement, this represents the actual income experience of the property over the period of the report. In a forecast of future cash flows, effective gross income represents the receipts an owner might reasonably expect to receive during the period.

Operating Expenses

Operating expenses represent cash expenditures necessary to maintain the property in sufficient condition to generate the effective gross income. The following are representative of typical operating expenses:

Supplies	Management Fees
Services	Painting and redecorating
Insurance	Maintenance and repairs
Real estate and other taxes	Trash removal
Payroll and payroll taxes	Advertising
Utilities	Rental commissions
Heat	

Expenditures which are *not* included in operating expenses include capital improvements, debt service (payments made incident to mortgage indebtedness), and income taxes.

Capital expenditures are designed to increase the market value or useful life of a property and are more in the nature of an investment than an operating expense. Such expenditures do, of course, affect net cash flow from the property and must, therefore, be included elsewhere on the statement. They reflect a management decision not incident to actual operation of the property, however, and should be omitted from the calculation of net operating income.

Payments on a promissory note secured by a mortgage on the property are called *debt service.* They result from a decision to utilize financial leverage (that is, to use borrowed money to supplement personal funds available for investment). Leverage affects the return to an investor, expressed as a rate of return on personally invested funds, but it does not have an impact on the operating results of the property itself. Therefore, debt–service payments on mortgage indebtedness are not included in operating expenses.

Income taxes are levied against the owner rather than the property. The amount of the tax obligation is more a function of an owner's personal tax position than of the revenue generated by operation of this particular property. Consequently, the income tax liability arising from ownership and operation of a property is excluded from the operating section of the financial statement. (We shall see, however, that income tax consequences are included in the nonoperating section of the statement and thereby deducted from net operating income to arrive at net cash flow to the investor.)

Replacement Reserves

Certain expenditures arising from operation and maintenance of real estate occur periodically, rather than on a regular basis. These include expenditures to repair or replace such items as mechanical equipment (refrigerators and garbage disposals, for example,) and water heaters, which have a relatively short life, and which tend to require extensive replacement funds over a short time period. No funds may be needed for these items during the first few years of the life of a building. Then, all the garbage disposal units, for example, may require replacement or major repair over the next 4 years.

To meet these periodic needs, many investors maintain a *replacement reserve* of funds set aside in relatively liquid investments. These funds can be drawn upon as needed to avoid a liquidity crisis arising from unexpected expenditures for replacements. To ensure their ready availability, replacement reserves must be invested in securities which are readily marketable and which do not fluctuate widely in market value.

Having made an estimate of the amount and timing of needed funds for repairs and replacements, the investor makes level annual deposits into the replacement reserve so that deposits plus accumulated earnings on the fund will be sufficient to meet projected needs.

Whether deposits to a reserve for replacement should be included as an expenditure depends on whether the investor actually intends to set such funds aside, rather than simply use the calculation as an accounting convenience. Since our purpose is to track the actual projected flow of funds, we include the deposits if, and only if, there is an expectation that such deposits will in fact be made. The alternative is to attempt to estimate actual periodic outlays required for repairs and replacements and to include them in cash expenditure projections for the appropriate years.

Net Operating Income

The actual cash–flow consequences of owning and operating a property, as opposed to the manner of financing its acquisition, is called the *net oper-*

ating income. Readers familiar with generally accepted accounting procedures are, by now, aware that this is a radically different use of the income concept than that used in the accounting profession.

Net operating income, then, is simply effective gross income less operating expenses requiring cash outlays. It represents the cash flow expected to result from operating the property, before providing for payment of mortgage indebtedness and before provision for income taxes.

Cash Flow before Income Tax

If a property is acquired on a free-and-clear basis (that is, without the use of mortgage indebtedness), then net operating income approximates the cash flow available to the investor before provision for income taxes. Rarely, however, will an investor fail to make use of borrowed funds to supplement his available equity investment. The presence of mortgage indebtedness implies a need to allocate some portion of net operating income to service the debt. Only the residual after debt service accrues to the equity investor.

Cash flow before income taxes, then, is the net operating income minus the annual debt service requirement. It is sometimes called *cash throw-off, equity dividend,* or simply *cash flow.* By whatever name, it represents the cash flow accruing to the equity investor, before provision for state and federal income taxes.

Income Tax Consequences

Unless the investor is a tax-exempt organization, the income tax obligation arising from an investment requires an additional periodic cash outlay. If, as is often the case, the investor's total income tax obligation is reduced as a consequence of ownership, the taxes thus avoided represent an additional cash inflow from the investment. The income tax aspects of investing in real estate are covered more fully in chapter 6.

Net Cash Flow

The "bottom line" to an investor is neither the net operating income nor the cash throw-off. His attention should be riveted to the amount of "bankable cash" flowing from an investment. This is the balance remaining after satisfying *all* prior claims. These claims most emphatically *do* include any obligation for state and federal income taxes. It is this after-tax cash flow, after all debt service, that investors generally refer to as *net cash flow.*

Estimating Current Operating Results

The preceeding section summarizes the cash-flow statement used in real estate investment analysis. Figure 3-1 illustrates the format for such a statement, variously called an *operating statement*, an *income statement*, or a *cash-flow statement.* Nomenclature aside, the format presents the net cash flow from ownership and operation of the property, either as a statement of historical fact or as a forecast of what the future portends.

The past may be interesting in its own right, but its significance to investment decisions is limited to what it suggests about the most probable course of future events. Investors buy only the right to *future* cash flows, and only sheer coincidence will make these correspond exactly with past experience.

An early task for the analyst, therefore, is to forecast future after-tax net cash flows from a prospective investment. The immediate past history of a property is taken as a starting point for this effort, but forecasting must not be viewed as a simple mechanical extrapolation of past trends, nor as a precise prediction of future occurrences. Rather, forecasting is an estimate of what the future holds, taking as a basis the recent past and modifying the observed trend according to what is known or suspected about the future environment in which property will be operated.

Conventions and Innovations

In primitive form, real estate investment analysis has been around for a long time. Certain conventions have been adopted over the years, some of which facilitate analysis, and some of which have outlived their usefulness.

Cash-flow projections are made on a periodic basis. The length of the period is an arbitrary decision and can be varied without significant impact on the outcome of the analysis. Twelve months is the period conventionally chosen, and there is no sound reason to deviate from this established practice. Semiannual, quarterly, monthly, or even daily forecasts could just as well be used, but this would contribute little, if anything, to the analysis and would greatly complicate interpretation and communication.

A less benign convention is something called *stabilizing* the forecast. This is a process of adjusting, or smoothing, projections so that cash-flow figures become a "typical" cash flow for a "typical" period. The motivation is to facilitate discounting. There was perhaps some justification for such expediency before the advent of computers and inexpensive, high-speed handheld calculators. No more. The additional precision involved in discounting uneven cash-flow forecasts certainly justifies the slight additional calculational effort involved.

Ready access to high-speed computers renders the question of whether to use uneven cash flows in the discounting process a nonissue. The computer can handle uneven cash flows as readily and easily as even flows. Reliance on handheld calculators makes uneven cash flows only slightly more bothersome. The bother is certainly justified in view of the significantly different annual after-tax cash flows resulting from the application of current tax law.

All receipts and disbursements are conventionally treated as having been made at the end of each period. This facilitates analysis by making possible the use of standard present-value tables in which the assumption is incorporated. Alternative assumptions about the pattern of receipts and disbursements, while more realistic, do not substantially alter the outcome of analysis, as reflected in the discounted present value of the forecasted cash flows.

Gross Income

Estimating gross income for the projection period is the first step in forecasting net cash flows. There are actually two "gross incomes" to be projected. The first, potential gross, is adjusted for vacancies and bad-debt losses, and for expected income from other sources, to arrive at effective gross income.

As explained earlier, potential gross income is that which would result from 100 percent occupancy at market rental rates. If, however, the property is currently under a long-term lease, contract rent should be used rather than market rent. *Market rent* is defined as that which the real estate would most probably command if placed on the market during the period for which the forecast is being made. *Contract rent*, in contrast, is the rent actually being paid by tenants in possession.

If the recent history of the property is to be used as a basis for estimating current gross income, at least 3 years of experience is required so that a trend can be established. If good reliable data for several additional years are available, the analyst is doubly blessed.

Such information, however, is generally not to be had. Even when it is available, it is seldom reliable. It should always be viewed with suspicion. If the current or recent owner of a property has something to gain by overstating the rental record, it must be assumed that he will do so. Therefore, all such data should be considered of doubtful validity until its reasonableness is verified by reference to rents on comparable properties.

Market rental inference by reference to comparable properties requires access to information on other properties providing the same services and amenities as the property under analysis. Locational influences and other major market factors must be approximately equal. Unit rental rates of comparables may then provide a guide for estimating the current market rental for this type of property.

Time and budget constraints place practical limits on the number of comparable properties about which information is gathered. The greater the number of properties included in a sample, and the more truly "comparable" they are, the more reliable will be the resultant estimate of market rental value.

Because real estate included in a sample of comparable properties will seldom correspond exactly in size and amenities with the property under analysis, some common unit of measurement must be employed to make rental rates more directly applicable. This can be done by expressing rents in a common denominator, such as dollars per room, per apartment, or per square foot.

Example 3-1 illustrates use of a small sample of comparables to estimate the market rate of rent attributable to a property under analysis. The date from this example will be carried over and used as a continuing illustration of many of the principles expounded in later chapters.

Example 3-1: The property to be analyzed is a forty-eight–unit apartment building containing twenty two-bedroom units, each having 900 square feet of living area; twenty one-bedroom units, each containing 650 square feet of living area; and 8 studio-type units, each with 500 square feet of living space.

Management permits inspection of the rental role for the past 3 years, which reveals the following:

	Rental Rates and Vacancies		
	Two Bedroom	*One Bedroom*	*Studio*
Latest 12-month period:			
Monthly rent	$250	$205	$160
Vacant units	None	1	2
Previous 12-month period:			
Monthly rent	$235	$200	$160
Vacant units	1	2	2
Earliest 12-month period:			
Monthly rent	$215	$190	$150
Vacant units	1	2	3

Inspection of the rental role also reveals that some tenants are on 24-month leases, some on 12-month leases, and some rent on a month-to-month basis. Most month-to-month tenants are in studio-type apartments. Further complicating matters, a variety of terms have been available to tenants. Some received special decorating allowances as an inducement to sign a lease. Others received special parking-fee concessions. The concessions seem to be related to periods when vacancy rates were particularly high, but this is impossible to verify because management refuses to confirm the concessions reported by tenants.

There are in the neighborhood several apartment complexes offering comparable accomodations. Services provided are essentially the same as those at the property being analyzed.

Data on comparable units have been obtained from a property-management firm having no interest in the property under analysis and is judged to be reliable. The data are as follows:

Comparable A has a total of fifty units. Thirty-five two-bedroom units with 890 square feet of living area rent for $240 per month. Ten single-bedroom units with 625 square feet rent for $180 per month. Five studios with 500 square feet rent for $155 per month. Currently, one two-bedroom unit and three studios are vacant. All the one-bedroom units are under lease.

Comparable B has fifteen two-bedroom units, fifteen one-bedroom units, and seven studio units. The two-bedroom apartments have 925 square feet of living area and rent for $260. The one-bedroom units have 650 square feet of living area and rent for $200. The studios have 510 square feet and rent for $160. There are currently two vacant one-bedroom units and three vacant studios. All the two-bedroom units are currently occupied.

Comparable C consists of seventy-two units, of which forty-five are two-bedroom units and fifteen are one-bedroom units. The remaining twelve units are studios. The two-bedroom units have 870 square feet of living area and rent for $235. The one-bedroom units have 630 square feet of living area and rent for $190. The studios, which have 495 square feet of living are, rent for $150. The complex currently has one vacant two-bedroom unit and three vacant studios. All the single-bedroom units are rented.

Comparable D has twenty two-bedroom units, twenty-five one-bedroom units, and fifteen studios. The two-bedroom units have 895 square feet of living area and rent for $245. The one-bedroom units have 655 square feet of living area and rent for $200. The studios rent for $165 and have 550 square feet of living area. There are two vacant one-bedroom and two vacant studio apartments.

The analyst notes that all the units in the comparable properties have only one bath, and all have a kitchen-dining room combination rather than a formal dining room. This conforms to the observed facilities in the property being analyzed.

To facilitate comparison and analysis, gross rental and vacancy data on comparable apartment buildings in example 3–1 are arrayed according to type of rental unit. The results are shown in tables 3–1 and 3–2.

Based on the data from the comparables, as arranged in tables 3–1 and 3–2, potential gross rent and estimated vacancy rates for the forty-eight-unit apartment building are estimated as indicated in table 3–3. The esti-

Table 3–1

Derivation of Market Rental Rates on Properties Comparable to Forty-Eight–Unit Apartment Building

	Comparable Property			
	A	B	C	D
Two-bedroom units				
Monthly rental	$240	$260	$235	$245
Square feet	890	925	870	895
Rental per square foot per month	$.27	$.28	$.27	$.27
One-bedroom units				
Monthly rental	$180	$200	$190	$200
Square feet	625	650	630	655
Rent per square foot per month	$.29	$.31	$.30	$.31
Studio units				
Monthly rental	$155	$160	$150	$165
Square feet	500	510	495	550
Rent per square foot per month	$.31	$.31	$.30	$.30

Table 3–2

Derivation of Vacancy Factors on Properties Comparable to Forty-Eight–Unit Apartment Building

	Comparable Property				
	A	B	C	D	"Market"
Two-bedroom units					
Number	35	15	45	20	115
Vacancies	1	0	1	0	2
Percent vacant	2.9%	0	2.2%	0	1.7%
One-bedroom units					
Number	10	15	15	25	65
Vacancies	0	2	0	2	4
Percent vacant	0	13.3%	0	8.0%	6.2%
Studio units					
Number	5	7	12	15	39
Vacancies	3	3	3	2	11
Percent vacant	60%	42.9%	25%	13.3%	28.2%

mates are taken from a very small sample and therefore contain a large margin of error. Ideally, a much larger sample would be used, which would permit application of formal statistical sampling techniques. But a larger sample often will be either unavailable or prohibitively expensive. Analysts

Table 3-3
Estimated Potential Rent and Vacancy Rates for Forty-Eight-Unit Apartment Building

Estimated Potential Gross Rent

	"Market" Value per Square Foot		Square Feet per Unit		Rental Value per Unit
Monthly potential gross rent					
Two-bedroom units	$.27	×	900	=	$243
One-bedroom units	.30	×	650	=	195
Studio units	.30	×	500	=	150
Annual potential gross rent					
Two-bedroom units	(20 units x $243 × 12)				$ 58,320
One-bedroom units	(20 units x $195 × 12)				46,800
Studio units	(8 units x $150 × 12)				14,400
Total potential gross rental revenue					$119,520

Estimated Vacancy Factor

	Potential Gross Rent		"Market" Vacancy Rate		Vacancy Loss Estimate
Two-bedroom units	$58,320	×	1.7%	=	$ 991
One-bedroom units	46,800	×	6.2%	=	$2,901
Studio units	14,400	×	28.2%	=	$4,061
Total rental loss estimate					$7,953
Vacancy loss as percent of potential gross					6.7%

must at all times weigh the relative benefits and costs of obtaining a marginally higher degree of accuracy in their estimates.

Where vacancy loss estimates are drawn from a very small sample, as in example 3-1, they cannot be unquestioningly applied. An unusually high rate in one of the comparable properties will have a disproportionate impact on the average for the sample. The vacancy rate in the nonconforming comparable, however, may be an aberration caused by some temporary problem with the property, or by imcompetent management, or by some other unusual influence not reasonably expected to be present in the property being analyzed.

If the experience of the subject property for recent years closely approximates estimates derived from a sample of comparables, this serves to more nearly validate the data in the sample. If the experience of the property being evaluated reflects a more favorable vacancy record than that suggested by the market sample, however, prudence dictates placing greater weight on the market indicator than on records of the property.

If a larger sample of comparable vacancy records can be collected, this provides a much more reliable estimate of standards applicable to the market. Such data are often available from local property-management firms, brokers, appraisers, and property owners. In larger metropolitan areas, the results of reasonably current market surveys by lenders or professional research groups are occasionally available.

For large properties, and for those of a specialized nature, such as major hotels, resort properties, and large office buildings, professional trade associations often publish standards that are helpful indicators of the reasonableness of the reported experience of the subject properties.

Operating-Expense Estimates

As with gross income, the most appropriate starting point for estimating operating expenses is the experience of the subject property. At least 3 years of historical data are needed to establish a trend. Continue to keep in mind that all data from the subject property are suspect if the current owner has a vested interest in overstating gross revenue and understating operating expenses.

Revising the Owner's Operating Statement

An early step in evaluating reported operating results is to convert the owner's or manager's statement into a more useful format. Example 3-2 presents a statement one might receive from existing owners or managers. Such a statement is typically prepared for accounting purposes, with an eye to satisfying record-keeping requirements of the Internal Revenue Service. It is thus likely to be based on different concepts of revenue and expenses from those used in investment analysis.

The owner's statement in example 3-2 includes only the rent actually received, with no reference to potential gross rental income and offsetting allowances for vacancy and income losses. To form a basis for forecasting, these additional data must be included in the current statement. Revising the statement to reflect the potential gross from example 3-1, with attendant provision for vacancy and rent losses, yields the effective gross income reflected in table 3-4.

Example 3-2: The owner of the forty-eight-unit apartment under analysis in example 3-1 provides the following statement of his most recent annual operating results:

Apartment Owner's Income Statement
for Year Ended June 30, 19--

Total receipts:
Rent receipts		$118,260
Parking and concession income		1,800
Total receipts		$120,060

Expenses:
Management fee (at 5 percent)	$5,913	
Salary expenses	9,500	
Utilities	4,500	
Insurance	9,600	
Supplies	750	
Advertising	195	
Maintenance and repairs	12,300	
Mortgage payments	38,780	
Depreciation expense	12,200	$ 93,738
Net income for the year		$ 26,322

Questioning the owner about the maintenance and repair charge in his statement reveals that it includes $8,580 for replacement of several refrigerators. The balance of $3,720 seems rather low for a building of this size and age. Further inquiry reveals that the owner keeps costs down by doing much of the repair and maintenance work himself. Comparison with similar buildings in the area suggests that a proper maintenance and repair charge, including all routine costs, but excluding replacements and major repair items, is approximately $10,000.

Investigating the need for a replacement reserve, the analyst determines that the only major appliances provided by the landlord are refrigerators and ranges. These cost approximately $250 (for refrigerators) and $180 (for tabletop ranges). An Appropriate replacement reserve, assuming an average life of 8 years for refrigerators and 12 years for ranges, is

Refrigerators ($250/8 × 48)	$1500
Stoves ($180/12 × 48)	720
Annual reserve deposit	$2220

The other operating-expense items appear reasonable for the building, based on the experience of comparable properties. Revised operating

Table 3–4

Reconstructed Operating Statement for Forty-Eight-Unit Apartment Building

Potential gross income		$119,520
Less: Allowance for vacancy and rent loss		
(at 6.7 percent)		7,953
		$111,567
Plus: Other income		1,800
Effective gross income		$113,367
Less: Operating expenses:		
Management fee (at 5 percent)	$ 5,580	
Salary expenses	9,500	
Utilities	4,500	
Insurance	9,600	
Supplies	750	
Advertising	195	
Maintenance and repairs	10,000	
Replacement reserve	2,220	$ 42,345
Net operating income (annual)		$ 71,022

expenses total $42,345. These items, along with resultant revised net operating income, are illustrated in table 3–4.

An alternative approach to estimating operating expenses, and one frequently employed when adequate reliable data are not otherwise available, is to use a "typical" operating-expense ratio. For many smaller properties, particularly those which are owner-operated, there simply are no reliable records of actual expenses. In such cases, analysts assume expenses have the same relationship to potential gross as have expenses of similar properties in the locality. If the ratio is derived from a substantial sample of comparables, the resulting expense estimate is more useful than one drawn from the actual experience of the property, since it includes a measure of variance which can be used for analysis of risk, a topic introduced in a later section of the book.

A major advantage of the "typical ratio" approach is that it eliminates the effect of current management as a variable in projected operating results. Since actual experience reflects the relative effectiveness of management as well as market factors and the physical condition of the building, use of actual historical cost data requires adjustment for atypical management influences. In most cases, the new owner will not inherit the old management structure. We have a distinct preference for use of "typical ratios," carefully constructed to reflect market conditions, stratified for type, size, and age of property, and modified to reflect any nonconforming aspect of the property under analysis.

Estimating Nonoperating Cash Flows

After estimating net operating income for a property, the analyst must estimate the first year's nonoperating cash flows. These generally consist entirely of debt-service payments and income tax consequences.

However, on occasion there will be additional items of nonoperating cash receipts and disbursements. Examples include additional expenditures for capital improvements, for cure of deferred maintenance, and for back property taxes. They might also include cash inflows from projected partial dispositions.

The amount of forecast annual cash expenditure for debt service depends on the availability and cost of borrowed funds and on the client's projected use of such funds. Having arrived at an estimate of the interest rate and amortization period currently effective in the mortgage-loan market, and having determined the extent to which the client intends to use available mortgage funds, the application of standard mortgage amortization tables to determine the projected debt service obligation is a simple mechanical process. It is explained fully in chapter 5.

Estimating the income tax consequences associated with an investment proposal is a complicated issue that requires extensive information about the investor's expected taxable income and other investments, as well as additional data too extensive for inclusion at this point. Income tax factors are explored more fully in chapter 6.

The Uncertain Nature of Future Cash Flows

Current cash-flow expectations are but the first step in analyzing an investment opportunity. Similar forecasts must be made for each year of the proposed ownership period. Only then can the total quantity, timing, and certainty of expected cash-flow consequences be evaluated.

Estimating problems are multiplied many times over when the forecast is pushed further into the future. Without some systematic procedure, the uncertainty surrounding the future of an investment opportunity would form an impenetrable haze in which the most astute analyst would become lost.

Estimating future effective gross income creates the most vexing problems in any projection extending over several years. The other items of cash flow—operating expenses, debt service, and income tax obligations—present a much less troublesome problem. This chapter discusses only these latter issues, leaving the more difficult problem of income forecasts for chapter 4.

Forecasting Operating Expenses

Having estimated operating expenses for a single year, a forecast for a number of additional years usually involves little more than including an inflation factor and "guessing" whether management will face some extraordinary expense such as major salary increases.

Were generating an accurate inflation factor as simple as the previous paragraph implies, many well-paid economists would become unemployed overnight. Indeed, the most often demonstrated characteristic of inflation is its unpredictability.

Two factors act to mitigate the seriousness of this problem. The first is that the analyst need not be extremely precise. Having estimated an inflation factor of 6 percent when the appropriate factor proves to be 7, for example, will seldom have fatal consequences on the usefulness of the analyst's recommendation. The second mitigating factor is that any misstatement of the inflation rate with respect to expenses is likely to be offset by an equally great misstatement of the rate applicable to rental revenue and terminal market value of the property. In practice, analysts generally rely on published estimates from sources recognized as authorative.

Forecasting Nonoperating Cash Flows

Debt service and income taxes are the two most common elements of non-operating cash flows. The debt–service element remains constant from the time a property is acquired until it is either disposed of or refinanced.[2]

Income tax estimates are somewhat less tractable than estimates of debt service. The major complication involves determining the proper marginal tax rate to be applied to taxable income from the property. This, in turn, depends on what happens both to the tax laws and to the client's taxable income from other sources. Frequently, the best an analyst can do is to state his assumptions at the time of the forecast and to note the impact of error in the assumptions.

Projecting Effective Gross Income

The preceding issues pale into insignificance when compared with the problem of projecting rental income over a number of years. This estimate requires knowledge of trends already established in the neighborhood and of their likely influence on the relative desirability of rental space in the future. It requires, also, an estimate of future additions and subtractions in the number of competing rental units, and of changes in the population making up the appropriate market segment. These issues are the subject of the next chapter.

Summary

Real estate ownership has investment value only because it confers the right to receive anticipated future cash flows from the property. Investment decisions require a forecast of the amount and timing of anticipated cash flows, and the degree of certainty attached to the forecast.

The starting point for cash-flow forecasts is the current operating statement. Because reliable information on the operating history of a property is seldom available, it becomes necessary to generate estimates from indirect sources. Data are gathered from the experience of the property itself, from the experience of comparable properties, and from aggregate statistics generated by various financial institutions and trade groups.

After-tax cash flows accruing to ownership are the aim of the analysis. Estimates are needed of the likely operating outcome for each year of the prospective ownership period. The first step is to forecast rental revenue and miscellaneous other income. Forecasted operating expenses are subtracted therefrom to arrive at forecasted net operating income. From net operating income there is subtracted an estimate of cash expenditures to service mortgage indebtedness and to satisfy income tax obligations arising from the investment. In many instances, there will actually be a net income tax *benefit* during the early years of ownership. If such benefits are forecast, the amount of the benefit is added to forecast net operating income. The bottom line is the forecast of net cash flow to the equity position.

Sources of intelligence for forecasting gross rental revenue and operating expenses include both the experience of the property under analysis and that of comparable properties. Data from the property being analyzed must be confirmed from a reliable source. Data from comparables must be adjusted for noncomparable factors.

Notes

1. While depreciation is not included by analysts as an operating expense, it is recognized as a tax-deductible item in calculating the income tax obligation arising from a venture. Analysts do recognize the depreciation allowance, therefore, but do not include it as a cash-flow item in itself.

Many legislators share the view of investment analysts in their description of depreciation allowances as "artificial accounting losses."

2. The advent of variable-rate mortgages will introduce new complications if extended to financing of investment properties. Secondary financing or planned refinancing also presents forecasting complications.

4 Forecasting Revenue in an Uncertain Future

Forecasting cash flows for future periods is a far more complex task than merely calculating a property's present ability to generate such flows. The current operating statement, as explained in the previous chapter, is only a starting point for developing the information critical to all investment decisions: the ability of the property to generate net cash flows over the prospective holding period.

Chapter 3 addresses the issue of estimating current earning potential of a property. It also explains that the most uncertain aspect of cash-flow forecasting is the estimate of a property's ability to command rent over the projection period. Other dimensions of the forecast—expenses, debt service, and income taxes—are far more precisely predictable than is effective gross income.

This chapter discusses major determinants of a property's ability to generate rental revenue in the future. Location factors dominate all other considerations. Important locational considerations include both the desirability of the location as perceived by potential space users and the degree and strength of associated monopoly elements. Secondary determinants include the existence and physical condition of amenities provided by the physical structure. This chapter addresses the problem of anticipating future levels and direction of change in these key variables.

The Basis for Gross-Income Forecasts

Factors influencing a property's ability to command rent include both the desirability of the space being offered and the desirability and price of competing space. Future changes in these same factors determine the ability of a property to continue generating rental income. Gross rent forecasts must therefore, start with an estimate of the movement of these causal factors over the projection period.

Quality, or desirability, of space refers to the availability of those amenities desired by present or prospective tenants and to the physical condition of the property. The more nearly a property contains all the amenities generally desired by prospective tenants, the greater will be its marketability and the better it will be able to compete with similar properties in the same market.

Property location in relation to the desires of tenant groups to whom

47

the property is to be marketed is a prime factor in a property's ability to command rent. Because location is fixed, economic and social trends in the neighborhood have a strong impact on a property's marketability as rental space. A forecast of gross rental revenue, therefore, must also include an estimate of the ability of the neighborhood to retain its attractiveness over the projection period.

Physical features can be altered through time at the discretion of management, but locational elements are less amenable to manipulation and control. Yet location is a major factor in the ability of a property to command rent. Locational factors include the economic and social status of the immediate neighborhood, ease of access to closely linked activities, and the prestige of the specific site. Gross rent forecasts must include an estimate of the direction and rate of change in these key locational variables.

Because availability and cost of substitutes are strong influences on the market value of rental space, the nature of the competition, both present and potential, must be thoroughly analyzed. This requires consideration not only of existing properties catering to the same clientele, but the potential for additions to the existing stock during the projection period. Relevant factors include availability of properly zoned building sites, likelihood of significant zoning changes, and probable cost and availability of construction loans.

Beyond the question of availability of competing space, future revenues depend on the relative degree of prestige associated with a property. The physical amenities and locational convenience of New York's Rockefeller Center are not appreciably greater than those of surrounding properties, yet the center commands premium rents. The distinction lies solely in the perception of space–time consumers who desire indentification with this specific address. Economists refer to this as a *monopoly element.* Marketing specialists prefer the more neutral term *product differentiation.*

Reviewing briefly the discussion from chapter 2, remember that owners of rental property sell the right to occupy a three–dimensional space for a specified time period. As a matter of semantic convenience, their product is called space–time.

Chapter 2 also develops the concept of *utility*, or want–satisfying power, as the basis of demand for space–time. In the final analysis, the market value of any product, including space–time, depends on its ability to generate utility and its relative scarcity. Scarcity, in turn, depends on subtractions from and additions to the total supply of the good.

Productivity and the Demand for Space–Time

Forecasting the ability of property to generate rental revenue is in reality a process of estimating the market value of space–time at a particular location, incorporating a specific set ot physical amenities. The price space-time can command is in turn based on its capacity to provide utility for the user and the relative scarcity of competitive properties.

Ability to provide utility is called the *productivity* of a property. Productivity depends on both natural and man-made features of the space and on its location on the urban landscape. Productivity elements may be classified as *physical characteristics* and *locational characteristics*. Some authorities include a classification called *transfer characteristics*, but these are subsumed by the more inclusive term, *locational characteristics*.[1]

Physical Characteristics

Physical characteristics are those which affect the efficiency with which a site can be used for its intended purpose. They may be either natural or man-made. They include such considerations as makeup of the soil, drainage, subsoil minerals, and so forth. They also include man-made improvements such as sewers, landscaping, buildings, and roads. Because almost all productive land has been improved in some fashion, sites can be accurately described as a manufactured product.

Limited useful life is an important aspect of almost all physical characteristics. As the usefulness of these characteristics wanes with the passing of time, a property becomes less desirable to potential users, in comparison with other newer or better maintained properties. This inexorable decline in competitive posture must be carefully estimated if a reasonably accurate projection of effective gross income is to be made.

Analytically, the impact of physical characteristics may be considered in two separate categories: functional efficiency and durability.

Functional Efficiency

How well a structure does its intended job is the acid test of *functional efficiency*. Because the very concept of functional efficiency is related to use, it can be judged only in that context. Houses are tested against the requirements of modern family lifestyles, factories against the demands of contemporary manufacturing technology, and so on.

As structures become less able to meet current standards of acceptability and less able to render intended services, they generally experience a corresponding diminution in ability to command previous levels of rent and may experience increased vacancy rates. This decline in acceptability resulting from defective or dated design or engineering characteristics is called *functional obsolescence*. At the extreme, it may result in a succession of uses or abandonment.

Functional absolescence is an inherent characteristic of structures. It is a consequence of continual evolution of social, business, and industrial life and concomitant changes in the desired functional form of the buildings housing these activities. It reflects the perception of potential users regarding actual versus ideal layout, space, structural specifications, and amenities which contribute to productive capacity.

Examples are readily available. Recent trends in family lifestyles have resulted in a preference for residences with large, well-equipped family rooms and the capacity to accommodate complex, power-absorbing mechanical equipment such as air conditioners, washers, and dryers. This renders many older, differently equipped residences functionally obsolescent.

In the industrial and commercial area, obsolescence has resulted from changes in manufacturing procedures, storage and shipping technology, and sales methods. Modern industrial technology favors single-story manufacturing plants, thus rendering older, multistoried facilities obsolescent. Other common items of functional inadequacy include ceilings with insufficient clearance, floors with inadequate load-bearing capacity, and unacceptably narrow spans between load-bearing walls.

Some buildings can be modified to accomodate rather drastic changes in style and technology; other structures or other changes in use might require modifications which are prohibitively expensive. This places a premium on the ability to foresee the rate and direction of change in the nature of activities for which a structure is designed. Analysts must evaluate the ease and cost of altering existing structures to accommodate potential changes required during the projection period.

Physical Durability

Analysis of a structure's *physical durability* is required for estimating how long it will continue to be productive. Structural design and the current condition of foundations, exterior walls, partitions, floors, ceilings, and roofs form a basis for evaluating a structure's durability.

Comparing the physical appearance of a building with that of other structures of approximately the same age provides some clues to inherent defects, to past abuse to which the structure may have been subjected, and to the rate at which future deterioration is likely to proceed. Some knowledge of structural design and building techniques is required to adequately evaluate physical durability. Analysts lacking this knowledge are wise to seek competent outside counsel, particularly when evaluating a vintage building.

Locational Characteristics

Urban growth both creates and destroys locational advantage. Because of the inherent characteristic of immobility, locational factors have a pervasive influence on the value of urban land. Urban complexes exist in response to the economic and social needs of inhabitants. The city's internal organization reflects these needs as they originally were and as they evolved over time. Changes in perceived needs of inhabitants cause alterations in the structure of urban space and in the value of urban locations.

Our concern is with the contribution locational factors make to real estate productivity. Location itself is a geographic phenomenon, but it has social, economic, and institutional dimensions as well.

A major aspect of the economic dimension relates to the cost of moving goods or people between sites. Any relationship between land–use activities which generates such movement is called a *linkage*. Fixity of location makes any site vulnerable to social and economic influences from surrounding properties. These environmental factors which impact on site value are called *neighborhood influences*. Governmental and social forces which limit or enhance the value of a site for a particular use are sometimes referred to as *institutional factors*.

Linkages

We live in a society characterized by economic specialization and interdependence. Activity at one site often initiates a complex set of economic and social interactions generating movement of goods or people between that and other sites. This requires transportation between sites and is called *linkage*. Linkages give rise to costs associated with overcoming the problem of spacial distance between linked activities.

A worker who commutes between home and employment creates a linkage between a residence and a workplace. Goods moving from warehouse to store or a person going from work to a restaurant for lunch are examples of important linkages. Other significant examples include movement of food products from farm to market and movement of manufactured goods from factory to consumer via retail outlets.

The costs of moving people or goods between linked sites are called *transfer costs*. Of course, if all social and economic activities which are in any way linked could take place at a single location, there would be no transfer costs. The nature of space, however, is such that this is obviously impossible. The necessary movement of people and goods through terrestrial space creates friction. Transfer costs are the costs of overcoming such friction.

Were this the only consideration, the optimal location for any social or economic activity would be that which minimizes total transfer cost. Locational choice is constrained, however, by physical characteristics of potential sites, by desirable or undesirable neighborhood influences, and by institutional arrangements. Moreover, firms compete for the more desirable sites, and those firms for which transfer costs are most significant generally can outbid other firms for the more nearly optimal locations.

Transfer costs associated with overcoming the friction of space are not always amenable to simple quantification. Those costs which represent direct outlays for vehicle operation or commercial fares can, of course, be measured directly. But transfer costs also include the value of time lost due to travel between linked sites, as well as the personal disutility of dealing with the inevitable frustrations associated with movement through urban areas. Total transfer costs per unit of time are the product of the cost per trip (measured to include both explicit and implicit costs) and the frequency of such trips.

Economists who study the impact of transfer costs are fond of demonstrating that these considerations explain the proclivity of natural resource processing firms to locate near their source of raw material, of retail outlets to locate near their customers or on major transportation arteries used by their customers, of service firms to locate adjacent to major users of the service, of labor-intensive firms to locate near major labor pools, and so on. In each instance, locational decisions represent an attempt to minimize the transfer costs associated with an industry where such costs are significant in comparison with other costs affected by a location decision.

Neighborhood Influences

Site usages which are not linked may nonetheless be attracted to proximate locations, just as linked establishments may be mutually repelled and so choose to incur substantial transfer costs in order to avoid proximity. Locational arrangements unrelated to linkage considerations may result from a number of causal factors or they may be simple historical accidents.

Two major sources of locational decisions not directly related to minimization of transfer costs are institutional constraints and neighborhood influences. The first of these represents attempts of individuals or political units to restrict certain types of activity to specified locations for reasons which are not necessarily economic (though they often are motivated in part, at least, by economic considerations). Such institutional factors are considered in a subsequent section of this chapter. The latter factor, neighborhood influences, includes a number of elements which are all related in some manner to what urban economists term *externalities.*

Externalities may be favorable and thus attract people or businesses making locational choices, or they may be unfavorable and so act as a repelling influence. The influence of externalities, or neighborhood factors, stems from real estate's long life and physical immobility. Since a firm, once established, cannot easily move to escape undesirable external factors or to capture desirable ones, the nature of neighborhood influences is a powerful factor in initial locational choice.

Favorable Externalities. Important advantages often stem from particular locations, even when no movement of people or goods is involved. These advantages, or favorable externalities, are sometimes of sufficient import to justify a location, even when significant additional transfer costs may thereby be incurred.

Special value often attaches to sites in a neighborhood considered to reflect favorably on the character of residents, for example. For many residential users, and for certain types of businesses, prestige is a powerful influence on locational choice. Thus in Chicago, a Gold Coast residential address implies a certain socioeconomic status, as does a Park Avenue address in Manhattan. For similar reasons, legal firms often desire to locate near other law firms which have achieved a high level of professional recognition, financial firms tend to seek the favorable aura of location in established financial districts, and so forth.

Favorable externalities include aesthetic considerations. For residential users, and for many commercial purposes, a pleasing view is considered particularly important. Locations adjacent to golf courses, near attractive parks, or with an impressive view of a large body of water or of the cityscape often command a premium price unrelated to the issue of transfer costs.

Unfavorable Externalities. Just as residences and business establishments are attracted by desirable neighborhood factors, so are they repelled by undesirable or incompatible conditions or activities. These objectional influences include noise, smoke, odors, and unsavory neighbors. A favorable location shields one from these objectional influences, whether by physical barriers, by distance, or by law.

Institutional Factors

Protection from unfavorable influences may be assured by the existence of physical barriers, such as a river, unbuildable terrain, or the existence of intervening compatible structures and uses. Frequently, in urban places, reliance is placed on private or public land–use–control provisions for such protection.

Private restrictions on land utilization are created by including special provisions in a deed of conveyance transfering title to land. A subdivision developer may, for example, include in all deeds of conveyance a restriction against usage thought to be incompatible with the intended purpose of the subdivision. Generally, these restrictions enhance the value of subdivision sites because potential purchasers value protection from obejctional neighborhood influences.

Increasingly residents have come to place reliance on special public land-use restrictions and other land-use-control ordinances to protect them from inharmonious or incompatible usages. These ordinances include zoning regulations, subdivision controls, and building codes, all of which are designed and intended to regulate the nature and quality of structures erected at a locality or the nature of the activities therein, or both. Public control over land use, which constitutes the exercise of the police power of the state, exerts a pervasive influence on the type and intensity of property use, and thus on its power to command rents.

A Program of Locational Analysis

Because it results from the actions of human beings in a social setting, site value can truly be said to be a manufactured product. Most site value is also incident to aggregate and largely uncoordinated socioeconomic activity. For this reason, many argue that site value is a socially created phenomenon which should not accrue to individuals solely because of their (often accidental) ownership of the land.

Site value can be destroyed as well as created by social and economic events beyond the control of the owner of the affected land. Therefore, analysts must carefully assess present and projected locational factors and their probable impact on the productivity of a site.

Careful locational analysis remains important regardless of the intended use of an urban site, but the need is amplified if a proposed use depends on anticipated changes in locational factors to enhance the profitability of the venture. Examples include speculative holding of land in the expected path of urban growth, rehabilitation of property in older neighborhoods in the expectation of imminent revival of the area or a major rehabilitation or renewal effort in an attempt to spark renewed economic growth in a stagnant downtown business district.

The first step in locational analysis is to identify the linkages which characterize existing or planned land use. The analyst then judges the relative importance of each linkage. He also locates linked establishments in terms of their geographic relationship to the site under analysis. This permits an assessment of the transfer costs associated with the proposed usage and the contribution of linkages to the potential profitability of that usage.

Determining the Linkages

Analysis of an improved property begins with a study of the activity therein to determine major geographic points with which the property has important linkages. If an alternative use is contemplated, the study assumes a hypothetical enterprise involved in the proposed activity.

Evaluating the Linkages

Not all linkages are created equal. Remember the proposition that total transfer costs include both the explicit cost of getting from one location to another plus the "cost" in terms of frustration and bother in so doing. Remember also that total cost is the product of the cost per trip and the number of trips made per period of time.

Examples of implicit costs which are difficult to quantify include the risk of children having to cross a busy highway to travel to and from school or of a housewife having to navigate an extremely disreputable neighborhood to reach the most convenient shopping center.

Futurity in Locational and Physical Analysis

Locational choice is meaningless without reference to a time element. Those factors which affect relative desirability of a site must be considered in the context of a specified use, a particular geographic location, and a specified time period. All the elements other than geographic location are in a constant state of flux. Analysis of locational desirability must therefore consider the probable future trend of change in locational factors.

Because locational factors dominate the ability of a site to produce income, investors must rely heavily on their own or an analyst's ability to interpret existing locational factors and their impact on present and future productivity. The analysis must be done in the present, but the focus is on the future. Not only are locational factors themselves subject to change, but even the importance of given factors vary through time. Forecasting the nature and the probability of these future changes is an essential step in the analysis.

An important but often overlooked aspect of properties embodying questionable physical or locational characteristics is the contribution these characteristics make to the vulnerability of the property to marginal changes in demand for space-time. Total demand in the relevant market might change only minutely during a projection period, yet the impact of the change is felt disproportionately by properties on the fringe of the market classification.

Social, technological, and economic changes often create new, or destroy old, site values. Because causal elements are diverse and interrelated, analysis of probable change in locational benefits must take into account probable future changes, not only in the factors themselves, but also in their interrelationships.

Changes in Linkages

Changes in lifestyles, patterns of business, or technology can sever existing linkages and create new ones. For example, the shift from urban to suburban living, combined with the popularity of the automobile as a private transportation mode, created linkages between communities and regional shopping centers while severing the old linkage between residential neighborhoods and the central business district.

Other examples abound. A decline in importance of public transport facilities has reduced the locational value of housing and retail stores along major public transportation arteries such as commuter railways and major bus routes. Concomitantly, mass ownership of automobiles has greatly increased the locational value of residential sites convenient to major highways. Shifting transportation patterns have diminished the locational significance of industrial sites adjacent to rail sidings, while the increased congestion of urbanization has magnified the value of industrial sites outside the central urban place yet convenient to it.

Changes within Linked Establishments

Old linkages grow less important as locational decision factors, lifestyles, or production modes reduce the value of ready access to the linked locations. Television, for example, has decreased the importance of existing linkages to community entertainment centers. Home food preservation systems have reduced the frequency of shopping trips and have weakened the need for quick and convenient access to grocery stores and restaurants.

Changes in Transportation Arteries

Modification of existing transport systems, such as the rerouting of major highways, the closing of railway spurs, or alterations in the cost and availability of parking facilities, can render an existing linkage insignificant. The construction of a bridge over a previously impassable river or the construction of a new limited–access highway can destroy the locational advantage of a site by providing ready access to the linked locations from competing sites.

In recent years, freeway construction has provided many graphic examples of unanticipated alterations in traffic patterns which have destroyed existing linkages and created new ones. The locational value of proximity to a desirable environmental factor, such as a park or beach, can be completely destroyed by having ready access severed by the creation of a controlled-access highway or by construction of an interveining railway or canal.

Changes in Neighborhood Influences

Destruction of physical barriers or the creation of previously nonexistent barriers drastically alters neighborhood influences. Removal of a railroad bed or public building complex which previously separated a highly desirable residential area from an area of decay or slum housing, for example, may foster a decline in a previously stable area. The same outcome might result from alteration of a barrier which is more psychological than physical. A small park or neighborhood shopping area, for example, might be a symbol of neighborhood solidarity and uniqueness, setting the residents apart from those in surrounding areas.

Altering the location of ancillary services such as schools or churches can have the same effect. Consolidating school districts or simply destroying the traditional linkage between place of residence and location of school attendance can result in massive and often unforeseen shifts in the relative desirability of residential neighborhoods.

Without protective zoning and building codes, inharmonious or incompatible land usage can quickly destroy the locational value of a neighborhood. Recent successful court challenges to existing zoning laws deemed to be unfairly exclusionary serve to emphasize the danger of relying on these institutional arrangements as a major element in preserving locational value.

The Supply Factor in Rental Value

Both desirability (productivity) and the relative scarcity and price of close substitutes affect the exchange value of any good or service, including space-time. Therefore, analysis of future ability to command rents must include a forecast of changes in the supply of comparable space-time during the projection period.

Demonstrably, the supply of land is far in excess of current needs. The

1970 census reports that 72.8 percent of the population occupies only 14.2 percent of the space in the United States. Moreover, more than 65 percent of the exurban space is uncultivated and available for uses other than agriculture. Clearly, there is abundant room for urban expansion.[2]

Moreover, there is adequate room for expansion at the fringes of most cities. As outer fringes expand arithmetically, the space within city boundaries expands geometrically. It is therefore true that the total supply of developable land is virtually unlimited.

What *is* limited is land well suited for specific uses. Most available undeveloped land lies on the urban fringe, but that is not the optimum location for many activities. Since only one parcel of land can occupy any particular location on the urban landscape, the supply of land with specific site characteristics is necessarily limited to one unique parcel.

Of course, while it may be true that there is "one best" location for many economic activities (because of the location of other urban economic and social activities and the unique physical characteristics of a particular site), it is equally true that there are almost always several alternative sites that are nearly as good. These substitute sites may yield slightly less total utility, but several may adequately fulfill the basic requirements for most urban economic activities.

To summarize the question of supply, sites are what economists call a *differentiated product.* That is, they have some characteristics which differentiate them from all others, but the differences are generally not so great that several slightly different sites will not serve *almost* as well. The choice between the ideal site and a close substitute will be made by potential users based on the relative market values of the sites and the relative present values of the anticipated future flow of benefits from their use.

Futurity in Supply Analysis

Were it possible to actually plot demand and supply relations as depicted by economists' graphs, analysts would live a less stressful, if also less interesting, life. Although the illustrations from chapter 2, in their entirety, cannot be constructed with real-life numbers, they nevertheless provide valuable information about the behavior of markets.

There must be some level of vacancies to provide an inventory of rentable space. Imperfect information makes it impossible for all space to be rented at all times at market-clearing prices. Orderly functioning of markets in the face of imperfect information requires an inventory to compensate for this imperfection.

When vacancy rates drop significantly below the historical average (that which experience has demonstrated generally prevails in the market), it is safe to infer that there is "excess demand" at currently prevailing prices. The price level for space-time can then be expected to move upward toward a new equilibrium over the short run. Conversely, when vacancy rates are running significantly above "normal", there is insufficient demand for available space. This suggests a moderation in prices until demand shifts sufficiently to absorb the available supply.[3]

Having estimated the *current* relationship between demand for space-time and the available supply, the analyst faces the task of forecasting changes in this relationship over the time period he contemplates the investor will be holding the property. This requires estimating the possible impact additional units of rental property will have on the market value of space-time and how this will interact with shifts in the demand curve over time.

Earlier the distinction was made between short-term and longer-term supply functions. The time frame for estimating supply will be the projected holding period of the property under analysis. Thus, if the property is expected to be held for 6 to 8 years, the analyst must consider the relationship between rents and supply over this period. Toward that end, it is useful to consider the long-term supply function as a series of points on a succession of short-run functions.

Remember, at any one point in time, the supply of rental units is relatively fixed. Thus the short-run supply function will always be essentially unresponsive to changes in price. This is depicted as a vertical line on a supply graph. Between short-run time periods, however, construction will continue, so that at a later time the short-term supply function will be fixed at a greater total supply. A series of point estimates of the short-run supply function through time results in an estimate of the location of the longer-term supply function.

The starting point in estimating a long-term supply function is to observe that additional rental units will continue being produced as long as the cost of production is less than the present value of the expected stream of future rents. Supply changes, therefore, are dependent on future rates of change in construction costs, on the cost and availability of appropriately zoned land, and on developers' perceptions of the direction and rate of changes in demand.

Monopoly Element in Supply Analysis

As with other products, space-time that has a prestige image can command a premium price. In market terms, product differences—whether real or spurious—desensitize buyers to price differentials. The distinction may lie in unique architecture, quality construction, luxurious appointments, or any other element that creates a compelling image for potential space–time consumers.

Product differences which exist only in the perception of buyers are even more valuable than physical differences. Styling, quality, and functional features can often be duplicated by competitors, but reputation is unique to individual properties and is often generated consciously to appeal to a specific class of tenants. Depending on the image associated with an address, space–time may consistently command a premium price or sell at a discount from prevailing rates for properties similarly located and outfitted.

Management that successfully cultivates and protects a particular property image captures some of the monopoly advantages associated with unique location. The power of such an image to command rent is far less vulnerable to future variations in the supply of space–time.

Summary

Forecasting rental revenue is a marketing research problem. Demand at a specific location is a function of the want–satisfying power of the space–time in question, and of the price and availability of competing units of space–time offering approximately the same level of want–satisfying power. Analysts often refer to the want–satisfying power of real estate as *productivity*.

Real estate productivity depends on both physical and locational characteristics. *Physical characteristics* include both geological features and man–made improvements. *Locational characteristics* relate to how well a location is suited for its intended use.

Desirability of physical characteristics varies over time because of changes in the physical characteristics themselves and because of altered needs or tastes on the part of space–time consumers. As improvements age, they become less suitable as a result of a decline in their attractiveness and increased maintenance costs. Technological innovation or variation in style and tastes may render existing physical characteristics less desirable than before, even when the characteristics themselves have remained virtually unaltered.

Locational desirability depends on the nature of *linkages,* on *neighborhood influences*, and on *institutional factors*. Linkages are relationships which require movement of goods or people between properties. Linkages result in *transfer costs*. The greater the transfer costs relative to total costs associated with an intended use, the greater the importance of choosing a site which minimizes transfer costs. These include both explicit costs of transportation and implicit costs, such as the value of time spent in transit and the bother and frustration of providing for transportation.

A location might be subject to either desirable or undesirable neighborhood influences. Whether a particular influence is considered malignant or benign varies with intended property use. Such influences are particularly important from the perspective of a property owner, since the immobility of his assets prohibits moving to escape the influence of neighborhood factors.

Private and governmental restrictions on land use are called institutional factors. They include contractual agreements between parties, such as those agreements often found in deeds of conveyance which prohibit certain site uses or require specific actions. In addition, they include government regulations such as zoning ordinances, building codes, fire regulations, and other federal and state statutes and local ordinances impinging on an owner's freedom to determine the use of his property.

Revenue forecasts involve estimating both demand for and supply of a particular class of space-time during the forecast period. This in turn requires estimating probable changes in site linkages, in neighborhood influences, and in institutional factors influencing either demand or supply. The supply factor is less troublesome if a property embodies significant monopoly elements. Monopoly elements may result from unique physical or locational factors, or they may exist only in the perception of potential consumers of space-time.

Notes

1. This entire chapter, including the terminology, is based on my interpretation of the writings of Richard U. Ratcliff. I most emphatically acknowledge my intellectual debt. I, of course, bear sole responsibility for the interpretation, including my errors or heresies. For a more lengthy exposition of these ideas, and for introduction to a most rewarding and innovative original source, read Ratcliff's own work, with special attention to *Real Estate Analysis* (New York: McGraw-Hill, 1961).

2. U.S. Bureau of the Census, *Statistical Abstract of the United States* (Washington: U.S. Government Printing Office, 1977).

3. Classical demand and supply analysis leads to the expectation of a drop in prices (rents) under these circumstances. In real life, prices tend to be "sticky" on the downside. Suppliers resist reductions in rents in the expectation of better opportunities in the future. Reductions which do occur are often hidden in the form of rent concessions which are not apparent to the casual observer. Close investigation is necessary to determine whether market rents are actually less than that suggested by current contract rates because of the existence of widespread rent concessions.

5 Financial Leverage and the Investment Decision

Because real estate is characterized by relatively large economic size, investors have traditionally relied on third-party financial institutions for a significant portion of the funds required for investment. Control of large parcels of real property is difficult to achieve without access to borrowed funds, which have, consequently, become a ubiquitous factor in real estate investment decisions.

Outside financing is generally desirable even where not absolutely necessary. Investors can, by extensive use of such funds, control more projects with the same total personal financial commitment. Spreading personal resources over several projects in this manner reduces the risk of catastrophy caused by local and unforeseen developments. The principle of diversification to reduce aggregate risk is widely recognized as valid and is a major factor in informed investment decisions.

In addition to reducing aggregate risk, third-party financing can amplify the rate of return on equity funds. This strategy can greatly magnify an investor's rate of return, although it may also significantly increase the financial risk associated with an investment position.[1]

Federal and state income tax laws have contributed greatly to the attractiveness of using borrowed funds. Interest payments are generally deductible from taxable income on a dollar-for-dollar basis. That is, one dollar of interest reduces taxable income by one dollar. But a gain on property disposal is generally taxed at a more favorable capital gains rate.

Also, investors are allowed a deduction from taxable income for an estimate of the wearing away of their investment in the improvements to real estate, whether or not any actual reduction in market value is evident. This allowance—called depreciation—is based on the total purchase price of a property, without reference to the source of funds used for acquisition.

Nature and Consequences of Financial Leverage

Financial leverage refers to the use of borrowed funds to finance an equity position. The greater the ratio of borrowed funds to equity, the greater is the degree of financial leverage employed. So long as the rate of return on assets exceeds the cost of borrowing, leverage increases return on equity funds. The difference between the rate of return on assets and the cost of

63

borrowing is often called the *spread.* Because of the typically high portion of invested funds acquired by borrowing (high leverage), even a small favorable spread greatly magnifies return on equity. This much-desired outcome is termed *favorable financial leverage.*

That leverage can "cut both ways" is more than a mere truism: it is an issue critical to investment survival. When the cost of borrowing exceeds the rate of return on assets, the spread is negative, and financial leverage is said to be unfavorable. In a highly leveraged real estate investment, even a small negative spread (unfavorable leverage) can result in a negative rate of return to the equity position.

Measures of Financial Leverage

A frequently used indication of financial leverage is the relationship between equity investment and total market value of assets acquired. This may be expressed as a ratio between debt and equity or between debt and total value. The *debt-to-equity ratio* is commonly used in corporate finance. For historical reasons having more to do with the origin of terminology than with its current use, a more common measure of this relationship in real estate circles is the *loan-to-value ratio.*

The loan-to-value ratio was initially developed as a tool of analysis for mortgage lenders. It provides them with information on potential loss if a mortgage note results in default and foreclosure. Foreclosure in most states is by sale to the highest bidder. Should the winning bid be less than the amount of the outstanding loan (plus administrative costs associated with the foreclosure sale), the lender is unlikely to recover the remaining balance. Expressing loans as a percentage of a property's market value provides some indication of risk of loss in the event of foreclosure.

From an investor's perspective, loan-to-value ratios serve an entirely different function. They provide a measure of the dollar amount of real estate which can be controlled with a given amount of equity funds. If, for example, the available loan-to-value ratio is 0.75, then the investor can control $1/(1 - 0.75)$, or \$4 of real estate for every \$1 of equity funds invested.

While leverage can amplify potential return to the equity position, it also magnifies risk. Greater leverage increases the portion of anticipated net operating income required to meet the debt-service obligation. Thus, if actual income is significantly below the amount anticipated, there is a possibility that it will be insufficient even to cover debt service. The greater the amount of financial leverage employed (and so the greater the required debt service), the greater is the risk that equity investors will have either to invest additional funds or default on a mortgage note.

Risk that cash flow from investments will be insufficient to service mortgage debt is called *financial risk*. It is a direct consequence of employing financial leverage. A useful measure of this relationship is the *debt-coverage ratio*, which relates cash flow before debt service to the amount of associated debt service. This ratio provides an indication of the extent to which actual cash flow can fall below the forecast amount before becoming insufficient to service mortgage debt.

The debt-to-equity ratio in example 5-1 is $750,000 to $250,000, or 3 to 1. This expresses the fact that an investor can borrow $3 for every $1 of equity funds invested. The loan-to-value ratio ($750,000 to $1 million = 0.75, or 75 percent) expresses the fact that, in the event of immediate default, the property could sell for as much as 25 percent below its current value before the lender would suffer a significant loss. It also can be used to express the observation that a borrower can control $4 of real estate for every $1 of equity funds invested.

The debt-coverage ratio in example 5-1 is 2.16, calculated by dividing the net operating income ($175,000) by the annual debt-service requirement (12 × $6,748 = $80,976). This expresses an expectation that annual cash flow before debt service will be slightly more than twice that required to service the debt. It indicates a substantial cushion for underestimated expenses or overestimated revenues before actual net operating income falls below that required to service the mortgage indebtedness.

Effect of Financial Leverage

The dramatic impact of financial leverage on both risk and expected return can be illustrated by further reference to example 5-1. In that example, cash flow before debt service is 17.5 percent of the market value of the property. This total amount flows through to the equity investors if they elect to use no financial leverage. In that case, their equity investment will be $1 million, and they will expect to receive $175,000 per annum before income taxes.

But as a consequence of the decision to borrow $750,000, not all of the $175,000 of net operating income accrues to the equity position. Of this

---

Example 5-1: A property with a market value of $1 million is expected to generate net operating income of $175,000 per annum. There is available a $750,000 note calling for level monthly payments of $6,748 for 20 years, including both principal and interest (interest at 9 percent).

amount, $80,976 is remitted to the mortgage lender. Only the balance of $94,024 is available to equity investors.

If the investors can achieve even greater financial leverage, this will, of course, reduce both the required equity investment and the cash flow to the equity position. To illustrate the principle, assume that there is also available an 80 percent loan ($800,000) on the investment in example 5-1. This loan would be for the same period and at the same interest rate as the lesser loan set forth in the body of the example. The monthly debt service would be $7,180, and the annual debt service would be 12 times this amount, or $86,160. Thus the cash flow to the equity position would be reduced to $88,840, while the equity investment would be reduced to $200,000. The impact on cash flow to the equity position, expressed as a percent of the initial equity investment, is illustrated on table 5-1.

What conclusion can be drawn from the data in table 5-1? The fundamental principle illustrated is that as long as the *debt-sevice constant* (the annual debt service expressed as a percentage of the amount borrowed) is less than the rate of return on total assets, additional financial leverage increases cash flow to equity, expressed as a percentage rate on the equity investment. In table 5-1, the rate of return on total assets is seen to be 17.5 percent; on the other hand, the debt-service constant is only 10.8 percent.

But the salutary effects of financial leverage are easy to overemphasize. Remember that the operating results in example 5-1 are mere *expectations*. The actual outcome might be much less attractive. If net operating income, as a percent rate of return on assets, drops below the debt-service constant, then using financial leverage will *reduce* the current return on equity.

To illustrate, consider again the data in example 5-1. The expected net operating income of $175,000 notwithstanding, assume the *actual* net operating income to be just $100,000. The consequences of having used financial leverage based on an overoptimistic cash-flow forecast are illustrated on table 5-2.

The Cost of Financial Leverage

Most mortgage loans require monthly payments designed to pay all interest currently and to retire the principal amount of the loan over a specified period. Such a loan is said to be *fully amortized*. Each payment will include interest accrued since the last preceding payment and a portion of the remaining principal balance. The principal portion of the payment is called the *amortization payment*.

While fully amortized loans generally call for monthly payments, quarterly payments are not uncommon, nor are annual payments unheard of. The point is that there is no such thing as a standard loan. Each proposal

Table 5-1

Impact of Favorable Financial Leverage on Return to Equity Position

			Expected Cash Flow to Equity	
Loan-to-Value Ratio	Expected Net Operating Income	Debt Service	Dollar Amount	Percent of Equity Investment
0	$175,000	0	$175,000	17.5%
75%	$175,000	$80,976	$ 94,024	37.6%
80%	$175,000	$86,160	$ 88,840	44.4%

Table 5-2

Impact of Variations in Net Operating Income on Cash Throw-Off from a Leveraged Investment

			Actual Cash Flow to Equity	
Loan-to-Value Ratio	Actual Net Operating Income	Debt Service	Dollar Amount	As Percent of Equity
0	$100,000	0	$100,000	10%
75%	$100,000	$80,976	$ 19,024	7.6%
80%	$100,000	$86,160	$ 13,840	6.9%

stands on its own merit, and variations are limited only by the inventiveness of the parties to the transaction.

As noted earlier, most loans are fully amortized. But partly amortized loans and term loans are sometimes employed. A *term loan* generally calls for payments of interest only during the term of the loan, with the entire principal amount becoming due and payable when the loan matures. A partly amortized loan will include some repayment of principal during the loan period, with a remaining balance due at the end. This remaining balance is called a *balloon payment.*

Determining the Debt Service

The size of the required debt service depends on the loan amount, the interest rate, and the repayment provisions. The various possibilities are best demonstrated by use of an example.

Example 5-2: A $100,000 loan with interest at 8 percent per annum requires monthly debt-service payments. The available loan provisions include

Alternative A: Level monthly payments to fully amortize the loan over 25 years.

Alternative B: Level monthly payments of principal and interest based on a 40-year amortization schedule, with the balance of the principal to be repayed after 25 years.

Alternative C: Interest only (in monthly payments) for 10 years, with the principal amount due and payable after 10 years.

To find the monthly debt service associated with Alternative A in example 5-2, turn to the amortization table in appendix D. Move down the left-hand column of the page to the row marked "25 years." Read across to the column headed by an interest rate of 8 percent. The number found at the intersection of the 25-year row and the 8 percent column is the monthly payment required to fully amortize an 8 percent loan of $1 over 25 years (.007718). The monthly payment on the $100,000 loan in example 5-2 will simply be 100,000 times this amount, or $771.80.

Alternative B in example 5-2 is an illustration of a partially amortized loan. The monthly payment over the period of the loan is $695.30, determined by reference to the factor located at the intersection of the 40-year row and the 8 percent column of the amortization table in appendix D. This factor (.006953) is multiplied by $100,000 to find the monthly payment on the note.

Since payments under Alternative B are made for only 25 years, though based on a 40-year payout, there will remain a balance due on the principal after 25 years. The amount of this *balloon payment* is the present value of an annuity for the remaining years at the contract rate of interest.

In the example, the contract rate is 8 percent. The remaining life of the payout period is 15 years (40-year payout period, less 25 years during which payments are actually made). The remaining balance (balloon) after 25 years is therefore the present value (at that point) of a 15-year annuity of $695.30 per month, discounted at 8 percent.

Annuities are explained more fully in chapter 8. For the present, simply accept that the present value of an annuity of $1 is the reciprocal of the amortization payment on a loan of $1 at the same rate of interest. The present value of a 15-year annuity of $1 per month can therefore be determined by reference to the monthly payment to retire a $1 debt over 15 years, at 8 percent. The reciprocal of the debt–service factor (1/.009557) is the present value of a \$1 annuity. Multiplying this value by the amount of the annual debt service will yield the remaining balance of the note:[2]

$$\$104.64 \times \$695.30 = \$72,752.95$$

Monthly debt–service payments on Alternative C are simply one-twelfth of the annual interest on the loan. Thus the amount is

$$(0.08/12) \times \$100,000 = \$666.67$$

Since payments are comprised entirely of accrued interest, none of the loan will have been amortized over the payment period. The remaining balance after 25 years will therefore be the entire \$100,000 face amount of the note.

The Annual Constant

Debt–service requirements are often expressed as a *debt–service constant*. The most common way of expressing the constant is as a percent of the face amount of the loan. The monthly constant associated with Alternative A in example 5–2 is

$$\$771.80/\$100,000 = .007718 \qquad \text{or} \qquad .7718 \text{ percent}$$

Alternatively, the constant may be expressed as the debt–service obligation per \$100 of indebtedness. This is nothing more than the percentage calculation expressed in dollar terms. The 0.7718 percent in the preceding calculation therefore becomes \$7.718.

The debt service may be expressed as an *annual constant* or a *monthly constant*, depending on the use to be made of the information. Since the annual constant is simply 12 times the monthly constant, the distinction is trivial.

Other Benefits of Financial Leverage

Conventional wisdom states that rational investors will not knowingly accept unfavorable financial leverage. This is demonstrably untrue. During periods of very high interest rates and rapid inflation, financial leverage, as traditionally measured, is almost certain to be unfavorable. Yet many astute investors do in fact enter into highly leveraged deals during such periods.

This seeming paradox is rooted in the conventional practice of computing rates of return on a before-tax basis and ignoring the change in market value of an asset over the holding period. Income tax effects are so pervasive that any investment calculation which ignores them is virtually useless. During periods of rapid inflation, the increase in market value over the holding period constitutes a significant portion of the expected return on investment. Intelligent investors are, of course, aware of these considerations and factor them into their calculations.

Amplifying the Tax Shelter

Federal and state income tax aspects of real estate investment, including depreciation deductions, are discussed in chapter 6. Briefly, depreciation is the decline in value or useful live of a capital asset because of wear, tear, obsolescence, or action of the elements. Federal income tax rules provide for a depreciation allowance to be offset against gross income each year, to account for the expected decline in the value or useful life of improvements to real estate.

Rules for calculating depreciation allowances vary with the type property involved, but in all instances, the initial basis for the calculation is that portion of property cost attributable to the improvements on it. Cost, however, and thus the initial basis, is not limited to equity capital invested. It includes any funds borrowed to finance the acquisition or any existing mortgage indebtedness assumed by the purchaser.

Financial leverage can, therefore, amplify the tax shelter provided by depreciation allowances. Tax savings from depreciation deductions may, in a matter of only a few years, exceed an investor's total initial cash outlay.

Example 5-3 illustrates the point. If Bucksaver makes the contemplated

---

Example 5-3: Bill Bucksaver intends to purchase a building having a market value of $100,000. Eighty percent of the value is attributable to the improvements, which are estimated to have a remaining useful life of 20 years. The property is expected to generate annual gross rental income of $23,000 and to require an annual cash outlay for tax-deductible operating expenses of $13,000. Bucksaver is in the 40 percent marginal tax bracket.

investment, his annual depreciation deduction (assuming he uses the straight-line method) will be $4,000, calculated as follows:

Total cost of property	$100,000
Less portion attributable to land (20 percent)	20,000
Basis for depreciation allowance	$ 80,000
Annual depreciation ($80,000/20 years)	$ 4,000

From the net cash flow generated in example 5-3, Bucksaver deducts the depreciation allowance to determine the impact of the investment on his taxable income. Assuming that the purchase is made on a strictly cash basis (without the use of borrowed funds), the income tax consequences of the venture will be

Gross rental income	$23,000
Less operating expenses	13,000
Net operating income	$10,000
Deduct depreciation allowance	4,000
Taxable income	$ 6,000
Times marginal income tax rate	.40
Income tax consequences	$ 2,400

After-tax cash flow from Bucksaver's investment is simply the before-tax cash flow (net operating income) minus the income tax consequences. This amounts to $7,600, calculated as follows:

Net operating income	$10,000
Less income tax consequences	2,400
After-tax cash flow	$ 7,600

All calculations so far have incorporated the assumption that the investment is made on 100 percent equity basis. That is, no financial leverage is employed. Therefore, the initial equity investment is the market value of the property—$100,000. This first year's after-tax cash flow, expressed as a rate of return on initial cash outlay, is $7,600 divided by $100,000 or 7.6 percent.

Assume now that an $80,000 loan is available with interest at 8 percent, using the real estate as security. Assume further that the loan is to be repaid in equal monthly installments over a period of 25 years. This implies a monthly debt payment of $617.44, including both principal and interest. For simplicity, assume no prepaid interest or loan fees are required. Total first-year debt service is therefore $7,409. Of this amount, approximately $6,355 represents interest on the debt, with the balance representing repayment of principal. Over the life of the loan, the portion of the payments representing interest regularly declines as the loan balance is reduced by periodic payments.

If Bucksaver borrows the $80,000, his first year's net cash flow from the investment in example 5-3 will be reduced by the amount of the annual debt service. The revised cash flow before taxes is

Gross rental income		$23,000
Less: Operating expenses	$13,000	
Debt service	7,409	20,409
Before-tax cash flow from investment		$ 2,591

Financial leverage also alters the income tax consequences of the investment. That portion of debt service attributable to payment of interest is tax deductible in the year paid. The first year's income tax consequence of the investment, if the available financial leverage is employed, is as follows:

Net operating income		$10,000
Less: Depreciation allowance	$4,000	
Interest expense	6,355	10,355
Taxable income (loss) from investment		$ (355)
Times marginal income tax rate		.40
(Tax saving) from investment, first year		$ (142)

As before, the after-tax cash flow from the investment is simply the before-tax cash flow, adjusted for income tax consequence. The first year's after-tax cash flow is $2,847, calculated as follows:

Net operating income	$10,000
Less debt service	7,409
Before-tax cash flow	$ 2,591
Add income tax saving	142
After-tax cash flow	$ 2,733

During subsequent years, the income tax consequence will increase as the portion of debt service attributable to tax-deductible interest payments declines.

Using financial leverage causes Bucksaver's after-tax cash flow to decline from $7,600 to $2,733. The initial cash outlay also decreases, however, from $100,000 to $20,000. The first year's after-tax cash flow, expressed as a percentage rate of return on the initial cash outlay, is now $2,733 divided by $20,000, or 13.7 percent. Financial leverage has almost doubled the rate of return.

The expected results of the investment in example 5-3, with and without the use of financial leverage, are summarized below:

	Without Financial Leverage	With Financial Leverage
Income tax consequence:		
Gross rental income	$23,000	$23,000
Deduct:		
Operating expenses	$13,000	$13,000
Depreciation	4,000	4,000
Interest expense	0	6,639
Taxable income (loss)	$ 6,000	$ (639)
Times tax rate	.40	.40
Tax (tax saving)	$ 2,400	$ (256)
Cash flow from investment:		
Gross rental income	$23,000	$23,000
Add tax savings	0	256
Subtotal	$23,000	$23,256
Less cash outlays:		
Operating expenses	$13,000	$13,000
Debt service	0	7,409
Income tax	2,400	0
After-tax cash flow	$ 7,600	$ 2,847
Return on initial cash outlay		
Initial cash outlay	$100,000	$20,000
First-year cash flow	7,600	2,847
Cash flow/initial outlay	7.6%	14.2%

Amplifying the Capital Gain

Provisions for accelerated depreciation allowances, as discussed in chapter 6, are somewhat anomalous in view of what generally happens to the market value of "depreciated" real estate. Instead of a decline, most real estate experiences a steady increase in value through time.

Of course, this is not a universal experience. Speculative buying sometimes drives prices in a neighborhood or other local above all reasonable indices of value. The thinking of participants in these speculative binges seems to be based on the "bigger fool" theory. Buyers knowingly pay more than the use value of a property in the expectation that they can subsequently sell at a profit to an even "bigger fool." Such speculative bubbles eventually burst. They leave the unlucky holder of the property in a sadder but wiser financial position and provide lecturers with rich anecdotal material.

Aside from such economic aberrations, the pressure of population growth and urban sprawl has made land in most parts of the United States experience a more-or-less continuous increase in value during the post-World War II period. This has been particularly true during periods of rapid monetary inflation such as we have experienced without significant relief since the latter part of the 1960s.[3]

Investors can multiply the potential gain from market appreciation by judicious use of financial leverage. Disregarding for the moment the income tax aspects of the situation, consider the case of a parcel of undeveloped land that is expected to increase in value at an average annual rate of 15 percent because of favorable locational characteristics, and note how favorable financial leverage can amplify the expected rate of return on equity.

Such a situation is illustrated in example 5–4. If Foxx makes the contemplated investment, his expected rate of return will differ significantly with the choice of available financing terms. Because the interest rate on the purchase–money mortgage is less than the expected rate of increase in the market value of the property, leverage is expected to be favorable. The expected annual rate of return on equity, calculated on a pretax basis under both of the available financing alternatives, is presented below:

	Cash Purchase	Purchase–Money Mortgage
Proceeds from sale after 5 years	$60,000	$60,000
Less balance due on note	0	36,236
Net proceeds, before tax	$60,000	$23,764
Initial cash outlay	30,000	7,500
Annual rate of return	14.9%	25.9%

The $36,236 balance due on the purchase–money note in the preceding calculation represents the value, after 5 years, of a $22,500 deposit (the face amount of the note) drawing interest at a compound rate of 10 percent per annum. The annual rates of return to Foxx (14.9 and 25.9 percent) represent compound annual growth rates which will make the initial cash outlays under each of the alternative financing arrangements equal to the net proceeds from sale after 5 years. These type of calculations are explained in more detail in chapter 8.

When income tax effects are considered, potential benefits of favorable financial leverage become even more obvious. This is so because interest on

---

Example 5–4: A tract of land situated in the most probable path of urban growth can be acquired for $30,000. Wylie Foxx, who is contemplating purchase, expects that the land will double in value during the next 5 years, at which time he would sell. During the interim, the land can be leased to a goat rancher for an annual rental which just covers the property tax liability, so there will be zero annual cash flow before consideration of debt service and income tax consequences.

Foxx can purchase the property for cash, or he can pay 25 percent down and sign a note and purchase–money mortgage for the balance. Both the principal and the accumulated interest on the note will be due and payable at the end of the fifth year, with interest accumulating at a compound annual rate of 10 percent.

borrowed funds reduces an investor's income tax obligation at his marginal tax rate, whereas the gain on property disposal increases taxes at less than one-half the regular tax rate. Income tax considerations are explored more thoroughly in chapter 6.

Mechanics of Mortgages

A mortgage is a contract which pledges a specific asset as security for the repayment of a debt or a promise to perform. The mortgage itself is not evidence of indebtedness. Rather, there is usually a promissory note acknowledging the amount of the debt and the terms. The two instruments are sometimes combined, but in most jurisdictions, there will be both a note and a mortgage associated with loans secured by real estate.

Alternatives to mortgages include deeds of trust and land contracts. A *deed of trust* transfers title to a third person "in trust," to be reconveyed upon satisfaction of debt. A *land contract,* sometimes referred to as a *contract for deed* or an *installment contract*, involves a promise by the seller of real estate (the *vendor*) to deliver a deed to the purchaser (the *vendee*) upon satisfaction of the terms stipulated in the contract.

First Mortgages and Junior Mortgages

Filing notice of the existence of a mortgage with the proper public official (recording) serves as constructive notice of the existence of a mortgage claim against property encumbered by the instrument. In most cases, the public official is the county recorder, and filing must be done in the county in which a property is located.

Recording a mortgage establishes its priority as a claim against the property. In most instances, the priority of a lien is established strictly on the basis of when the mortgage was presented for recording. A first mortgage is simply the first to be filed with the county recorder, a second mortgage is the second to be filed, and so on. Exceptions to this priority rule include tax liens and liens for labor or materials associated with construction on a property.

Default and Foreclosure

A borrower is said to be in *default* at any time he fails to abide by the terms of a loan agreement. This might involve failure to make a scheduled payment, failure to maintain the property in good condition, nonpayment of taxes, or noncompliance with any other term of the agreement.

The most common remedy available to a lender in case of default is a foreclosure action. Foreclosure involves the extinguishment of whatever right or interest the mortgagor has in a property. The exact procedure varies between states, but generally it involves a public sale of the mortgaged property under court supervision. Funds from the sale are distributed to creditors in the order of priority of their liens. That is, the claim of the holder of a first mortgage must be satisfied first, those of a second mortgagee second, and so on. Should there remain any proceeds after satisfaction of all lienholder claims and after covering the costs of the foreclosure sale, the balance generally accrues to the defaulting mortgagor.

Summary

Financial leverage is the use of borrowed money in connection with an investment position. Borrowed funds enable an investor to acquire a much more expensive property than would otherwise be possible or to spread his available equity over several properties and thus to reduce business risk by gaining geographical diversification.

Financial leverage can also increase the rate of return on equity funds. This occurs when the rate of return on assets exceeds the rate of interest paid on mortgage debt. When annual debt service, expressed as a percentage of the amount borrowed, is less than the rate of return on assets, financial leverage is said to be favorable. It is unfavorable if the rate of return on assets is less than the rate of payment on borrowed funds.

Financial risk is the risk that cash flow from an investment will be insufficient to meet associated mortgage–debt payments. Increasing the amount borrowed, therefore, means increased financial risk. The borrowing decision involves weighing, offsetting elements of increased earnings and increased financial risk.

Income tax laws encourage use of financial leverage. The deductibility of interest expense reduces the after–tax cost of borrowing. Borrowing enables control over much larger financial investment, with the consequent possibility of claiming greatly increased income tax deductions for depreciation expense. There also results an increased probability of ultimately realizing a substantial gain on disposal of the property. The gain is taxed at a much more favorable rate than is regular income.

Mortgages are pledges of specific assets as security for repayment of a loan or satisfaction of a promise to perform. Alternative security instruments include deeds of trust and land contracts.

Recording mortgages at the county records depository constitutes constructive public notice of the existence of the underlying debt and establishes the priority of the lien in case of foreclosure. Mortgages generally have priority according to the order in which presented for recording. Exceptions include tax liens, materialmen's liens, and mechanics' liens, all of which often take precedence over claims recorded before them.

Borrowers who fail to fulfill their obligations are said to be in *default*. A lender's remedy is to file a suit, asking the court to foreclose the borrower's right to reclaim his property by subsequent settlement of the debt obligation. Foreclosure is commonly by public sale, but the procedure varies according to state law.

Notes

1. Increased financial risk attendant to use of high debt-to-equity ratios may be more than offset by the reduction in aggregate risk resulting from increased diversification thereby made possible. Part 3 explores this topic in greater detail.

2. The calculations involve some rounding error, but are approximately correct. In this instance, the rounding error is less than $5.

3. Concluding that land investment is universally, or even generally, a wise investment would be premature. An investment is desirable only if the rate of return exceeds that available on alternative ventures embodying the same degree of risk. From this perspective, many land-investment opportunities are ill-advised.

6 Income Tax Factors in Investment Decisions

Since their relatively innocuous initiation to finance the World War I, federal and state income taxes have become increasingly important in business and investment transactions. Today no rational financial decision is made without considering tax consequences. Tax specialists have joined attorneys and CPAs as shamen of modern commerce.

This chapter does not pretend to displace competent tax counsel. It aims to alert analysts and investors to the more common income tax issues associated with real estate investment and to illustrate how tax factors affect the analysis. The chapter will be successful if readers are convinced of the need for more intensive study of federal and state tax codes.

From an initial overview of the relationship between real estate investment and federal income taxes, the chapter moves to a discussion of the tax basis of real property. It then explains depreciation allowances, which represent a provision for capital recovery over an investment's useful life. There follows an analysis of the minimum tax liability on preference items. The chapter concludes with a look at the potential capital gains tax liability arising from property disposal.

Overview of the Tax Problem

Critical to an understanding of the importance of income tax considerations is a clear distinction between taxable gains and tax-deductible losses on the one hand, and cash receipts and expenditures on the other. Tax laws focus on accounting flows—income, expenses, and capital gains and losses—whereas investment analysis is concerned with cash receipts and disbursements. Accounting conventions and tax law often prescribe treatment of income and expenditures in a manner not even remotely related to these cash flows. One result is that tax liabilities are often a consequence more of how paperwork is processed than of the economics of an investment.

Making the Investment

To illustrate this point, consider the typical cash-flow pattern of a real estate investment. The greatest cash outflow generally occurs when the property is being acquired. Yet this event has little or no immediate tax consequences. No tax deduction is allowed for the cash disbursement, even though income from the investment will be taxed when earned.

While the purchase price is not an item of direct immediate tax consequence, it does affect the tax impact of subsequent events. Taxes during the holding period and in the year of disposal will be strongly influenced by the amount paid for the property, whether or not payment was made in cash.

Taxes during the Holding Period

Most cash receipts from property will be taxable income during the holding period. Likewise, cash expenditures will generally represent tax-deductible expenses. Two important exceptions to this correspondence between cash disbursements and tax-deductible expenses are debt-service payments and capital expenditures.

Generally, property acquisition involves a considerable amount of outside financing. Expenditures for repayment of mortgage indebtedness are comprised of both interest payments and amortization of principal. Chapter 5 addresses this issue in more detail. The interest portion of a debt-service obligation is tax deductible in the year of payment, but capital amortization generally has no income tax consequences.[1]

Cash disbursements to maintain property in "normal operating condition" are generally tax deductible as repair and maintenance expenses. But outlays increasing a property's value or useful life are *capital expenditures* and are not deductible in the year incurred. Instead, capital expenditures are added to the tax basis of the property and are reflected in the depreciation allowance or the gain on disposal.

Tax Consequences of Property Disposal

Sale or exchange of real estate is usually a taxable event, but the tax obligation often bears little relationship to before-tax cash flow from disposal. The taxable gain (or tax-deductible loss) is based on the original cost and all subsequent capital outlays, adjusted for all depreciation allowances claimed during the holding period. The transaction price includes both equity outlay and all borrowed funds, plus anything else of economic value included in the deal.

Determining the Tax Basis

Acquisition cost and all subsequent capital expenditures form the owner's *tax basis*. This basis determines the amount of annual depreciation expense which can be claimed as a deduction from taxable income, as well as the portion of proceeds from eventual property disposal which is reported as a taxable gain. A property's tax basis, therefore, has pervasive income tax consequences.

The Initial Basis

The cost of newly acquired real estate is called the *initial basis*. *Cost* includes all expenditures for obtaining and defending title to a property. Included, for example, are purchase commissions (where payed), legal fees, and title insurance purchased in connection with the acquisition and not deductible as a current expense.

The purchase price, and thus the initial basis, includes not only the equity cash paid by a purchaser. It includes, also, any mortgage debt assumed or to which the property remains subject, as well as any purchase-money mortgage or third-party financing involved in the acquisition (see example 6-1).

Property acquired in an exchange of assets generally has an initial basis equal to the market value of assets tendered. A major exception to this rule is an exchange which qualifies under Section 1031 of the tax code, as "like-kind." The special rules for like-kind exchanges are discussed later.

Example 6-1: An investor purchases an apartment building on the following terms: he pays $20,000 in cash, signs a note and purchase-money mortgage for $40,000, and assumes the $350,000 balance of an existing first mortgage note. He pays $350 for legal representation at the closing, $120 for an owner's title insurance policy, and $320 for a lender's title policy.

The investor also pays the following amounts at the closing: $500 into a tax and insurance escrow, $40 for the seller's prepaid water bill, $3 for deed recording, and $28 for state documentary stamps.

The investor's initial tax basis is $410,501, computed as follows:

Purchase price:		
Cash down payment	$ 20,000	
Purchase-money mortgage	40,000	
Note assumed	350,000	$410,000
Attorney's fee		350
Owner's title policy		120
Recording fee		3
Documentary stamps		28
Total		$410,501

All other outlays represent costs of obtaining financing or are incidental to property ownership and are, therefore, not properly includable in the initial basis.

Allocating the Basis to Land and Improvements

Only a portion of the tax basis is charged off as depreciation expense over a property's useful life. The portion attributable to the land itself will be carried intact until the property is disposed of, at which time the basis of the land, together with any remaining basis attributable to improvements, comprise the portion of the sales price treated as a tax-free recovery of capital.

If the relative values of land and improvements are specified in the purchase contract, the initial basis is allocated accordingly. So long as the purchase is an arms-length transaction, the Internal Revenue Service is inclined to accept such a contractual allocation for tax computation purposes. This approach is usually acceptable because the interests of the parties are assumed to be antithetical.

If there is no contractual allocation of the purchase price, an alternative method must be employed. A common solution is use of the ratio of values attributed to land and improvements by the tax assessor. Property tax assessors typically appraise land and improvements separately. The assessed values themselves may bear no identifiable relationship to the actual market value of the property, but they nevertheless provide an acceptable basis for allocation.

A second generally accepted alternative is to have an independent appraiser estimate the relative values of land and improvements. The values so estimated may differ from the purchase price, but they nevertheless provide a ratio for allocating the investor's cost. In most cases, an appraisal will have been ordered in connection with third-party financing, so this method entails no additional expense.

Adjusting the Basis

There may be several adjustments to an owner's initial basis during his holding period. The resulting *adjusting basis* is important in determining the gain or loss on eventual property disposal.

All capitalized expenditures increase the basis. Generally, any cash disbursement for property improvements which is not currently deductible is a capital item.

Theoretically, currently deductible outlays for maintenance and repairs are unequivocably distinguished from capital outlays which must be included in the adjusted basis. The basic rule is that outlays required to maintain property in proper operating condition but which neither extend useful life or materially add to current value may be deducted currently; all other outlays must be capitalized and charged off over the period in which benefits are enjoyed. Practically, this rule is sufficiently ambiguous to have spawned legal arguments providing lucrative employment for a legion of lawyers. Treasury regulation 1.162-4 attempts to clarify the rule with instructive examples of expenditures which may and may not be charged off as currently deductible operating expenses.

Real estate taxes paid or accrued on vacant or unproductive land may, at the option of the taxpayer, be capitalized. Alternatively, they may be charged off as a current expense. These alternatives are also available for interest accrued on funds secured by, and used to acquire, vacant or unproductive property. Usually taxpayers prefer the option of claiming such outlays as current expenses. Occasionally, however, prudent tax management dictates their capitalization, in anticipation of higher future marginal tax brackets or to avoid problems associated with investment interest limitation rules.

Adjustments which reduce a property's basis include depreciation allowances and other forms of capital recovery, such as property insurance proceeds or tax deductions for uninsured casualty losses. Depreciation deductions are by far the most significant downward adjustment to the basis, however. The imporance of depreciation rules warrants more extended coverage.

Depreciation Allowances

Because improvements to real property have a limited lifespan, a portion of revenue generated from their use is more appropriately considered capital recovery than operating income. To accomplish this, taxpayers are permitted to claim *depreciation expense* based on the estimated reduction in value or useful life of income-generating assets during the tax period.

Generations of committee work, lobbying, and special-interest legislation have created depreciation tax rules bearing only a remote relationship to actual changes in the value or useful life of depreciable assets. In fact, during periods of persistent inflation, most real estate consistently increases in monetary value (though not necessarily in *real* value, after adjusting for purchasing-power losses) while being systematically written off via depreciation allowances.

Liberal provisions for depreciation allowances have traditionally made real estate a favored investment for people in high-income tax brackets. Recent rule changes have drastically reduced the amount of depreciation an investor may claim in any one taxable year and have increased the minimum income tax liability he incurs as a consequence of owning depreciable real property.

Investor Benefits

Depreciation is a tax-deductible expense requiring no current cash outlay. Provisions for accelerlated depreciation allowances during the early years of ownership sometimes result in a substantial net cash flow from an asset with little or no accompanying income tax liability. Indeed, attractive cash flows have often been accompanied by substantial "losses" for tax purposes.

Investors benefit from these special provisions in two ways: net "losses" (sometimes called *artificial accounting losses*) can be offset against taxable income from other sources, thus reducing the total tax obligation below what it would have been in the absence of real estate investment. At the same time, judiciously chosen real estate may actually appreciate in value. Depreciation deductions reduce the adjusted basis of the property and thus increase the taxable gain upon disposal. However, such gains may be afforded preferential tax treatment.

Much of the allure of accelerated depreciation was erased with the 1976 Tax Reform Act, which places special minimum tax obligations on taxpayers who utilize accelerated depreciation in association with real estate investments. For many investors, accelerated depreciation no longer proves advantageous. But the special benefits associated with claiming currently deductible depreciation allowances while incurring no current cash expenditure remain, albeit in reduced form.

Who May Claim Depreciation Deductions

A reasonable provision for the wasting away of income-generating assets is provided by the tax code where an asset is useful over more than one taxable period. Thus a depreciation deduction is allowed on improvements to all realty held for production of income, whether or not such income is in fact realized. The basic requirements are than an investor have a capital interest in the property, that improvements have a finite life, and that ownership be intended to generate income.

Estimating Useful Life

Useful life is limited by both physical and socioeconomic phenomena. It is the period over which an asset may reasonably be expected to yield economic benefit to the owner. Because social and economic factors can render property useless for its intended purpose long before it deteriorates physically, useful life is seldom synonymous with physical life.

Notable inconsistency has been the hallmark of the Internal Revenue Service's approach to the question of selecting useful life estimates. The government has wavered between giving taxpayers wide latitude to choose their own estimates and stipulating rigid rules regarding minimum acceptable useful-life estimates for specific classes of assets.

Current rules have remained substantially unchanged since 1971. They provide specific "guideline" lives for various classes of depreciable real property. The list in table 6-1 has been extracted from Treasury regulations.

Taxpayers need not subscribe to the government's guideline periods. A defensible estimate shorter than that included in the class-life guidelines is advantageous because it results in greater annual deductions from taxable income. The class-life guidelines are estimated average physical lifespans for each class of asset and may differ significantly from the facts associated with a specific asset.

Table 6-1
Guideline "Lives" for Various Classes of Depreciable Real Property

Description of Assets Included	Asset Guideline Period
Building services:	
Shelter, space, and related building services for manufacturing and for machinery and equipment repair activities:	
Factories	45
Garages	45
Machine shops	45
Loft buildings	50
Building services for the conduct of wholesale and retail trade, includes stores and similar structures	60
Building services for residential purposes:	
Apartments	40
Dwellings	45
Building services relating to the provision of miscellaneous services to businesses and consumers:	
Office buildings	45
Storage:	
Warehouses	60
Grain elevators	60
Banks	50
Hotels	40
Theaters	40

Component Method of Estimating Useful Life

Taxpayers have the option of estimating useful life for each of various components of a building and depreciating each component separately. Since components generally have useful lives much shorter than that of an entire building, the aggregate effect of using the component method might be greatly increased annual depreciation deductions. This approach is particularly advantageous where a substantial portion of a building's cost is comprised of relatively short-lived components, such as heating and air-condition units, carpets, paneling, and miscellaneous mechanical systems.

Allowable Depreciation Methods

Allowable methods of calculating depreciation allowances differ depending on whether depreciable improvements are new or used and on whether they are intended for residential or nonresidential use. The tax code specifies methods which generate the maximum allowable depreciation for each class of depreciable asset. It then permits taxpayers to choose any consistent method which does not, during the first two-thirds of an asset's useful life, result in cumulative depreciation deductions in excess of those allowable under the method specified for that class of asset.

Generally, residential income property is allowed a more accelerated depreciation method than is nonresidential property of the same type, that is, new residential as compared with new nonresidential and used residential as compared with used nonresidential. New property is also permitted a more accelerated rate than is used property intended for the same use. The code specifies the following methods:

Straight-Line Method. This method may be used with any depreciable property, since it does not result in cumulative deductions in excess of those from any other specified method during the first two-thirds of an asset's useful life. This is the *only* method permitted for use in calculating depreciation on used, nonresidential income property.

Simplicity of application is the hallmark of the straight-line method. Merely subtract any estimated salvage value from the asset's initial basis.[2] The balance is charged off in equal annual increments over the estimated useful life of the asset (see example 6-2).

Sum-of-the-Year's-Digits Method. This method may be used only for new residential income property. A property is considered residential if at least 80 percent of the rental income is from residential rents. The 80 percent test must be applied separately each taxable year.

Example 6-2: A property whose improvements are estimated to last 40 years and have a salvage value of $12,000 is acquired for $150,000, 20 percent of the purchase price being attributable to the land and the balance to the improvements. Using the straight-line method, the annual depreciation deduction is calculated as follows:

Depreciable base:

Cost of improvements (80 percent of total)	$120,000
Less: Estimated salvage value	12,000
Depreciable base	$108,000
Annual depreciation deduction:	
Depreciable base (from above)	$108,000
Times 1/40 (1/useful life)	0.025
Annual deduction	$ 2,700

To determine the depreciation allowance, multiply the cost of improvements (less salvage value) by a fraction whose numerator is the number of years remaining in the asset's useful life as of the beginning of the current year, and whose denominator is the sum of the digits in the original useful-life estimate. The product of this calculation is the current year's depreciation allowance.

This confusing explanation of the sum-of-the-year's-digits method belies its simplicity of application. The procedure is easily understood when demonstrated, as in example 6-3.

Example 6-3: A property which qualifies for the sum-of-the-years-digits depreciation method costs $160,000, of which $20,000 is applicable to purchase of the land. The improvements have an estimated useful life of 40 years and an estimated salvage value of $12,000. The annual depreciation deduction is calculated as follows:

Step 1. Compute the depreciable base:

Cost		$160,000
Less: Site value	$20,000	
Salvage value	12,000	32,000
Depreciable base		$128,000

Step 2. Compute denominator by summing the year's digits. Digits representing the years of useful life range from 1 through 40. The summation of the digits $(1 + 2 + 3 + \cdots + 39 + 40)$ equals 820.

Step 3. Compute the year's depreciation allowance. Multiply the (original) depreciable base from step 1 by a fraction whose numerator is the number of years remaining in the useful life at the beginning of the current taxable year and denominator is the constant derived in step 2:

Year	Fraction	Depreciable Base	Annual Depreciation
1	40/820	$128,000	$ 6,244
2	39/820	128,000	6,088
3	38/820	128,000	5,932
.	.	.	.
.	.	.	.
.	.	.	.
39	2/820	128,000	312
40	1/820	128,000	156
Totals	820/820	128,000	$128,000

To simplify the work of summing the year's digits, multiply the useful life by (1 + useful life), and divide the product by 2. The quotient is the sum of the year's digits. In example 6-3, the sum of the year's digits can be derived as follows:

$$\frac{(\text{Useful life}) (1 + \text{useful life})}{2} = \frac{(40) (41)}{2} = 820$$

200 percent Declining-Balance Method. Like the sum-of-the-year's-digits method, the 200 percent declining-balance method can be used only for new residential income property. Taxpayers using this method apply a constant percentage rate each year to the remaining unrecovered basis of their depreciable assets. Since there is always a remaining balance with this method, no adjustment need be made for estimated salvage value. The cumulative depreciation, however, may never exceed cost less salvage value.

The constant by which the unrecovered basis is multiplied each year is 2 × (1/useful life). The procedure is illustrated in example 6-4, using property with a 40-year useful life. Thus the constant for the example is (2 × 1/40), or 0.05.

150 percent Declining-Balance Method. The procedure is the same as the 200 percent method, except that the constant used as a multiplier is 1.5 × (1/useful life). Therefore, in example 6-4, the appropriate multiplier for this rate is (1.5 × 1/40), or 0.0375. The 150 percent declining-balance method is the maximum rate allowable for new nonresidential income property.

125 percent Declining-Balance Method. Specified as the maximum rate allowable for used residential income property, the 125 percent declining-

Example 6–4: Improvements to a certain property have a depreciable basis of $200,000. The improvements have an estimated useful life of 40 years. The annual depreciation allowance for each of the first 5 years of ownership is as follows. Using the 200 percent declining-balance method:

Year	Declining Balance	×	Rate	=	Depreciation
1	$200,000		5%		$10,000
2	190,000		5%		9,500
3	180,500		5%		9,025
4	171,475		5%		8,574
5	162,901		5%		8,145

Using the 150 percent declining-balance method:

Year	Declining Balance	×	Rate	=	Depreciation
1	$200,000		3.75%		$7,500
2	192,500		3.75%		7,219
3	185,281		3.75%		6,948
4	178,333		3.75%		6,687
5	171,646		3.75%		6,437

Using the 125 percent declining-balance method:

Year	Declining Balance	×	Rate	=	Depreciation
1	$200,000		3.125%		$6,250
2	193,750		3.125%		6,055
3	187,695		3.125%		5,865
4	181,830		3.125%		5,682
5	176,148		3.125%		5,505

balance method differs from other declining-balance approaches only in the multiplier applied to derive the constant, which is 1.25 × (1/useful life). This method also is illustrated in example 6–4.

Switching Depreciation Methods

Taxpayers are permitted to change from an allowable declining-balance method to the straight-line method at any time. They need only inform the Internal Revenue Service of their intent. Any other switch is considered a change in accounting method and requires prior approval of the Commissioner of the Internal Revenue Service.

Disposal of Investment Property

The sale or exchange of income or investment property (other than like-kind exchanges, discussed later in the chapter) is a taxable event. A portion of the proceeds may be a nontaxable return of capital, but the balance represents a taxable gain on disposal. The gain may be taxed as ordinary income, or it may receive preferential treatment as a long-term capital gain.

Calculating Gain or Loss

Remember that the adjusted basis of a property is its initial cost, increased by the amount of any capital improvements and reduced by all depreciation deductions claimed. There may also be other adjustments. The gain or loss on disposal is the amount realized minus the adjusted basis.

The amount realized from disposal is the market value of all goods and services received in exchange, all cash received, and any net debt relief resulting from the transaction minus all selling costs (see example 6–5).

Example 6–5: A taxpayer conveys an apartment building in exchange for the following: cash payment of $20,000, a note and purchase-money mortgage for $30,000, and vacant land worth $15,000. The other party accepts the apartment building subject to an existing mortgage with a remaining balance of $210,000. The taxpayer pays a brokerage fee and closing costs totaling $15,000. He originally paid $200,000 for the apartment and subsequently claimed depreciation totaling $22,000. There have been no other adjustments to his basis.

The gain on disposal of the apartment building is $82,000. Here are the calculations:

Amount realized:		
Value received:		
Cash received	$ 20,000	
Note received	30,000	
Land received (at market value)	15,000	
Net debt relief	210,000	$275,000
Less: Transactions cost		15,000
Net realized		$260,000
Less: Adjusted basis:		
Cost	$200,000	
Less: Cumulative depreciation	22,000	$178,000
Gain		$ 82,000

Recapture of Excess Depreciation

If a taxpayer uses an accelerated depreciation method, then a part or all of any gain on disposal may be considered a recapture of excess depreciation. Any portion so considered will be taxed as ordinary income in the year of disposal.

The difference between depreciation allowances actually claimed in any taxable year and the allowances which would have been claimed had the taxpayer been using straight-line depreciation is considered *excess depreciation*. When property on which there have been excess depreciation deductions is sold, any gain on the transaction will be deemed to represent recapture of cumulative excess depreciation deductions, to the full amount of such cumulative excess. Recaptured excess depreciation is reported as ordinary income in the year of the sale. Any gain on disposal not treated as recapture of excess depreciation is reported as a capital gain (see example 6-6).

There are exceptions to the recapture rule. They relate to excess depreciation claimed prior to 1976 on residential income property, excess depreciation taken prior to 1969 on nonresidential income property, and all excess depreciation taken on residential income property intended for low-income tenants. There are stringent length-of-holding-period rules under which these exceptions take effect. Refer to a standard tax guide for details.[3]

Any gain on disposal comprising recapture of excess depreciation must be reported as ordinary income. Any portion representing a capital gain may be ordinary income or, under special circumstances, may receive preferential tax treatment. This preferential treatment is explained in the next section.

Example 6–6: From example 6-5, assume that cumulative depreciation would have totaled only $14,000 had the taxpayer been using the straight-line depreciation method. The balance of $8,000 is cumulative excess depreciation. The $82,000 gain on disposal is divided between recapture of excess depreciation and capital gain in the following manner:

Total gain on disposal (from example 6-5)		$82,000
Less: Recapture of excess depreciation:		
Cumulative depreciation	$22,000	
Less: Straight-line depreciation	14,000	8,000
Capital gain		$74,000

Capital Gains Rules

Capital gains (and sometimes losses) arise from the sale or taxable exchange of capital assets or certain noncapital assets that are treated as capital items. If the property on which such a gain is realized was held for more than 12 months, the gain is usually afforded preferential treatment as a long–term capital gain. The net effect of preferential treatment is a significant reduction in the attendant tax liability.

When the Capital Gains Rules Apply

Property held as an investment is considered a capital item if it has a life expectancy of more than 1 year. Long–lived assets of a personal nature (as opposed to investment property) are considered capital assets for purposes of computing a taxable gain on disposal, but there is no provision for recognizing a capital loss on personal items. Long–lived assets held for use in a trade or business (Section 1231 assets) are treated as capital assets when disposed of at a gain and as noncapital assets when sold at a loss. Long–lived assets held primarily for resale are never treated as capital items.

Minimum Holding Period

Gains from disposal of capital assets held for 12 months or less are considered short term. As such, the gains are taxed at the same rate as is ordinary income. Capital assets held for more than 12 months are considered long term, and gains are afforded preferential treatment under the long–term capital gains rules discussed earlier.

Capital Gains and Recapture Rules

When a portion of the gain on disposal of capital assets is treated as recapture of excess depreciation, this reduces the benefits of the preferential treatment accorded long–term capital gains. The capital gain is a residual, comprised of the total gain less the recapture of excess depreciation.

Accounting for Simultaneous Capital Gains and Losses

Taxpayers sometimes experience both capital gains and losses, both long–term and short–term, all in the same taxable year. When this occurs, capital gains rules provide for the following procedure:

1. Offset short-term losses and short-term gains against each other.
2. Offset long-term losses and long-term gains against each other.
3. If, after the offsetting process, there is a net loss in either the long-term or the short-term category and a net gain in the other category, offset the two categories against each other.

The net gain or loss, long-term or short-term, is then reported as taxable income or (in the case of a net loss) as an offset against taxable income.

Reporting Net Capital Losses

Net short-term losses are offset against ordinary income on a dollar-for-dollar basis. But net long-term losses offset ordinary income only on a 2 for 1 basis. That is, $2 of net long-term losses offset $1 of ordinary income. Only $3,000 of ordinary income can be offset by capital losses in any one taxable year. Losses in excess of those permitted to be offset are carried forward and treated as capital losses in future years. There is no limit on the number of years such losses may be carried forward.[4]

Net Short-Term Capital Gains

If, after the offsetting process just discussed, there remains a net short-term capital gain, it is included in ordinary income on a dollar-for-dollar basis. The effect on an investor's tax obligation is the same as if the net short-term capital gain had been ordinary income.

Net Long-Term Capital Gains

Should there remain a net long-term capital gain after the offsetting procedure previously discussed, only 40 percent of the gain need be included in ordinary income for the year. The other 60 percent is excluded from the tax calculations and therefore has no ordinary income tax implications.

But the excluded 60 percent is treated as an "alternative" tax preference item and subjected to tax rules described in the next section.

The Alternative Minimum Tax

Taxpayers claiming long-term capital gains, and those who have itemized deductions in excess of the standard deduction, must compute an alternative minimum tax, and they are liable for the greater of the alternative minimum tax or the tax calculated in the regular fashion.

The basis for the alternative minimum tax is the sum of (1) regular taxable income (after adjustments for certain net operating losses), (2) 60 percent of long-term capital gains, and (3) the amount of itemized deductions exceeding 60 percent of adjusted gross income.[5] Twenty thousand dollars of this sum is excluded from the tax calculation. The balance is subject of a minimum tax at the following graduated rates:

Amount Subject to Alternative Minimum Tax	Tax Rate
First $40,000	10%
$40,000 to $80,000	20%
Over $80,000	25%

Actual tax liability is the greater of the alternative minimum tax or the normal tax liability (including the add-on preference tax).

Applying the alternative minimum tax rules to the data from example 6-7 indicates that the taxpayer in that example has an alternative minimum tax liability of $5,412. Since this is less than his normal income tax liability of $12,150, he is liable for the normal rather than the alternative minimum. His alternative minimum tax is calculated as follows:

Basis for alternative minimum tax computation:

Regular taxable income	$38,659
60 percent of long-term capital gain	20,400
Excess itemized deductions	8,000
Total	$67,059
Less Statutory exclusion	20,000
Amount subject to minimum tax	$47,059
Alternative minimum tax:	
On first $40,000 at 10 percent	$ 4,000
On balance at 20 percent	1,412
Total	$ 5,412

Example 6-7: An individual taxpayer has a regular income tax liability of $12,000 before including his preference tax. The liability results from taxable income of $38,659. He claims total long-term capital gains of $34,000 (40 percent of which is included in taxable income), and he claims excess itemized deductions of $8,000. He claims depreciation deductions of $23,000, whereas he would have claimed only $12,000 had he been using the straight-line depreciation method.

The Add-On Preference Tax

Taxpayers claiming accelerated-depreciation deductions, as well as those claiming certain other deductions deemed *preference items* by the tax code, may incur liability for an additional tax on these items. The tax is called *add-on* because it is added to the regular income tax liability.

Items subject to the add-on preference tax include the portion of accelerated-depreciation deductions which exceeds the deduction that would have resulted from using the straight-line depreciation method from the beginning of the ownership period. Other items, of less immediate concern to the real estate investment decision, are also subject to the add-on preference tax. These items are

1. The difference between the exercise price and the fair market value of stock received under a qualified-stock-option plan.
2. Certain intangible drilling costs deducted by drillers of oil and gas wells.
3. The excess of accelerated depreciation over straight-line depreciation claimed on personalty under a net lease.
4. Excess amortization allowable for certain assets.
5. Additions to reserve for bad debts in excess of actual bad-debt losses for the current year, allowed as a tax-deductible item for certain financial institutions.

Taxpayers are allowed to exempt a portion of their preference income from the add-on tax. Corporations may exempt an amount equal to the greater of total income tax liability (before inclusion of the add-on tax and after specified other adjustments) or $10,000. Individuals may exempt the greater of $10,000 or one-half their total income tax liability (before including the add-on tax and after specified other adjustments). The tax rate on preference items subject to the add-on tax is 15 percent, for both individual and corporate taxpayers (see example 6-7).

The taxpayers in example 6-7 incurs liability for an add-on preference tax of $150, computed as follows:

Preference items:		
Current depreciation deduction		$23,000
Less straight-line deduction		12,000
Excess depreciation		$11,000
Less exemption:		
a. Minimum exemption	$10,000	
b. 50 percent of tax before add-on	6,000	
Greater of *a* or *b*		$10,000
Amount subject to add-on tax		$ 1,000
Add-on tax at 15 percent		$ 150

Tax Preferences and "Maxitax" Rules

Taxpayers earning sufficient income from performance of personal service to move them above the 50 percent marginal income tax bracket face a particularly pernicious consequence of preference tax provisions. Their problem springs from the interrelationship between preference income and the minimum tax on personal service income.

Qualifying income from personal service is taxed at a maximum rate of 50 percent. This compares favorably with the maximum rate of 70 percent applicable to income from other sources. Taxpayers whose income from personal service is sufficiently great to move them above the 50 percent marginal tax rate in the absence of the special maximum tax provision therefore benefit substantially from the maxitax rules.

But that portion of personal service income subject to a maximum tax rate of 50 percent is reduced by the amount of any preference item included in the add-on tax computation plus the excess itemized deductions included in the alternative minimum tax computation. Minitax benefits are reduced by these items whether or not the taxpayer actually incurs a preference tax liability. In this fashion, preference items may increase the tax on a portion of personal-service income well above the 50 percent rate.

Special Income Tax Rules

Space precludes discussing all income tax issues of significance to real estate investors. Two particular rules, however, are so important that their exclusion must be explicitly noted. Their potential benefits justify considerable effort in their mastery.

Installment-Sales Method

Sellers receiving only part payment for their property in the year of the transaction may be able to defer recognition of a portion of the taxable gain until they collect the balance of the sales proceeds. Tax liability for the gain is incurred under this provision on a pro-rata basis as the proceeds are received each year.

Some of the advantages of installment-sales reporting are obvious. Because of the time value of money, it is usually advantageous to defer recognition of taxable income where the costs of so doing are less than the appropriate discount rate. By spreading the income tax obligation over several periods it is often possible to avoid being elevated into a higher marginal tax bracket and to avoid or minimize the preference tax obligation.

Stringent rules exist for qualifying for installment-sales reporting of casual sales of real estate. These rules must be scrupulously followed or the installment method will be disallowed, and the entire income tax obligation will be incurred in the year of the transaction, without regard to when sales proceeds are actually received.

Basic requirements are that not more than 30 percent of the sales price be received during the year of the sale, and that payment be received in 2 or more subsequent installments. Application of these seemingly simple rules is fraught with technicalities and legal pitfalls. Competent legal and tax counsel is needed before attempting to use the installment-sales method.[7]

Like-Kind Exchanges

Section 1031 of the tax code provides that no taxable gain or loss may be recognized when like-kind assets are exchanged. *Like-kind* is a confusing concept. It includes most real estate held for investment or business purposes, but not that held for personal use or for resale.

Instead of recognizing a gain or loss when the like-kind exchange occurs, taxpayers adjust the basis of the newly acquired asset so that any deferred gain or loss will be recognized when the substitute asset is subsequently sold.

Benefits available from like-kind exchanges include deferral of income tax obligation for capital gains and possible avoidance of a preference-tax obligation altogether. Under certain very limited circumstances it may also be possible to use this provision to avoid the recapture of excess depreciation.[8]

Summary

Tax rules affecting ownership and disposal of real estate have been presented in necessarily sketchy fashion. Each of the subheadings could easily be expanded into a lengthy chapter in its own right. The objective here has been to make readers aware of the rules. Recommended readings provide additional information essential for intelligent investment decisions.

Important points to be drawn from the chapter include the significance and determination of the initial basis and the adjusted basis, the treatment of various expenditures and allowances during the property holding period, and the tax consequences of disposal by sale or exchange.

The initial basis is the constructive cost of acquiring and defending an ownership interest. It includes everything of value tendered in exchange for property, including cash, other assets, relief from debt obligations, and services rendered. Adjustments to the basis include capital improvements and betterments, depreciation allowances, casualty losses, and partial conversions. The outcome of the adjusting process is the owner's adjusted tax basis, which determines the portion of the eventual sales price representing a taxable gain.

The initial basis, and certain subsequent adjustments, must be allocated between land and improvements on the land. The portion attributed to improvements forms the basis for computing allowable depreciation. Depreciation allowances are tax-deductible "expenses" which do not represent actual cash outlays in the period in which they are claimed. They thereby have the salutary effect of reducing the income tax obligation without reducing before-tax cash flow.

When taxpayers dispose of business or investment property, the difference between the amount realized from disposal and the adjusted basis represents a gain or loss on disposal. Gains on disposal are divided between ordinary income and capital gains, depending on the existence of excess depreciation subject to recapture.

If cumulative depreciation deductions exceed those which would have accumulated from using the straight-line method, the difference represents excess depreciation. With certain exceptions, gains on disposal will be taxed as ordinary income to the extent of any such cumulative excess depreciation. This amount will be considered a recapture of the excess depreciation rather than an actual increment in the capital value of the asset.

Gains on disposal of investment and business property not attributed to recapture of excess depreciation are considered capital gains. If the property is held for more than 12 months, the gain is a long-term capital gain and is afforded preferential income tax treatment. Gains on property held for 12 months or less are considered short-term and are taxed at the same rate as ordinary income.

Both straight-line and accelerated methods of calculating depreciation may be allowable, depending on whether depreciable improvements are new or used and on the use to which the property is to be put. Claiming accelerated depreciation may have untoward preference-tax consequences which more than offset savings on the regular income tax obligation. For most investors, accelerated depreciation is no longer desirable on real estate other than that intended to house low-income tenants.

Tax-preference items are divided into two categories. The first category is called add-on preference items because the resultant tax is added to the regular tax obligation. This category includes the excess of accelerated-depreciation deductions over straight-line depreciation, as well as a number of other items not directly related to real estate investment. The second category, alternative minimum tax preference items, includes the portion of long-term capital gains not included in regular taxable income plus itemized deductions exceeding 60 percent of adjusted gross income. The taxpayer is liable for the greater of the alternative minimum tax or the income tax obligation computed in the normal way.

An additional untoward consequence of preference-tax rules for individuals is the possible reduction in that portion of service income subjected to a maximum tax rate of 50 percent.

Special tax rules of particular interest to investors in real property but not covered in the present text include the installment method of reporting property rules and the tax-free exchange of like-kind property under code Section 1031.

Notes

1. Only interest paid as accrued or in arrears is currently deductible. Prepaid interest is generally not deductible until actually earned by the lender.

2. *Salvage value* is the estimated market value of the improvements at the end of their useful life to the taxpayer, minus the estimated cost of demolition and removal. In most cases, the estimated salvage value of real property will be zero.

3. See, for example, Gaylon E. Greer, *The Real Estate Investor and the Federal Income Tax* (New York: Wiley-Interscience, 1978), pp. 163–168.

4. These rules apply only to individual taxpayers. Corporate taxpayers may not offset capital losses against ordinary income. Corporate capital losses may, however, be carried back 3 years or forward 5 years and used to offset capital gains in the years to which they are carried.

5. Before making the comparison, both itemized deductions and adjusted gross income are reduced by medical expenses, casualty losses, state and local tax deductions, and estate tax deductions relating to income from the estate of a decedent.

6. These rules apply only to individual noncorporate taxpayers. For a discussion of corporate income tax rules, and for detailed calculations for individual taxpayers, see Greer, *The Real Estate Investor and the Federal Income Tax.*

7. Ibid., pp. 169–178.

8. Ibid, chapter 10.

Part II
Measures of Investment Worth

Cash-flow forecasting is a mere first step in the investment-analysis process. The forecast is the expected benefit from investment, but its worth has yet to be considered. Part II begins discussing the evaluation process in chapter 7 by summarizing techniques traditionally employed for this purpose. It explains why these techniques are almost universally inadequate and sketches alternatives which eliminate the most objectional element of traditional approaches. Chapter 8 provides the arithmetical tools necessary for use of contemporary evaluation techniques. It sets forth both the theoretical basis and operational techniques for deriving compound interest and present-value operators. Chapter 9 applies the tools from chapter 8 to concrete problems of investment analysis.

7

Comparative Measures of Investment Worth

Real estate markets encompass a bewildering array of investment alternatives. Investors must choose from among myriad combinations of opportunities that differ not only in the amount of required initial cash investment, but also in the timing and amount of expected future cash flows and in the degree of confidence which can be placed in the expectations.

Making rational choices from such a diverse menu presents formidable challenges, even to those educated, trained, and experienced in real estate analysis. Approaches range from snap judgments based on little more than "hot tips" or ill-formed hunches to carefully calculated decisions backed by expensive and time-consuming analysis. While most investors are sufficiently rational to reject the snap-judgment approach, they seldom have the skill for extended analysis. They often compromise by using rules of thumb which provide references to either past experience or benchmark measures of profitability based on market observation.

After reviewing appropriate terminology, this chapter introduces the most commonly used benchmark measures and rules of thumb. It also explains the most generally employed measures of profitability encountered among investors attempting more detailed analysis.

The chapter proceeds from popular ratios measuring profit/price relationships and operating results to more complex evaluation techniques extensively employed by those educated in traditional real estate investment analysis. It then introduces the more rational and advanced techniques to be explored in subsequent chapters.

Review of Terminology

Many of the terms employed in chapter 2 to present the operating statement are used also in analysis of profitability. A review of the more significant terms will enhance understanding of both traditional and contemporary evaluation techniques.

Particularly important is a clear understanding of the meaning of various measures of profitability. Confusion reigns because the word *profit* has an entirely different meaning in real estate analysis than in conventional accounting. Analysts are concerned with measuring net cash inflows per period of time relative to the amount of cash an investor must initially expend. Their interest in profit as defined by accounting conventions is limited to its significance for determining an investor's income tax liability.

Financial leverage and income tax effects can create a significant divergence between before-tax and after-tax cash flow. For investors in very high income tax brackets, the latter might actually exceed the former. One consequence of this is the production of several measures of return, depending on the extent to which the impact of financial leverage and income tax factors have been considered.

Net Operating Income

As explained in chapter 2, *net operating income* is the total of rental revenues and other income expected to be generated by a property (effective gross income), minus the cash expenditures required to maintain the property in sufficient condition to generate the gross income.

Cash Throw-Off and After-Tax Cash Flow

To reiterate, in the absence of financial leverage and income tax consequences, net operating income will represent the net amount of cash flowing to an investor. But financial leverage reduces both net cash flowing to investors and the required initial cash outlay. To measure the desirability of financial leverage, the consequences of these alterations in cash outlay and periodic net cash inflows must be evaluated. The debt-service obligation resulting from use of borrowed funds is discussed in chapter 5. Expressing this amount as an annual cash expenditure and subtracting it from net operating income leaves the cash available to an investor before considering income tax consequences. This measure is often called *cash throw-off.*

There are also, of course, income tax consequences that attach to most real estate investment ventures. There may result an increase in the investor's income tax liability, or perhaps a net tax decrease. The latter outcome is called *tax shelter,* and it increases the cash flow generated by an investment.

Referring to figure 3-1, the relevant portion of the operating statement expressing these relationships is

Net operating income	$XXX,XXX
Less: Debt service (annual mortgage payment)	XX,XXX
Cash throw-off (before tax cash flow)	$ XX,XXX
Less: Income tax liability (or plus benefit)	X,XXX
After-tax cash flow	$ X,XXX

Taxable Income

Tax effects are considered at length in chapter 6. To move from net operating income to taxable income, subtract any tax-deductible item which is
not reflected as an operating expense (and thus previously deducted).
Generally, these items are interest expense on borrowed funds and allowance for depreciation. Note that while interest expense is a part of the
annual debt service, and thus deducted from net operating income to arrive
at cash throw-off, it is not subtracted prior to arriving at the estimate of net
operating income. The sequence of calculations is

Net operating income		$XXX,XXX
Less: Interest expense	$XX,XXX	
Depreciation expense	XX,XXX	XXX,XXX
Taxable income (or tax deductible loss)		$ X,XXX

Tax Shelter

Because of the high leverage generally employed by real estate investors,
and because of the significance of the allowance for depreciation (depreciation expense), real estate investments often show a net loss for tax-computation purposes. These losses can be offset against income from other
sources, thus reducing an investor's total income tax liability below what it
would have been in the absence of such an investment.

Of course, nobody is anxious to lose money on their investments. Tax
losses, however, are often distinct from actual negative cash flows. Large
deductions for interest and depreciation often enable investors to claim
losses for tax-computation purposes, even though positive cash flows are
being generated by their investments.[1]

Some tax shelter, of course, results whenever any tax-deductible item
exceeds the actual cash outlay associated with that item. The shelter produced may not exceed income from the investment and thus will not carry
over to shelter income from other sources, but it does shelter some of the
income from the investment generating the tax loss. It therefore reduces the
investor's tax liability (and thereby increases his after-tax cash flow) to
some extent.

Ratio Analysis

Strictly speaking, ratios are not indices of profitability. They are, rather,
tests of the reasonableness of reported relationships between various cash-
flow items and between income and the market value of a property.

Income Multipliers

One of the more ancient techniques simply relates expected income to a property's market price. This permits application of either a rule of thumb or a comparative analysis. The rule of thumb involves comparing the relationship to some benchmark index and rejecting all opportunities offering a less favorable relationship. Comparative analysis, one step further in sophistication, relates the relationship between price and expected return to that observed to be available from comparable real estate investment opportunities.

Income multipliers may express the relationship between price and either gross or net income. While neither is an ample tool of analysis in isolation, both can play a valuable role in determining a property's desirability. The most important role of multiplier analysis is to weed out obviously unacceptable opportunities in an inexpensive and timely manner, reserving more extensive (and expensive) analysis for properties more likely to meet an investor's predetermined criteria.

To use multiplier analysis as a preliminary filter, first determine the relationship prevailing in the market area of interest for properties comparable to that being investigated. Then automatically reject all opportunities with multipliers above this benchmark figure. Opportunities passing the preliminary filter are subjected to further analysis.

The *gross–income multiplier (GIM)* is also often referred to as the *gross-rent multiplier.* It represents the relationship between the purchase price of a property and its effective gross income. Using data from example 7-1, the gross income multiplier is

$$\text{GIM} = \frac{\text{market price}}{\text{effective gross income}}$$

$$= \frac{\$100,000}{25,000}$$

$$= 4$$

The *net–income multiplier (NIM)*, a less frequently employed ratio, is calculated in the same fashion, using net income instead of effective gross income. For example 7-1, the net income multiplier is

$$\text{NIM} = \frac{\text{market price}}{\text{net operating income}}$$

$$= \frac{\$100,000}{\$\ 12,000}$$

$$= 8.33$$

Gross–income–multiplier analysis is generally more useful than net–income–multiplier analysis, because substantial research may be necessary to determine the appropriate measure of net operating income. This obviates the major benefits of multiplier analysis: timeliness and economy.

When the GIM is used as a preliminary screening mechanism with respect to prospective property acquisitions, generally, in the interest of economy and speed, it is necessary to use potential gross income rather than effective gross income. Adjusting the reported gross (which is generally potential gross, perhaps with an average vacancy factor for the area) for realistic vacancy and credit losses represents more of an investment in investigative time than a preliminary screening operation justifies.

Financial Ratios

Intraproperty comparisons are facilitated by reference to the percentage of gross income consumed by operating expenses. This measure, called the *operating ratio*, will be lower for relatively more efficient properties. Generally, there is a tendency for operating ratios to rise as a property ages, because property becomes relatively less efficient with age. The ratio can be

---

Example 7-1: An investment opportunity having a market price of $100,000 and requiring a 25 percent downpayment is expected to yield the following operating results during the first year:[a]

Effective gross income	$25,000
Less: Operating expenses	13,000
Net operating income	$12,000

Other relevant information includes:

1. There is available a $75,000, 25–year mortgage loan requiring equal monthly payments with interest at 9½ percent.
2. Land accounts for 20 percent of total property value. Improvements (80 percent) are depreciable over 30 years, using straight–line depreciation. Salvage value is estimated to be zero.
3. Best estimates indicate that the property will increase in market value at a compound rate of about 5 percent per annum during the immediate future.
4. The investor is subject to a marginal income tax rate of 40 percent.

---

[a]Calculations for effective gross income, operating expenses, and net operating income are explained in chapter 3.

misleading, however, because it reflects in part the efficiency of management as well as of the property itself. Some investors, in fact, look for properties with high operating ratios, intending to reduce the ratio through efficient management techniques and thereby increase the indicated property value. The operating ratio for example 7–1 is

$$\text{Operating ratio} = \frac{\text{operating expenses}}{\text{gross income}}$$

$$= \frac{\$13,000}{\$25,000}$$

$$= 52 \text{ percent}$$

Two very useful ratios expressing the margin of safety associated with financial operations are the *breakeven ratio* and the *debt-service coverage ratio*. The breakeven ratio is most useful when expressed on a before-tax cash throw-off basis. It indicates the relationship between cash inflows and cash outflows. The lower the breakeven cash throw-off ratio, the greater can be the decline in gross revenues (or the increase in operating expenses) before an investor experiences a negative cash flow from his project. Applying the formula to the project in example 7–1, the ratio is

$$\text{Breakeven cash throw-off} = (\text{fixed expenses} + \text{operating expenses} + \text{debt service}) / \text{gross income}$$

$$= (\$13,000 + \$7,863)/\$25,000$$

$$= 83.5 \text{ percent}$$

The debt-service coverage ratio provides an indication of safety associated with the use of borrowed funds. It expresses the extent to which net operating income can decline before becoming insufficient to meet the debt-service obligation. This index, the ratio of net operating income to the debt-service obligation, with respect to Example 7–1 is

$$\text{Debt-service coverage} = \frac{\text{net operating income}}{\text{annual debt service}}$$

$$= \frac{\$12,000}{\$7,863}$$

$$= 1.5$$

Traditional Profitability Measures

Investors and analysts who reject the snap–judgment approach need some technique with which to impose order on the seeming chaos of market choices. A shared characteristic of all traditional approaches has been an attempt to relate cash investment to expected cash returns in some systematic fashion. The techniques differ in the degree to which they incorporate available data into the analysis. They differ also in that some ignore the question of perceived risk, while others make rudimentary attempts to adjust for risk differentials.

Overall Capitalization Rate

This technique, also known as the *free–and–clear rate of return*, expresses the first year's expected net operating income as a percentage of market price. The overall capitalization rate in example 7-1 is

$$\text{Rate} = \frac{\text{net operating income}}{\text{market price}}$$

$$= \frac{\$\ 12,000}{\$100,000}$$

$$= 12 \text{ percent}$$

Recall that the net–income multiplier is market price divided by net operating income. The overall capitalization rate, therefore, is simply the reciprocal of the net–income multiplier. Thus, in example 7-1, 1/0.12 equals 8.33, which is the net income multiplier for the example.

Usefulness of overall capitalization rates is limited by the nature of typical financing arrangements, and by the approach most investors take to arrive at an acceptable sales price. In a typical negotiating session there is an acknowledged tradeoff between price and financing terms. Since this tradeoff is not reflected in the overall capitalization rate, comparison of rates between properties with significantly different financing arrangements can be very misleading.

Equity Dividend Rate

Because few properties are purchased without using borrowed funds, and because the availability and cost of mortgage financing differs between investment opportunities, the overall capitalization rate (free–and–clear return) is not a very useful measure either for an accept/reject decision or for choosing between investment alternatives. A more useful measure compares spendable income from a project with the investor's equity investment. Such a measure is often called the *equity dividend rate.*

The equity dividend rate, as generally calculated, expresses before–tax cash flow (net operating income minus debt service) as a percentage of the required initial cash outlay. The equation is

$$\text{Equity dividend rate} = \frac{\text{NOI less debt service}}{\text{market price less mortgage}}$$

Calculating the equity dividend rate for the property in example 7–1 requires prior determination of the equity dividend (NOI less debt service) and the initial equity (price less mortgage). These calculations are

Equity dividend (cash throw–off):

Net operating income	$12,000
Less: Debt service on $75,000 mortgage	7,863
Equity dividend (cash throw–off)	$ 4,137

Initial cash outlay:

Purchase price	$100,000
Less: Available mortgage	75,000
Initial equity	$ 25,000

Therefore, the equity dividend rate applicable to example 7–1 is, 16.5 percent, determined as follows:

$$\text{Equity dividend rate} = \frac{\$\ 4,137}{\$25,000}$$

$$= 16.5 \text{ percent}$$

While the equity dividend rate is useful in distinguishing between properties offering different financing structures, it suffers from failure to incorporate income tax considerations. Cash flow to the equity position (cash throw–off) becomes meaningful as a measure of return on investment only after deducting the applicable income tax liability (or adding back the income tax benefit). Where properties (and financing arrangements) involve significantly different income tax implications, the equity dividend rate will have limited usefulness as an analytical tool.

Cash-on-Cash Return

The equity dividend rate was originally developed as an appraisal tool. To render it more useful for investment analysis, the relationship embodied therein must be expressed on an after-tax basis. The modified expression is often referred to as the cash-on-cash rate of return.

Cash-on-cash return, then, is the first year's expected net spendable cash (after all financing costs and income taxes), expressed as a percentage of the initial cash investment. To determine the expected cash-on-cash rate of return, the first year's expected income tax effect must be known. This in turn requires estimates of depreciation and interest expense. For example 7-1, these latter estimates are

Depreciation expenses:	
Cost of property	$100,000
Less: Price of land	20,000
Cost of depreciable improvements	$ 80,000
Less: Estimated salvage value	0
Depreciable amount	$ 80,000
Annual depreciation ($80,000/30 years)	$ 2,667
Interest expense:	
Amount of initial mortgage loan	$ 75,000
Less: Remaining balance after 12 months	74,229
Principal reduction during year	$ 771
Total debt service during first year	$ 7,863
Less: Principal reduction (from above)	771
Interest expense, first year	$ 7,092

These data, combined with projected net operating income from example 7-1, permit an estimate of the first year's income tax obligation:

Net operating income		$12,000
Less: Depreciation expense	$2,267	
Interest expense	7,092	9,359
Taxable income from investment		$ 2,641
Times: Marginal income tax rate		.40
Income tax obligation		$ 1,056

After-tax cash flow to the equity position is the net operating income less debt service and income tax payments:

Net operating income		$12,000
Less: Mortgage payments (debt service)	$7,863	
Income tax obligation	1,056	8,919
After-tax cash flow		$ 3,081

With the preceding information, the cash-on-cash return can be calculated. For example 7-1, the computation is

$$\text{Cash-on-cash} = \frac{\text{after-tax cash flow}}{\text{equity investment}}$$

$$= 12.3 \text{ percent}$$

Broker's Rate of Return

Seeking to cast the best possible image of a property being offered for sale, brokers are inclined to argue that any measure of return which ignores the buildup of an investor's equity is misleading. *Broker's rate of return* adjusts the cash-on-cash rate to include equity buildup resulting from amortization of mortgage debt. This, of course, increases the indicated return to the equity position and thereby makes the property appear more attractive.

For the property in example 7-1, the broker's indicated rate of return is 15.4 percent, determined as follows:

$$\text{Broker's return} = \frac{\text{after-tax cash} + \text{equity buildup}}{\text{initial equity}}$$

$$= \frac{\$3,081 + 771}{\$25,000}$$

$$= 15.4 \text{ percent}$$

While the broker's rate of return is widely used, it is somewhat misleading. Equity buildup is not significant unless it ultimately results in added cash flow to the investor. The important measure of potential cash flow from disposal is the difference between market value and remaining balance on mortgage indebtedness, less estimated brokerage commission and other transaction costs. Since this cash flow is not realized on an annual basis, but only upon property sale, it is inconsistent and misleading to include the equity buildup in the measure of annual cash flow.

Payback Period

One of the simplest and perhaps most common rules of thumb is to estimate the number of years required to recoup the initial cash investment in a project. In *payback-period analysis,* alternative opportunities are ranked in accordance with the length of time required for the anticipated stream of cash proceeds to equal the initial cash investment. Presumably, if opportunities are perceived as embodying equal risk, the one with the shortest payback period is considered most desirable. For projects with differential risk factors, the maximum acceptable payback period will be inversely related to the perceived risk.

When anticipated cash flow from an investment is the same amount each year, the paycheck period can be calculated by simply dividing initial cash outlay by the expected annual cash flow. Thus, for a project requiring an initial cash outlay of $10,000 and expected to yield an annual cash flow of $2,500, the payback period is 4 years:

$$\text{Cash outlay/annual cash flow} = \$10,000/\$2,500$$

$$= 4 \text{ years}$$

Of course, expected cash flow from a real estate investment opportunity is seldom the same from year to year. The focus of the analysis is after-tax cash flow, and even if this were the only factor which did not remain constant from year to year, it would be sufficient to keep annual cash-flow estimates from being equal. Consequently, payback-period calculation is seldom as straightforward as the preceding example suggests. In most instances, the payback period must be determined by summing expected proceeds from year to year until the total equals initial outlay.

The appeal of payback-period analysis is its apparent simplicity and its adaptability as a policy tool. An investor can specify some maximum payback period for real estate of a specific type or in a given location based on his perception of associated risk.

The major shortcoming of this method is that it ignores what is often the most significant part of the return from a real estate investment: cash flow from disposal. This failure to consider cash flow beyond the payback period will cause assets with little appreciation potential to be chosen over those with almost certain large returns because of an increase in value over the holding period.

A second problem is that the method fails to discriminate between cash flows with different timing, even during the payback period. A project with all the benefits ''up front'' in terms of tax benefits from accelerated depreciation, for example, would not be chosen over one offering the same total benefit spread evenly over the entire payback period. The time value of money is thus ignored, and the project with the greatest potential return may not be chosen.

Failure to consider cash flows beyond the payback date and to discriminate between cash flows with different timing within the payback period make the payback-period approach unacceptable as a primary method of choosing between investment alternatives.

Toward More Rational Profitability Analysis

To understand the shortcomings of traditional measures of investment value, it is helpful to review the major components of expected return. There is, of course, an initial cash commitment on the part of an investor, for which he expects to receive cash flow from operations during the holding period and cash from disposal upon termination of his investment position.[2] Traditional approaches ignore differential cash-flow expectations during the holding period, concentrating instead on the first year or, at best, the first few years of operation. They also completely ignore cash-flow expectations from disposal. Yet this latter component may in some instances be the greater portion of the expected return from an investment.

There are five major aspects to the expected profitability of a real estate investment:

1. The cash amount invested.
2. Cash flow from operations.
3. Cash required to service mortgage indebtedness.
4. Income tax liability or tax shelter from the investment.
5. Cash flow from disposal.

The significance of the various elements in determining profitability will differ from project to project, depending on the nature of the venture and on the objectives of the investor. An investor needing current income, for example, will concentrate on cash flow from operations, net of debt-service requirements and income tax liabilities. Those subject to onerous income tax obligations because of income from other sources are likely to emphasize the tax-shelter aspects of investment proposals. Investors needing to build an estate or generate tax-deferred gains will be drawn to opportunities where cash flow from disposal comprises a major segment of total profitability.

Regardless of particular predispositions of the investor, however, benefits from investment must be adjusted for quantity, quality, and timing. *Quantity* refers to the amount of the net cash flows, after incorporating all income tax liabilities or benefits, and after adjusting for debt-service obligations arising from use of financial leverage. *Quality* refers to the certainty with which expectations are held regarding forecasted net cash flows. *Timing* refers to when the forecasted net cash flows are expected to be realized.

The moral is that an ideal measure of profitability not only will account for differences in the amount of expected net cash flows, on an after-tax basis, but also will reflect differences in the expected time of receipt. A common weakness of traditional measures of profitability is that they ignore the question of timing of net cash inflows. Time-adjusted measures have been introduced in recent years and are being consistently extended and refined by both theoreticians and practitioners. The most widely accepted and valuable of these techniques are introduced in the following section.

Time-Adjusted Measures of Return

Since timing of anticipated cash flows is at least as important as their amount, techniques which ignore the time value of money are universally inadequate as final measures of investment desirability. They serve, at best, as rough filters which are quick and inexpensive to apply and which eliminate obviously unacceptable proposals. Projects surviving a rough-and-ready filter test must be subjected to additional analysis to evaluate the significance of differences in timing of anticipated cash flows and to distinguish between different levels of attendant risk.

A common element in all time-adjusted techniques is that they discount expected future cash flows to make them more nearly comparable to those receiveable in the present. Some techniques adjust purely for the time value of money, while others include an adjustment for risk. Still others take the adjustment factor as a variable to be found in order to equate future and present cash flows. This latter approach contemplates comparison of the resulting adjustment factors as a basis for choosing between alternatives.

Present Value

The present-value approach adjusts all anticipated future receipts at a predetermined rate per period of time. The result is the present value of anticipated future cash flows. This is compared with the required immediate cash outlay. The basic idea is that if the required initial cash outlay exceeds the present value of the future net cash inflows, the project is not worthy of further consideration.

Net Present Value

An investor's total wealth consists of both current funds and the present value of all rights to future receipts. Real estate acquisition involves giving up current funds for the right to receive cash receipts from property in the future. If the present value of these future benefits exceeds the amount of current funds expended in their acquisition, the investor's wealth is enhanced. If, on the other hand, the initial cash outlay exceeds the present value of the right to receive future cash receipts, then the investor's wealth is diminished as a consequence of the investment.

The net-present-value technique is a simple application of this idea. Having discounted anticipated future receipts at the appropriate discount rate to arrive at their present value, subtract the amount of the immediate cash expenditure required. The result is *net present value,* which, if greater then zero, represents an increase in the investor's wealth. But if the cash outlay exceeds the present value of future receipts, then net present value is a negative figure, which represents a decrease in the investor's aggregate wealth.

Internal Rate of Return

Alert readers will have wondered at the constant reference to the "appropriate" rate for discounting future cash flows. Determining this rate is a matter of some controversy. Exposition of the problem, and a solution to it, is deferred to later chapters. Some analysts avoid the issue altogether by taking the discount rate as a variable to be determined in solving the arithmetic of the discounting equation.

This approach involves taking the known initial cash outlay and the expected future cash flows as constants and seeking the discount rate which will make the present value of the future cash flows exactly equal to the amount of the initial cash outlay. This means the net present value is set at zero and a discount rate is found to make the equation solvable. The equation itself is presented in several formats in chapter 8.

Financial Manager's Rate of Return

Critics of the internal-rate-of-return technique observe that it is unreasonable that cash generated from a high-yield investment can be reinvested at the extraordinary rate—an assumption built into the tables employed in the internal-rate-of-return calculation. Moreover, projected cash-flow patterns which include intermediate periods of negative cash flows create computational problems which may result in there being no unique solution to the internal-rate-of-return equation.

A major response to these problems associated with the internal-rate-of-return method has been a compromise approach generally referred to as the *financial manager's rate of return*. Intermediate cash flows are assumed to be reinvested at a predetermined "safe" rate. Subsequent negative cash flows are offset against the reinvested balance. Negative cash flows in excess of the cumulative balance of previous positive cash flows compounded at the "safe" rate are treated as being drawn from an initial deposit made by the investor and left to grow at the "safe" rate.

The Ellwood Method

In 1967, L.W. Ellwood introduced a set of financial tables which permit appraisers and analysts to capitalize projected income streams directly from figures on the tables. The tables provide for various assumptions about mortgage-loan terms and rates of growth in the terminal value of property under analysis.[3] Ellwood's tables, an adaptation of standard annuity tables, permit appraisers and analysts who are willing to accept compromises with actual operating projections to capitalize the expected cash flows without really understanding the principle of the time value of money. Ellwood's tables and the so-called Ellwood technique have been widely adopted by appraisers in the United States. However, the results (when the tables are properly applied) are approximately the same as those determined by use of standard annuity tables. Availability of mechanized computational facilities largely obviate the previous justification for use of the Ellwood technique.

Summary

Over the years, investors and analysts have developed a variety of investment evaluation techniques. These include ratios for comparing income to market price and ratios for evaluating profitability and financial risk. They also include several measures of profitability designed to compare anticipated cash flows with required initial cash expenditures.

Traditional profitability measures generally fail to consider the time value of money. This is a serious shortcoming because the timing of cash inflows and outflows is a major element in the comparative desirability of investment opportunities. Time-adjusted measures of return are an essential tool of rational investment analysis. Methods include present-value and net-present-value computations, and calculation of the internal rate of return.

Internal-rate-of-return analysis is intuitively appealing to many analysts and investors, but it contains two serious flaws. It assumes a (sometimes unrealistic) reinvestment rate equal to the internal rate of return, and the equation occasionally has two or more solutions. To compensate for these problems, analysts have developed a variant called the financial manager's rate of return. This eliminates the major shortcomings, but at the cost of increased complexity not necessarily justified by the benefits the technique offers.

As a computational aid, and to enable a "cookbook" approach to adjusting for the time value of money, L.W. Ellwood compiled a set of tables permitting ready solutions to a variety of discounting problems. The tables require an assumption of cash flows which are either steady or change at a constant rate over the discount period.

Elwood's tables were a valuable contribution to the investment-evaluation literature. Their usefulness has been greatly reduced by the advent of fast and inexpensive computers that permit ready discounting of uneven streams of cash.

Notes

1. Claiming depreciation expenses from real estate investment, while a property may in fact be increasing in value, has recently drawn the ire of legislators bent on modifying the federal income tax code to eliminate perceived inequities in what they have termed "artificial accounting losses." Advantages of accelerated depreciation methods have been eroded by increasingly onerous *minimum tax* rules. This topic is introduced in chapter 6. For more detailed analysis, and for a discussion of optimum tax strategies for real estate investors, see Gaylon E. Greer, *The Real Estate Investor and the Federal Income Tax* (New York: Wiley-Interscience, 1979).

2. Under rare circumstances, astute use of leverage techniques may enable an investor to "cash out," that is, to acquire an equity interest with no initial equity cash outlay.

3. L.W. Ellwood, *Ellwood Tables for Real Estate Appraising and Financing,* The American Institute of Real Estate Appraisers, 1967.

8 The Simple Mathematics of Real Estate Finance

Astute real estate investors are not interested in actual "sticks and bricks" except as they effect the financial return on an investment. Real estate is only a means to the ultimate end of financial gain or of some other benefit which can generally be measured in financial terms. It is useful therefore to view investments less in terms of the physical property acquired than in terms of the stream of benefits expected to accrue from them.

The futurity of investment returns can hardly be overemphasized. Investors must wait for their reward. Expectation of future benefit carries an associated degree of risk and uncertainty. Since the future is inherently unknowable, anticipated benefits may never materialize. Investors expect to be compensated for bearing this risk as well as for their patience.

Both anticipated waiting time and perceived risk affect the desirability of an investment and thus the amount investors are willing to pay. The relationship between anticipated future benefits and the present worth of an opportunity is the *discount rate*.[1]

This chapter explains the basic concepts of compound interest and discount and demonstrates how financial tables can simplify computational chores. It illustrates use of the tables to solve a variety of financial problems, including the present value of a single sum or a series of future payments or receipts, the future value of an amount left on deposit, and the amount of level periodic deposits required to have a specified sum available at a predetermined future date.

Readers quickly taxed by computational chores will find this chapter not to their liking. Those well educated in mathematics or finance will find it elementary and therefore somewhat boring. Both groups may be tempted to skip the chapter and go on in search of more interesting information. For the latter group this may be a profitable strategy; the former are urged to resist the temptation. Mastery of fundamental analytical skills is somewhat tedious, but pays massive dividends to those who persevere.

All of modern investment and financial theory rests firmly on the concept of compound interest and discount. Thus a thorough grounding in the subject is an essential prerequisite to understanding the investment decision-making processes. Failure to master the use of this analytical tool will render any modern investment text (including the balance of this book) utterly incomprehensible.

Conceptual Basis for Discounting

Two fundamental propositions form the theoretical basis for discounting: more is better than less, and sooner is better than later. The first proposition is so obvious that it needs little elaboration. The second becomes equally evident with a minimum of consideration.

Better More than Less

That more of a good thing is better than less is disputed only by philosophers and mystics. Economists have considered this a self-evident proposition since the dawn of their discipline. If one bottle of champagne is gratifying, two will be even more so; three are even more desirable than two, and so forth. Fundamental to the concept (and certainly to our example) is that one need not consume the greater quantity if one wishes not to do so. Increased gratification, therefore, stems from certain knowledge that more is readily available if desired. Two bottles thus provide the same option as one, plus the additional option of continued imbibition.

Better Sooner than Later

A preference for present over future consumption is only one step further into abstraction. Who would not (other things being equal) prefer $5 today to the certain promise of $5 next week? Choosing the promise of future receipt reduces one's option for present consumption without offering anything in return. Current receipt, in contrast, provides the option of consumption either now, next week, or any time in the distant future. Clearly, the want-satisfying power of a good is generally enhanced by current receipt.

Compound Interest

If a $1,000 loan for 1 year requires payment of $1,070 at the end of the year, the amount of interest is $1,070 less $1,000, or $70. The rate of interest is $70/$1000, or 7 percent per annum. This simple example incorporates all the mechanics of compound interest. The general relationship may be expressed as

Amount repayed = amount borrowed + interest

Since annual interest is usually expressed as a rate or percentage of the amount borrowed (the principal), the same relationship may be expressed as

Amount repayed = amount borrowed + (amount borrowed × interest rate)

Rearranging the terms on the right-hand side of the preceding equation yields

$$\text{Amount repayed} = \text{amount borrowed} \times (1 + i)$$

where i is the interest rate. In the earlier illustration of a $1,000 loan for 1 year at an interest rate of 7 percent, this becomes

$$\$1,070 = \$1,000 \times 1.07$$

Suppose that the previously mentioned loan of $1,000 was for a period of 3 years, with interest at 7 percent per year and with the entire payment of principal and compound interest to be remitted at the end of the third year. Table 8-1 illustrates how the compound interest accumulates so that the amount to be repaid after 3 years equals $1,225.04.

Expressing the calculations in table 8-1 in terms of the equation

$$\text{Amount repayed} = \text{amount borrowed} \times (1 + i)$$

The amount to be repaid after 3 years is

After 1 year: $1,000 × 1.07

After 2 years: ($1,000 × 1.07) (1.07) = ($1,000) (1.07)^2

After 3 years: ($1,000 × 1.07   1.07) (1.07) = ($1,000) (1.07)^3

$$= \$1,000 \times 1.22504$$

$$= \$1,225.04$$

Table 8-1
Accumulation of Compound Interest

Year	Amount Owed at Start of Current Year	Plus Interest at 7 percent	Amount Owed at Year-End
1	$1,000.00	0.07 × $1,000.00	$1,070.00
2	$1,070.00	0.07 × $1,070.00	$1,144.90
3	$1,144.90	0.07 × $1,144.90	$1,225.04

This relationship between principal, compound interest, and time is summarized in more general fashion as

$$V_n = P(1 + i)^n$$

where V_n is the amount to be received in the future, P is the initial amount deposited (or borrowed), i is the interest rate, and n is the number of time periods involved.

In the example illustrated on table 8-1 P is the initial amount of a loan, and V_n is the amount to be repaid at maturity. But the formula applies equally when P is the amount of a deposit or an investment of any kind, and V_n is the expected amount to be received at a future date. The only laborious arithmetic in the formula is raising $(1 + i)^n$ to the nth power. For the problem illustrated on table 8-1, there are only 3 periods over which to calculate the compound amount. But suppose there had been 75 periods. In the absence of a good calculator or a set of tables, the calculation of $(1 + i)^{75}$ would be tedious in the extreme.

Fortunately, tables are readily available which give solutions to $(1 + i)^n$ for various values of both i and n. An excerpt from such a table, for some representative values of i and n, is reproduced below as table 8-2. The time periods in the table are expressed as years, but they could just as well be days, months, quarters, or any other period appropriate to the problem being considered. A more complete set of values appears in the tables in appendix A.

The earlier problem of the amount to be repaid on an initial 3-year loan of $1,000 with compound interest at 7 percent per annum (see table 8-1) can be solved quickly by reference to table 8-2. Simply extract the value for $(1 + 0.07)^3$ by reading down the column in table 8-2 under the 7 percent rate and across the row indicating 3 years. That factor (1.2250) is the compound amount of $1 left on deposit for 3 years at 7 percent. Multiplying this factor by the initial payment P of $1,000 yields the value for V_n ($1,125.04). Example 8-1 further illustrates the procedure.

The equation to solve the question in example 8-1 is

$$V_n = (\$5,000) \times (1.10)^7$$

where V_n is expected value at the end of the seventh year. The factor $(1.10)^7$ can be read from table 8-2, at the intersection of the 10 percent column and

---

Example 8-1: A vacant lot in a local subdivision is available for $5,000. The lot is expected to increase in value at a compound rate of 10 percent per annum for the next several years. What is the expected value of the lot after 7 years?

Table 8-2
How $1 Left on Deposit at Compound Interest Will Grow

Period	Compound Interest Rate						
	6%	7%	8%	9%	10%	12%	14%
1	1.0600	1.0700	1.0800	1.0900	1.1000	1.1200	1.1400
2	1.1236	1.1449	1.0664	1.1881	1.2100	1.2544	1.2996
3	1.1910	1.2250	1.2597	1.2950	1.3310	1.4049	1.4815
4	1.2625	1.3108	1.3605	1.4116	1.4641	1.5735	1.6890
5	1.3382	1.4026	1.4693	1.5386	1.6105	1.7623	1.9254
6	1.4185	1.5007	1.5869	1.6771	1.7716	1.9738	2.1950
7	1.5036	1.6058	1.7138	1.8280	1.9487	2.2107	2.5052
8	1.5938	1.7182	1.8509	1.9926	2.1436	2.4760	2.8526
9	1.6895	1.8385	1.9990	2.1719	2.3579	2.7731	3.2519
10	1.7908	1.9672	2.1589	2.3674	2.5937	3.1058	3.7072

the 7-year row. This factor (1.9487) multiplied by the initial $5,000 market value of the property gives its expected value of $9,744 after 7 years.

Present Value of a Future Amount

The equation for the future value of an initial amount can easily be altered to solve for a known future value and an unknown initial amount. The restructured equation is

$$P = V_n \left[1/(1 + i)^n \right]$$

where the symbols have the same meaning as before, but the initial amount P is the unknown. In this form, the equation is used to solve problems involving the present value of known or estimated future amounts or the interest (discount) rate required to equate known present values with known or estimated future amounts (see example 8-2).

Substituting the known interest rate and future value from example 8-2 into the equation for determining the present value of a known or estimated future amount, we get

$$P = \$1,500 \, (1/1.12^5)$$
$$= \$ \, 851$$

Example 8-2: A parcel of land is expected to sell for $1,500 per acre when sewer lines are extended 5 years hence. What is the most an investor can pay for the land today if he expects to earn 12 percent annum on his investment?

Solving for the value of $1/(1 + i)^n$ would be laborious when n is a high number were it not for precalculated tables of values for this factor. The solution to $1/1.12^5$ can be read directly from table 8-3 by reading down the 12 percent column and across the 5-year row. The factor at the intersection of the column and row is 0.56743. Multiplying this factor by the expected future value of the land in example 8-2 ($1,500) gives the present value of $851 when the future value is discounted at 12 percent.

Note the distinction between tables 8-2 and 8-3. The first gives values for $(1 + i)^n$, while the latter gives values for $1/(1 + i)^n$. Because these are reciprocals of each other, separate tables are not really needed. All the values for either table can be derived by dividing the corresponding values from the other table into 1. Both tables are generally provided, however, because it is easier for most people to multiply than to divide.

A byproduct of the added convenience of two tables is the attendant problem of determining which to use. One way to keep this straight is to remember that the solution to factors on the future-value table $[(1 + i)^n]$ is always greater than that for the present-value table $[1/(1 + i)^n]$ for the same interest rate so long as the rate is greater than zero. This reflects the basic idea that an amount received in the present is always more valuable than the certain promise of receiving the same amount at a future date. A more extensive set of values for $1/(1 + i)^n$ is given in appendix B.

Annuities

Any series of periodic payments received or payed at regular intervals may be termed an *annuity*. Examples include pension checks from a retirement fund or payments on a fully amortized installment note. While all such regular periodic streams of cash technically qualify as annuities, not all are popularly known as such.

Present Value of an Annuity

The present value of an annuity is best thought of as the amount, which if invested today at a given interest rate, would provide the known periodic payments for the prescribed period.

Example 8-3: Funds placed on deposit with interest at 6 percent per annum (compounded annually) are to be withdrawn in $1,000 increments at the end of each year for 3 years. What must be the initial deposit if the balance of the account is to be exactly zero after the third annual withdrawal?

Table 8–3
Present Value of $1 Due at a Future Date

Period				Discount Rate			
	6%	7%	8%	9%	10%	12%	14%
1	0.9434	0.9346	0.9259	0.9174	0.9091	0.8929	0.8772
2	0.8900	0.8734	0.8573	0.8417	0.8264	0.7972	0.7695
3	0.8396	0.8163	0.7938	0.7722	0.7513	0.7118	0.6750
4	0.7921	0.7629	0.7350	0.7084	0.6830	0.6355	0.5921
5	0.7473	0.7130	0.6806	0.6499	0.6209	0.5674	0.5194
6	0.7050	0.6663	0.6302	0.5963	0.5645	0.5066	0.4556
7	0.6651	0.6227	0.5835	0.5470	0.5132	0.4523	0.3996
8	0.6274	0.5820	0.5403	0.5019	0.4665	0.4039	0.3506
9	0.5919	0.5439	0.5002	0.4604	0.4241	0.3606	0.3075
10	0.5584	0.5083	0.4632	0.4224	0.3855	0.3220	0.2697

Example 8–3 can be solved by reference to table 8–3. Doing so requires that the problem be divided into 3 subquestions:

Question 1: How much must be deposited today to provide $1,000 in 1 year?

To solve this question, first restructure the basic equation to solve for the present value P_1 :

$$P_1 = V_1 \times \frac{1}{(1 + i)^n}$$

where V_1 is the first periodic withdrawal, i is the interest rate, and there is just one compounding period. Substituting the appropriate numerical values into the equation, we have

$$P_1 = \$1,000 \times \frac{1}{1.06}$$

Question 2: How much must be deposited today to provide $1,000 in 2 years? Again, substituting the appropriate numbers into the basic equation, we have

$$P_2 = \$1,000 \times \frac{1}{1.06^2}$$

Question 3: How much must be deposited today to provide $1,000 in 3 years? Numerical substitution results in the following equation:

$$P_3 = \$1,000 \ \frac{1}{1.06^3}$$

The total amount to be deposited to provide for the three annual withdrawals is the sum of the three values just calculated. Therefore, the total present value P is

$$P = \$1,000 \times \frac{1}{1.06} + \$1,000 \times \frac{1}{1.06^2} + \$1,000 \times \frac{1}{1.06^3}$$

$$= \$1,000 \times \frac{1}{1.06} + \frac{1}{1.06^2} + \frac{1}{1.06^3}$$

Values for $1/1.06^n$, where n varies from 1 through 3, are found in the 6 percent column of table 8-3. Summing these three factors, we get

$$P = \$1,000 \times (0.9434 + 0.8900 + 0.8396)$$

$$= \$1,000 \times 2.6730$$

$$= \$2,673$$

The general form of the preceding computation can be expressed as

$$P = R \left[\frac{1}{(1 + i)} + \frac{1}{(1 + i)^2} + \cdots + \frac{1}{(1 + i)^n} \right]$$

where R is the amount of a level periodic receipt, P is the initial deposit, and i is the discount (interest) rate.

Alternatively, the same concept can be expressed as

$$P = R \sum_{t=1}^{n} \frac{1}{(1 + i)^t}$$

where t indicates time periods from 1 throuth n.[2]

The practical problem in solving these type of calculations is the time required to do the computations when the number of compounding periods [and thus the exponent for $(1 + i)^t$] is very large. Precomputed tables for

Table 8-4
Present Value of an Annuity of $1

Period	Discount Rate						
	6%	7%	8%	9%	10%	12%	14%
1	0.9434	0.9346	0.9259	0.9174	0.9091	0.8929	0.8772
2	1.8334	1.8080	1.7833	1.7591	1.7355	1.6901	1.6467
3	2.6730	2.6243	2.5771	2.5313	2.4869	2.4018	2.3216
4	3.4651	3.3872	3.3121	3.2397	3.1700	3.0373	2.9137
5	4.2124	4.1002	3.9927	3.8897	3.7908	3.6048	3.4331
6	4.9173	4.7665	4.6229	4.4859	4.3553	4.1114	3.8887
7	5.5824	5.3896	5.2064	5.0330	4.8684	4.5638	4.2883
8	6.2098	5.9713	5.7466	5.5348	5.3349	4.9676	4.6389
9	6.8017	6.5152	6.2469	5.9952	5.7590	5.3282	4.9464
10	7.3601	7.0236	6.7101	6.4177	6.1446	5.6502	5.2161

the troublesome factor again simplifies the problem. Example 8-3 can be solved quickly and simply by reference to the annuity factors in appendix C, an excerpt of which is presented in table 8-4.

To find the value for an annuity of $1, simply read down the column headed by the appropriate discount rate and across the row for the appropriate number of periods. The intersection of the column and row is the value of the summation of $1/(1 + i)^t$, where t ranges from 1 through n.

Using table 8-4 to solve example 8-3 involves finding the factor for a discount rate of 6 percent for 3 years. That factor (2.6730) multiplied by $1,000 gives the amount which must be deposited initially ($2,673).

Payments to Amortize a Loan

Some situations call for determining the amount of an annuity provided by a known initial deposit (payment). Consider, for example, receipt of a lump-sum grant of $10,000 to be spent by a student during 4 years of study at a university. How much can the student withdraw each year, in four equal annual installments, if the balance in the fund draws interest at (say) 6 percent? Recall the general expression for a level annuity, which is

$$P = R \sum_{t=1}^{n} \frac{1}{(1 + i)^t}$$

The difference in the present problem is that the initial payment P is known and the periodic receipt R is the unknown quantity.

The problem can be solved using factors from table 8–4. First, find the value from the table for the summation of $1/(1 + i)^t$, where the interest rate i is 6 percent, and the time periods range from 1 through 4 years. The factor is 3.4651. The problem can thus be expressed as

$$P = R \sum_{t=1}^{4} \frac{1}{1.06^t}$$

$$= R \times 3.4651$$

and since the value of P is known to be $10,000,

$$\$10,000 = R \times 3.4651$$

Solving for R yields

$$R = \$10,000 \times \frac{1}{3.4651}$$

$$= \$ 2,885.92$$

Note that the final solution involves the reciprocal of a factor from the annuity table. As a matter of analytical convenience, tables are available which incorporate these reciprocal values. Such a table is included in appendix D. An excerpt appears as table 8–5.

The factors in table 8–5 are often called *loan-repayment factors*, or *debt constants.* The table itself is then referred to as an *amortization table.* It gives the equal periodic payment necessary to repay a $1 loan, with interest, over a specified number of payment periods. Because table 8–5 gives repayment factors based on monthly payments, it is *not* reciprocal to table 8–4. A table of annual payments, however, would be. Example 8–4 presents a situation requiring an amortization table.

To solve example 8–4, first find the amortization factor for a $1 loan at 8 percent for 5 years with monthly payments. This factor (0.02028) is found at the intersection of the 8 percent column and the 5-year row on table 8–5. Multiplying the factor by the amount of the loan in example 8–4 gives the

---

Example 8–4: Determine the monthly payment necessary to retire a loan of $100,000, if equal monthly payments are made over a period of 5 years, with interest at 8 percent per annum on the unpaid balance.

Table 8-5
Installment to Amortize $1
(*Monthly Payments*)

	Interest Rate						
Years	6%	7%	8%	9%	10%	12%	14%
1	0.08607	0.08653	0.08699	0.08745	0.08792	0.08885	0.08979
2	0.04432	0.04477	0.04523	0.04569	0.04615	0.04707	0.04801
3	0.03042	0.03088	0.03134	0.03180	0.03227	0.03321	0.03418
4	0.02349	0.02395	0.02441	0.02489	0.02536	0.02633	0.02733
5	0.01933	0.01980	0.02028	0.02076	0.02125	0.02224	0.02327
6	0.01657	0.01705	0.01753	0.01803	0.01853	0.01955	0.02061
7	0.01461	0.01509	0.01559	0.01609	0.01660	0.01765	0.01874
8	0.01314	0.01363	0.01414	0.01465	0.01517	0.01625	0.01737
9	0.01201	0.01251	0.01302	0.01354	0.01408	0.01518	0.01633
10	0.01102	0.01161	0.01213	0.01267	0.01322	0.01435	0.01553

required monthly payment ($2,028). This is the monthly amount the lender must receive if he is to recover his initial outlay of $100,000 plus receive 8 percent per annum interest on the outstanding balance of the loan.

Suppose the loan payments in example 8-4 were to be made annually rather than monthly. The annual payment would be somewhat more than the total of twelve monthly payments. This is so because the interest on the outstanding balance would be increased as a result of the balance not having been "paid down" at monthly intervals during the year. In general, the more frequently payments are made, the less will be the average outstanding balance during the year, and thus the less the total interest payments.

Had the loan in example 8-4 called for annual payments, table 8-5 would not have been usable. No table of annual amortization payments is given, because loans seldom provide for this repayment pattern. But the amortization factor can be easily derived by calculating the reciprocal of the factor for an 8 percent, 5-year annuity. Divide the annuity factor (3.9927) from table 8-4 into 1. The quotient (0.25046) is the annual payment to retire a 5-year, 8 percent loan of $1. Multiplying this factor by the $100,000 amount of the loan in example 8-4 gives the annual payment necessary to retire the loan in 5 years.

Notice that, as suggested earlier, the $25,044 annual payment is somewhat more than the sum of twelve monthly payments ($24,336). To repeat, the difference is attributable to the smaller total interest involved when the more frequent payments reduce the average amount of the outstanding principal balance during the year.

Sinking Funds

A variant of the annuity problem involves periodic deposits to accumulate a specified total amount of funds in the future (see example 8-5).

The problem in example 8-5 is to determine the annual deposit, such that the deposits and cumulative interest on the growing fund will sum to $5,000 by the end of the fifth year. Remember that the deposits are to be made at the end of each year. Thus the last deposit will not draw any interest, since it will have been made at the end of the final year and will be withdrawn immediately. The initial deposit, made at the end of the first year, will have drawn compound interest for 4 years. The second deposit will have drawn interest for 3 years, and so forth. The pattern of deposits and growth in the fund is depicted graphically in figure 8-1.

A single sum placed on deposit at compound interest will grow so that it will eventually equal $R(1 + i)^n$, where R is the initial amount deposited, i is the interest rate, and n is the number of periods the money is left on deposit. Since the initial deposit in example 8-5 is left on deposit for 5 years, it will accumulate to $R_1 (1 + i)^4$. The second deposit draws interest for 3 years and accumulates to $R_2 (1 + i)^3$, and so on. Algebraically, the solution can be expressed as

$$\$5{,}000 = R_1 (1.07)^4 + R_2 (1.07)^3 + R_3 (1.07)^2 + R_4 (1.07) + R_5$$

Since the value of R_1 through R_5 (the periodic amount deposited into the fund) remains constant for each year, the expression can be regrouped as follows:

$$\$5{,}000 = R (1.07^4 + 1.07^3 + 1.07^2 + 1.07 + 1)$$

Substituting values from table 8-2 for the terms in parentheses gives

$$\$5{,}000 = R (1.3108 + 1.2250 + 1.1449 + 1.07 + 1)$$

$$= R (5.75074)$$

Therefore,

$$R = \$5{,}000/5.75074$$

$$= \$869.45$$

which is the amount to be deposited at the end of each year to accumulate a $5,000 fund in 5 years.

The final solution to example 8-5 is depicted in figure 8-2, which indicates a deposit of $869 per annum and a compound sum of $4,998. How

Example 8-5: The roof of a recently acquired warehouse will need replacing in approximately 5 years. How much must be deposited in a special replacement reserve fund to provide for the new roof, which is expected to cost $5,000, if deposits are made at the end of each year and draw interest at 7 percent per annum?

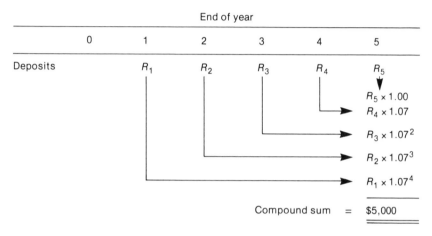

Figure 8-1. Periodic Deposit to Accumulate the Compound Sum of $5,000 after 5 Years, with Interest at 7 Percent.

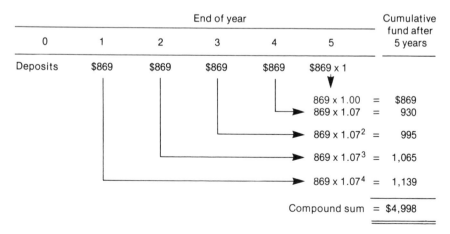

Figure 8-2. Periodic Deposit to Accumulate the Compound Sum of $5,000 5 Years, with Interest at 7 Percent.

does this reconcile with the earlier arithmetical solution? Rounding all amounts to the nearest whole dollar introduces a $2 error. However, because the data are approximations of what is expected to happen in the future, this is certainly precise enough for most decision-making situations.

A special fund set aside for a specific purpose such as that in example 8-5 is often called a *sinking fund*. This is a variation on the annuity problem, which is concerned with the present value of a known series of future payments or receipts. The generalized expression for the (compound amount) problem is

$$S_n = R[(1 + i)^{n-1} + (1 + i)^{n-2} + \cdots + (1 + i)^1 + 1]$$

$$= R \sum_{t=1}^{n-1} (1 + i)^t + 1$$

where S_n is the terminal value (compound amount) of the series of periodic deposits, R is the amount of the periodic deposit, i is the interest rate, and n is the number of periods.

The compound-amount equation is easily converted to solve for the periodic deposit required to yield a predetermined terminal value S_n. In revised form, the problem is expressed as a sinking fund. The revised equation is

$$R = S_n \sum_{t=1}^{n} \frac{1}{(1 + i)^t} - 1$$

where all the symbols have the same meaning as before.

Solving the preceding equation is simplified by using a special table of sinking-fund factors. Such a table is presented in appendix E. An excerpt appears below as table 8-6. To see how a sinking-fund table can simplify calculations, refer again to example 8-5, which can be expressed as

$$R = \$5,000 \times (IF)$$

where the term (IF) is the value from a sinking-fund table for five annual sinking-fund deposits drawing interest at 7 percent. This is found in table 8-6 at the intersection of the 7 percent column and the 5-year row. The factor replaces the term (IF), and the equation becomes:

$$R = \$5,000 \times 0.1739$$

$$= \$869$$

Table 8-6
Annual Payments to Create a Sinking Fund

Period	Compound Interest Rate						
	6%	7%	8%	9%	10%	12%	14%
1	1.00000	1.00000	1.00000	1.00000	1.00000	1.00000	1.00000
2	0.48544	0.48309	0.48077	0.47847	0.47619	0.47170	0.46729
3	0.31411	0.31105	0.30803	0.30505	0.30211	0.29635	0.29073
4	0.22859	0.22523	0.22192	0.21867	0.21547	0.20923	0.20320
5	0.17740	0.17389	0.17046	0.16709	0.16380	0.15741	0.15128
6	0.14336	0.13980	0.13632	0.13292	0.12961	0.12323	0.11716
7	0.11914	0.11555	0.11207	0.10869	0.10541	0.09912	0.09319
8	0.10104	0.09747	0.09401	0.00967	0.08744	0.08130	0.07557
9	0.08702	0.08349	0.08008	0.07680	0.07364	0.06768	0.06217
10	0.07587	0.07238	0.06903	0.06582	0.06275	0.05698	0.05171

Summary of Interest and Discount Factors

Five separate interest factor tables are explained in this chapter. Extended tables of values for the factors are presented in appendixes A through E. Before discussing how the tables can be employed to generate a variety of financial information, basic explanations of their use are summarized below.

Single Payment or Receipt

To find the future value of a single sum received or deposited, use the compound-amount factor from appendix A:

$$V_n = P(IF)$$

where V_n is the future value, P is the initial deposit or receipt, and (IF) is the factor for $(1 + i)^n$ taken from appendix A.

To find the present value of a single sum to be received or paid in the future, use the present-value factor from appendix B. The formula is

$$P = V_n(IF)$$

where P is the present value, V_n is the amount to be paid or received at the end of year n, and (IF) is the factor for $1/(1 + i)^n$ taken from appendix B.

Annuity Paid or Received

Use the annuity present–value factors from appendix C to find the present value of a level series of receipts or payments. Use the factors to solve the equation

$$P = R\,(IF)$$

where P is the present value of the annuity, R is the level periodic payment or receipt, and (IF) is the factor for the summation of

$$(1 + i) + (1 + i)^2 + (1 + i)^3 + \cdots + (1 + i)^n$$

The future value of a level series of deposits is found by solving for the accumulated future value S_n as follows:

$$S_n = R\,(IF)$$

where R is the level periodic deposit, and (IF) is the factor taken from appendix F.

If the desired future value is known and the required level periodic deposit is unknown, the appropriate (IF) factor comes from the sinking-fund table in appendix E. The equation to solve the problem in this form is

$$R = S_n\,(IF)$$

where R and S_n have the same meanings as before, and (IF) is the factor from the sinking-fund table.

Installment to Amortize a Note

Amortization tables are simply the reciprocal of those for the present value of an annuity. However, annuity problems generally involve the assumption of annual receipts, whereas most promissory notes require monthly payments. Using annual tables to solve problems involving monthly debt-service payments overstates both the annual interest payment and the remaining balance on the note. For these reasons, a separate table of *monthly* amortization factors is provided in appendix D.

Use the amortization factors to solve the equation

$$R = P\,(IF)$$

where R is the monthly payment required on a note, P is the face amount of the note, and (IF) is the factor taken from the amortization table for a specified contract rate of interest.

Extending the Use of the Tables

A variety of additional problems can be solved by use of the tables. Several such applications are explored in this section to demonstrate the versatility of the tables and to provide exercises in their use. Extended uses include

Finding values not included on the tables.

Valuing an uneven series of payments or receipts.

Valuing deferred payments series.

Determining effective rates of interest or yield.

Calculating the remaining balance on a note.

These extended uses are by no means exhaustive. They are intended rather to demonstrate the flexibility of the compound–interest and discount concepts, the total usefulness of which is limited only by imagination and inventiveness.

Finding Values not in the Tables

Interest tables give factors for values at intervals over a wide range. Sometimes the rate under consideration falls at an intermediate point between those in a table. When this happens, estimate the actual value by interpolating between table values most nearly approximating the rate being sought.

Interpolation involves assuming a linear relationship between tabular values. This introduces a degree of error, since the actual relationship is quadratic rather than linear. The convenient assumption greatly simplifies calculations, however, and the error will generally be insignificant if interpolation is between those tabular values closest to the unknown factor.

The problem is illustrated in figure 8–3. The curved line shows the relationship between the (IF) values from the annuity present–value table in appendix C for discount rates of 7 and 8 percent and for all intermediate discount rates. The intermediate points, however, are omitted from the table. Interpolation results in estimates of the intermediate values, as indicated by the straight line in the illustration. The distance between the curved (actual) function and the straight (estimated) line respresents error introduced by interpolation. Obviously, the wider apart the known values from which an unknown factor is estimated, the greater will be the error introduced by the assumption of linearity. Try example 8-6.

The annuity table in appendix C (and the excerpt in table 8-4) gives present-value factors for discount rates of 7 and 8 percent, but for no intermediate rates. Since 7.25 percent falls one-fourth of the way between these given factors, approximate the appropriate factor by moving one-fourth of the distance between the factor for 7 percent and that for 8 percent. The 7 percent factor is 4.1002, and that for 8 percent is 3.9927. Multiply the difference by 0.25, and subtract this amount from the factor for 7 percent. The result is a factor of 4.0733, determined as follows:

$$4.1002 - 0.25(4.1002 - 3.9927) = 4.0733$$

These calculations are diagramed in figure 8-4. The total number of percentage points between 7 and 8 percent is 8 minus 7, or 1 point. The distance between discount rates of 7 and 7.25 percent is 7.25 minus 7, or 0.25 point. Since 0.25 point is 25 percent of 1 point, the "target" discount rate lies 25 percent of the distance between the known values. Assume a linear relationship, and estimate the discount factor for the 7.25 percent rate by moving 25 percent of the distance between the discount factor for 7 percent and that for 8 percent.

The total distance between the factor for 7 percent (4.1002) and that for 8 percent (3.9927) is 0.1075. Twenty-five percent of this distance is 0.25 × 0.1075, or 0.0269. Moving this far from the 4.1002 value associated with the 7 percent discount rate results in an estimate of 4.0733 for the factor associated with a discount rate of 7.25 percent.

Having estimated the appropriate discount factor for example 8-6, there remains only to multiply this factor by the annuity payment of $1,000 to arrive at the present value of the annuity. The appropriate answer to the problem is $4,073.

Present Value of an Uneven Series of Payments

Annuity tables facilitate calculating the present value of level periodic payments, but they are not applicable to an uneven series. Faced with uneven

---

Example 8-6: Find the present value of a 5-year annuity of $1,000 per year if the appropriate discount rate is 7.25 percent.

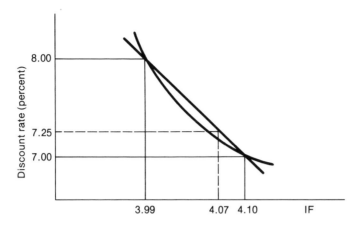

Figure 8–3. Interpolating between Known Present–Value Factors.

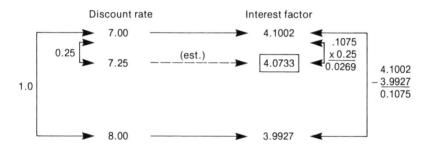

Figure 8–4. Interpolating between Known Present–Value Factors.

payments, the simplest approach is to treat each as an individual reversion (single sum) to be discounted with reference to the table in appendix B. Summing the resultant present values yields the present value of the entire stream of cash flows (see example 8–7).

To solve example 8–7, first find the present–value factors in the 8 percent column in appendix B for the years associated with each anticipated receipt. Multiply each cash amount by the appropriate factor from the table, and sum the products. The total present value is $1,301.20, determined as follows:

Example 8–7: Given discount rate of 8 percent, determine the present value of the right to receive $500 after one year, $700 after 2 years, and $300 after 3 years.

---

(1) Years until Receipt	(2) Amount to be Received	(3) Value Factor from Table	(4) Present Value of Receipt (col. 2 x col. 3)
1	$500	0.9259	$462.95
2	$700	0.8573	600.11
3	$300	0.7938	238.14
Present value of series of payments (summation of col. 4)			$1,301.20

Present Value of a Deferred Annuity

Tables of interest and discount factors may be manipulated a number of ways to determine the present value of a series of level payments or receipts (a level annuity) where the payments do not start for a number of periods. Alternative approaches to a solution are best illustrated with an example (see example 8–8).

Solution Method 1: Combine annuity and single-sum tables. This approach involves moving forward in time to determine the value of the annuity at the beginning of the sixth year (that is, the end of the fifth year). From this perspective, the problem is a simple 5–year annuity. The value at the beginning of the sixth year is then discounted for 5 years as a single sum.

The value of the 5–year annuity at the beginning of the first year in which a payment is to be received—the start of year 6—is determined with reference to the 5–year row and 8 percent column of the annuity table in appendix C, partially reproduced as table 8–4. Multiplying the annuity factor (3.9927) by the $400 annual receipt yields a $1,597.08 value for the annuity at that future point in time.

Remember that this $1,597.08 will be the value of the annuity 5 years from the present. (The solution is for the beginning of year 6, but that is necessarily the end of year 5.) This lump–sum value of $1,597.08 can therefore be treated as a reversion to be received after 5 years. Its present value is determined by reference to the 5–year row and 8 percent column of the table for the present value of a single sum in appendix B, an excerpt of which is reproduced as table 8–3.

From the table, observe that the present value of $1 due in 5 years, discounted at 8 percent, is 0.6806. The present value of the right to receive $1,597.20 is therefore 0.6806 times $1,597.08, or $1,086.97.

The same solution can be reached with one less calculation by first finding the value of a 5–year annuity of $1 per annum which starts after 5 years. This is simply the factor for a 5–year annuity multiplied by the factor for a single sum due in 5 years. The present value of a $400 annuity starting after 5 years will have a value exactly 400 times this amount. The solution, therefore, is

$$\$400 \, (3.9927 \times 0.6806) = \$1,086.97$$

Example 8-8: Using a discount rate of 8 percent, determine the present value of a 5-year annuity of $400 per annum, where the first payment is to be received at the end of 6 years.

Solution Method 2: Determine the difference between two annuities. Treat the problem as a 10-year annuity, but observe that the first 5 years will go to someone else. At an 8 percent discount rate, the present value of a 10-year annuity of $1 per annum is $6.7101, and the present value of a 5-year annuity is $3.9927. The present value of the *last 5 years* of a 10-year annuity of $1 is therefore $2.7174, determined as follows:

Value of 10-year annuity of $1	$6.7101
Less value of first 5 years	3.9927
Value of last 5 years	$2.7174

Since the annuity in example 8-8 is $400 per period, its present value is 400 times as great as an annuity of $1. Simply multiply the preceding factor by 400. The value of a 5-year annuity of $400 which does not start until the sixth year is therefore $400 × $2.7174, or $1,086.96.

Solution Method 3: Treat each receipt as a separate reversion, and sum the present value of each independent future receipt. The solution, using factors from the 8 percent column of appendix B (or the excerpt presented as table 8-3) is as follows:

Years until Receipt	Amount to be Received	×	Present Value Factor	=	Present Value at 8 percent
6	$400		0.6302		$ 252.08
7	$400		0.5835		$ 233.40
8	$400		0.5403		$ 216.12
9	$400		0.5002		$ 200.08
10	$400		0.4632		$ 185.28
Present value of all future receipts					$1,086.96

Effective versus Nominal Interest Rates

Effective interest rates are those actually paid for the use of borrowed funds. They often differ strikingly from rates quoted by lenders. Effective rates are a function of the amount borrowed and the amount and timing of the required repayment.

Common instances of differences between nominal interest rates (rates quoted by a lender) and effective rates on term loans occur when the lender charges a *loan-origination fee,* sometimes called *discount points* or simply *points.* The lender subtracts a percentage of the face amount of the note and disburses only the remaining balance. Alternatively, the lender may disburse the full face amount of the note but require the borrower to immediately remit a specified percentage of the face amount as an origination fee. The net effect is the same in either case: the borrower has the use of only a fraction of the funds stipulated in the promissory note. Interest and principal payments, however, are based on the full face amount of the note. Since the borrower is paying interest (and making amortization payments) on funds which he never receives, the effective interest rate exceeds the stated, or nominal, rate (see example 8-9).

The borrower in example 8-9 receives *net proceeds* of only $4,900 from the lender (the $5,000 face amount of the note less the 2 percent fee) but pays interest and principal based on the full $5,000 face amount of the note. When the note matures after 1 year, the required payment will be $5,350, determined as follows:

Face Amount of note	$5,000
Add: Interest at 7 percent for 1 year	350
Amount due at maturity	$5,350

To determine the total *effective* interest, subtract the net proceeds of the note (the amount actually received by the borrower, net of any required "front-end" payment) from the amount due at maturity. The difference is the cost of using the borrowed funds:

Amount due at maturity	$5,350
Less: Net proceeds from note	4,900
Total *effective* interest payment	$ 450

The maturity value of a note can be expressed by the equation

$$V_n = P(1 + i)^n$$

where V_n is the cumulative value of the note at the end of year n, P is the original investment (that is, the net proceeds of the note), i is the *effective* interest rate, and n is the number of periods the interest is left to compound. Because the number of years n in example 8-9 is only 1, the equation becomes

$$V_1 = P(1 + i)$$

$$= P + P_i$$

Example 8-9: A borrower signs a $5,000 promissory note due and payable in 1 year, with interest at 7 percent. The lender charges a loan-origination fee equal to 2 percent of the face amount of the note.

---

and may be expressed alternatively as

$$(V_1 - P)/P = i$$

Substituting the numerical amounts from example 8-9 into this final expression, we get

$$(\$5,350 - \$4,900)/\$4,900 = i$$
$$= 0.0918, \text{ or } 9.18 \text{ percent}$$

The values substituted into the variables of the equation are the total amount repaid and the net proceeds of the note, respectively. The solution is simplified by setting the term of the note at only 1 year. This eliminates the complication of compound interest. When a note is outstanding for more than one interest period, the solution is facilitated by reference to the interest-rate tables in the appendices. Now let's move on to example 8-10.

Only 98 percent of the face amount of the note in example 8-10 actually will be disbursed to the borrower. The net proceeds will thus be only $4,900, as in the preceding example. But both cumulative interest and principal payable on maturity will be based on the full $5,000 face amount of the note. This discrepancy between the basis for determining the repayment obligation and the amount actually received by the borrower results in an effective rate of interest in excess of the stated, or contract, rate.

The equation for determining the amount payable on maturity of the note is

$$V_n = P(1 + i)^n$$

where V_n is the principal and cumulative interest at maturity, P is the face

---

Example 8-10: Consider again the promissory note from example 8-9: a face value of $5,000, stated interest of 7 percent, and a 2 percent origination fee, with principal and accumulated interest upon maturity. Assume this time, though, that the term of the note is 3 years, with accumulated interest compounded annually.

---

amount of the note, i is the contract rate of interest, and n is the number of periods over which the interest is compounded. To use compound–interest tables, the equation is restated as

$$V_n = P(IF)$$

where (IF) is the value for $(1 + i)^n$, taken from appendix A. Substituting the factor from the 3–year line of the 7 percent column on the table, the equation becomes

$$V_n = P(1.2250)$$
$$= \$5,000\,(1.2250)$$
$$= \$6,125$$

Therefore, the borrower in example 8–10 will have to repay \$6,125 for the use of \$4,900 for 3 years. The effective interest rate this represents is found by repeating the preceding calculation, but letting the variable P represent the net proceeds of the note instead of the face amount. In this second calculation, the maturity value of \$6,125 is taken as given, and the unknown variable is the interest rate i, which will be the *effective* rather than the contract rate. To summarize, we solve for i in the equation

$$V_n = P(1 + i)^n$$

where V_n is the maturity value of the note, P is the net proceeds, n is the number of compounding periods, and i is the effective rate of interest. Replacing $(1 + i)^n$ with the now unknown factor (IF) and substituting the known values for V_n and P, we get

$$\$6,125 = \$4,900\,(IF)$$

Solving for the unknown variable (IF), we get

$$(IF) = \$6,125/\$4,900$$
$$= 1.2500$$

Having determined the only value for the factor (IF) that will equate the repayment obligation with the net proceeds from the note, the effective interest rate is found by reference to appendix A. The effective rate is the interest rate in the table which is associated with the 1.2500 value for the (IF) factor, and it is found by inspection of the 3–year row of the table.

Inspection reveals that this value for the (IF) factor lies between those associated with interest rates of 7 and 8 percent, because the factor for 7 percent (1.2250) is less than 1.2500, while the factor for 8 percent (1.2597) is larger. The rate which corresponds with a factor value of 1.2500 is estimated by the process of interpolation explained earlier in this chapter.

Note on the table that as the interest rate moves from 7 to 8 percent, the associated value factor moves from 1.2250 to 1.2597, a change of 0.0347. Note also that the change from the value factor associated with 7 percent to that associated with the effective interest rate (unknown) is 1.2500 minus 1.2250, or 0.0250.

This suggests that the effective interest rate lies approximately 0.025/0.0347 of the distance from 7 to 8 percent. In example 8–10, the effective interest rate is therefore approximately 7.7 percent, determined as follows:

$$i = 7 \text{ percent } + 0.025/0.0347$$

$$= 7 \text{ percent } + 0.7205$$

$$= 7.72 \text{ percent}$$

A similar problem exists in determining effective interest rates on fully amortized loans. For this, see example 8–11.

Reference to the 3–year row of the 8 percent column in appendix D reveals that the monthly payment to repay a fully amortized note of $1 is 0.03134. To repay a $6,000 note, therefore, the payment must be ($6,000 × 0.03134), or $188.04.

But the borrower in example 8–11 incurs an obligation to make monthly payments of this amount, while actually enjoying the use of only $5,760. This is the net proceeds of the $6,000 note, after deducting the 4 percent origination fee.[3] Consequently, the effective interest rate is greater than the 8 percent stated on the promissory note.

Returning to the basic equation for determining the amount of the periodic payment to amortize a note, we can estimate the effective interest rate by taking the amount of the monthly payments and the amount of the note as given, and solving for the amortization factor from the table which makes the required monthly payments correspond to the net proceeds of the loan. The basic equation, when using the amortization table, is

$$R = P\,(IF)$$

where, as before, R represents the monthly debt–service obligation, but this

---

Example 8–11: A $6,000 note with a contract interest rate of 8 percent is to be repaid in equal monthly payments over 3 years. There is a loan–origination fee equal to 4 percent of the face amount. There is no expectation that the note will be retired prior to the scheduled repayment dates.

time P is the net proceeds rather than the face amount of the loan; (IF) is the (unknown) amortization factor from the table, which is associated with the effective interest rate. Substituting the net loan proceeds and the monthly debt–service payments into the equation, we get

$$\$188.04 = \$5760 \, (IF)$$

Therefore,

$$(IF) = \$188.04/\$5,760$$

$$= 0.03265$$

Estimating the effective interest rate associated with this amortization factor is a matter of thumbing through the amortization table in appendix D in search of a factor in the 3–year row which approximates 0.03265. The factor associated with an interest rate of 10 percent is 0.0323. Interpolating between this and the factor for 11 percent reveals that a 0.03265 factor corresponds to an interest rate of approximately 10.8 percent.

Remaining Balance on a Note

Since annuity tables and amortization tables are reciprocal, either can be used to determine the amount required to retire an outstanding note prior to maturity. (see example 8–12).

The solution to example 8–12 is rendered simple by remembering that note payments represent an annuity whose present value must equal the original face value of the note when discounted at the contract (that is, the nominal) rate. We know this to be so because the payments themselves could have been determined by using the annuity table rather than the amortization table.

Annual debt service on the loan is $1,423.77. This could be determined by reference to an annual amortization table, were such a table available. In the absence of an annual table of amortization factors, the amount is calculated by reference to the reciprocal of the value factor from the annuity table.

The reciprocal of the annuity factor at 7 percent for 10 years is

---

Example 8-12: A $10,000, 7 percent note calls for equal annual payments of principal and interest to retire the note in 10 years. Payments are made at the end of each year. What is the remaining principal balance of the note immediately after the fourth payment?

1/7.0236, or 0.14238. This factor multiplied by the face amount of the note gives the annual debt-service payment.

After 4 years, there remains an obligation to make six annual payments. The remaining balance on the note at that time is simply the present value (at the start of year 5) of the remaining payments, discounted at the 7 percent contract rate:

Annual debt service payment	$1,423.77
Times 6-year annuity factor at 7 percent	4.7665
Remaining balance	$6,786.40

Had the problem in example 8-12 called for monthly amortization payments, the solution would have been similar, but the remaining balance somewhat different. Monthly debt service on the loan is $116.10, determined by referring to the monthly amortization table in appendix D. The remaining balance after the final payment of the fourth year is the value at that time of the remaining 72 monthly payments, discounted at the contract rate of 7 percent.

Absent monthly annuity tables, a precise calculation can be had by deriving the annuity factor from the amortization table. Since the tables are reciprocal, the annuity factor for a monthly annuity of 6 years at a discount rate of 7 percent is 1/0.01705, or 58.6510. The present value of the remaining payments is therefore $116.10 times 58.6510, or $6,809.38.

Notes

1. Some investors calculate the maximum price they will pay for a property by discounting both for time and for risk. Others discount only for time and deal with the risk element in other ways. Risk adjustments are discussed in Part III. The present discussion is limited to discounting expected future benefits based on the length of the waiting period and the time value of money.

2. The term $\sum_{t=1}^{n}$ simply means "sum the following variable for the number of periods 1 through n." Thus, it is a shorthand expression of the value shown as

$$\frac{1}{1+i} + \frac{1}{(1+i)^2} + \cdots + \frac{1}{(1+i)^n}$$

3. It makes no difference whether the origination fee is deducted from the note or paid by separate check. The final outcome is that the borrower receives $6,000 and immediately pays $240, for net receipts of $5,760.

Appendix 8A
Solved Problems

1. A mortgage loan of $75,000 has been made on a property valued at $125,000. The interest rate is 8.5 percent per annum, and the maturity date of the note is 15 years. Monthly debt-amortization payments, however, are based on a 22-year maturity.

    a. *Required:* Determine the loan-to-value ratio.

    Solution:

$$\$75,000/\$125,000 = 0.60, \text{ or } 60 \text{ percent}$$

    b. *Required:* Determine the monthly debt service obligation.

    Solution:

Face amount of note	$75,000.00
Times (*IF*) factor from appendix D	0.008384
Monthly payment	$ 628.80

    c. *Required:* Determine the remaining balance due on the notes after the last monthly payment at the end of the fifteenth year.

    Solution: The remaining balance is the value *at that time* of an annuity for the remaining years, discounted at the contract rate (8.5 percent), where the amount of the annuity is the monthly debt service:

Monthly debt service	$ 628.80
Times (*IF*) factor for monthly annuity of 7 years*	63.1473
Remaining balance	$39,707.02

    d. *Required:* Determine total interest paid over the life of the note.

    Solution:

Total payments made due to the note:	
Monthly debt service (180 payments at $628.80)	$113,184.00
Remaining balance paid after fifteenth year	39,707.02
Total	$152,891.02
Less amount borrowed	75,000.00
Interest paid	$ 77,891.02

---

*Number of years: 22-year term minus 15 years elapsed = 7; (*IF*) factor is reciprocal of factor for monthly amortization.

2. Alfred Freespender can buy land for $20,000 under the following terms: 25 percent cash down, with the balance payable in equal monthly payments over 8 years, with interest at 12 percent per annum. Freespender anticipates that in 10 years he can sell the land for $55,000 cash. During the interim he expects to rent the land to a Georgia peanut farmer at a rate just sufficient to pay real estate taxes.

    a. *Required:* Determine Freespender's *cumulative* debt-service expenditure before considering income tax consequences.

      Solution:

Face amount of mortgage note (0.75 × $20,000)	$15,000.00
Times (*IF*) factor for 96 monthly payments	0.016253
Monthly mortgage payments	243.80
Times number of payments (8 × 12)	96
Cumulative debt-service expenditure	$23,404.80

    b. *Required:* Determine total interest expense during the third year of the holding period, before income tax consequences.

      Solution:

Remaining balance after 2 years:		
Monthly mortgage note payments	$243.80	
Times (*IF*) factor for 72-month		
annuity at 12 percent*	51.1509	
Remaining balance		$12,470.59
Less: Remaining balance after 3 years:		
Monthly payments	$243.80	
Times (*IF*) factor for 60-month		
annuity at 12 percent*	44.9559	
Remaining balance		$10,960.26
Principal reduction during third year		$ 1,510.33
Total third-year payments (12 × $243.80)		$ 2,925.60
Minus principal reduction (from above)		1,510.33
Interest portion of third-year payments		$ 1,415.27

    c. *Required:* Determine the present value of the anticipated sales price, when discounted at 8 percent (disregard income tax effects).

---

*(*IF*) factor is reciprocal of monthly amortization factor.

Solution:

Anticipated sales price	$55,000.00
Times (*IF*) factor at 8 percent for 10 years, from appendix B	0.46319
Present value of anticipated sales price	$25,475.45

d. *Required:* Determine the *net present value* of the investment proposal, discounted at 8 percent (disregard income tax considerations).

Solution:

Present value of anticipated sales proceeds (from above)		
Less: Discounted value of total		$25,475.45
debt service:		
Annual debt service		
(12 × $243.80)	$2,925.60	
Times (*IF*) factor for 8 years from appendix C	5.7466	$16,812.25
Present value of all anticipated future cash flows		$ 8,663.20
Less: Cash down payment		5,000.00
Net present value		$ 3,663.20

e. *Required:* Determine the internal rate of return, based on the preceding cash-flow forecast (disregard income tax considerations).

Solution: Internal rate of return is the discount rate which results in a net present value of zero:

		Present Value	
Years	Expected Annual Net Cash Flow	at 10 percent	At 11 percent
1 to 8	($2,925.60)	$15,607.78	($15,055.43)
10	$55,000.00	$21,204.70	$19,369.90
Cumulative present value		$ 5,596.92	$ 4,314.47
Less: Cash down payment		5,000.00	5,000.00
Net present value		$ 596.92	($ 685.53)

Interpolation:

Discount Rate	Net Present Value	
11 percent	− 685.53	
IRR	0.00	596.92
10 percent	596.92	

$$596.92$$
$$+ 685.53$$
$$1,282.45$$

IRR = 10 percent + 596.92/1,282.45 = 10.5 percent

3. William B. Bucksqueezer acquires a certain parcel of land for $20,000, paying $8,000 in cash and signing a note for the balance. The note is payable in equal monthly installments over 10 years, with interest at 8 percent per annum. He sells the land after 10 years. During the holding period he rents the land to a turf farmer for an amount just equal to the property taxes and other expenses.

   a. *Required*: At what price must the property sell at the end of the tenth year for the internal rate of return to have been 12 percent before accounting for income tax consequences?

   Solution:

Annual debt–service obligation:	
Face amount of note	$12,000.00
Times (*IF*) factor for 10 years	
at 8 percent, appendix D	.012133
Monthly debt service	$ 145.60
Times number of months in year	12
Annual debt service	$ 1,747.20

Sales Price: If the IRR is 12 percent, then discounting at that rate will yield a net present value of zero for all anticipated future cash flows, both positive and negative. Net present value is present value minus down payment. Since the down payment made by Bucksqueezer is $8,000, the present value of debt service plus the present value of sales proceeds must equal $8,000 also. Therefore,

Net present value, discounting		
at 12 precent		0.00
Add: Required down payment		$8,000.00
Present value of future cash flows		$8,000.00
Less: Present value of debt service:		
Annual debt service		
(from above)	($1,747.20)	
Times 10-year annuity		
factor at 12 percent	5.6502	(9,872.03)
Present value of sales proceeds*		$17,872.03
Times 10-year (*IF*) factor at		
12 percent, appendix A		3.1059
Minimum sales price after 10 years		$55,508.74

---

*To subtract a negative number from a positive, change the sign and add.

b. *Required:* At what compound annual rate must the market value of the property increase for Bucksqueezer to sell at the price contemplated in part *a*.

Solution:

Anticipated sales price (from *a*)	$55,508.74
Times 10–year (*IF*) factor from appendix B	(*IF*)
Price paid by Bucksqueezer	$20,000.00

Therefore,

$$(IF) = \$20,000.00/\$55,508.74$$
$$= 0.36030$$

Rate of growth yielding this (*IF*) factor lies between 10 and 11 percent.

Interpolation:

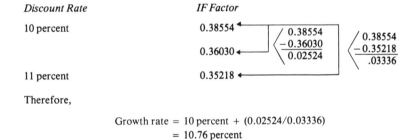

Discount Rate	IF Factor
10 percent	0.38554
	0.36030
11 percent	0.35218

Therefore,

$$\text{Growth rate} = 10 \text{ percent} + (0.02524/0.03336)$$
$$= 10.76 \text{ percent}$$

9 Discounted Cash Flows Revisited

Modern investment analysis is a practical application of the economic theory of the firm, which states that one should operate at the point where marginal revenue equals margin cost. This is a formalized way of observing that so long as the last dollar of revenue results in less than one additional dollar of cost, the additional revenue is worthwhile. It implies, of course, that *all* costs borne by a decision unit are included in the analysis, whether they be explicit accounting costs or merely implicit, such as the value of the decision maker's time.

Translated into the language of investment analysis, this means ventures are acceptable as long as the rate of return on investment exceeds the cost of investable funds. In corporate financial analysis, the concept is made operational by comparing the discounted value of anticipated cash flows from an investment, on an after–tax basis, but before consideration of interest costs on borrowed funds, with the cost of capital. In corporate analysis, *cost of capital* includes cost of both debt and equity funds and is usually calculated by using a "target" composition of sources of funds and computing the weighted average cost from all sources.

Applying this time–tested capital–budgeting technique to real estate analysis requires some modification in computational technique to adjust for differences in sources of funds and differing institutional arrangements. Generally, weighted–average cost of debt and equity funds is not an operational concept for real estate investment analysis. Nor is it generally possible to objectively calculate the cost of equity capital. Necessary modifications to the model therefore include substituting subjective cost of equity funds, or the opportunity cost of equity capital, and the use of projected cash flows net of debt service on borrowed funds. Investment evaluation, therefore, involves comparing the present value of anticipated future net cash flows with the initial equity cash outlay, or comparing rates of return on equity investment with the opportunity cost of equity funds.

Having made these alterations, the corporate capital investment–evaluation model is directly applicable to most real estate investment opportunities, regardless of the nature of the project of the form of the investment entity.

This chapter considers at length two common forms of the evaluation model, both of which were introduced in chapter 7. Each formulation involves discounting expected future net cash flows back to the present and comparing their present value with the required immediate equity cash expenditure. Both methods have merit as investment analytical techniques, both can be supported with compelling logical arguments, and several variations of the basic techniques have been developed in the literature. Equipped with the theory and analytical tools presented in this book, analysts and investors can evaluate all such model variants and indeed can develop their own variations to meet needs peculiar to their immediate circumstances.

Theoretical Basis for Discounting

Several traditional methods for evaluating investment proposals were considered in chapter 7. All were rejected because under at least one plausible set of circumstances they lead to less–than–optimal investment decisions. Common to all these rejected approaches is failure to properly account for timing as well as volume of anticipated future cash flows. Chapter 7 concludes with an introduction to methods designed to overcome this weakness of traditional analysis. Preparatory to more extensive consideration of these improved techniques, there follows a brief review and summary of the concept of the present value of future receipts as an analytical device.

Fundamental to all discounted cash–flow models is the concept of the time value of money, as discussed in detail in chapter 8. The models equate initial cash outlays with the present value of expected cash flows by discounting the expected flows through use of the appropriate discount rates. For a publicly held firm, this may be the "market" cost of equity funds. For other investment entities, it may be the opportunity cost of capital, as discussed earlier. A common (though not recommended) variant is to adjust the discount rate for perceived risk in excess of that embodied in the general portfolio of the investing entity. The issue of risk management is explored further in Part III.

The two most commonly employed models for discounting projected cash flows are the internal–rate–of–return (IRR) and net–present–value models. These variants of the discounted cash–flow approach generally yield the same decision criteria, but under certain circumstances they will give conflicting accept/reject signals. Moreover, there are important differences in underlying assumptions and adaptability of the models to the risk-management techniques discussed in Part III.

Internal Rate of Return

Since (as indicated in chapter 8) there is an inverse relationship between discount rates and present value, there must be some rate that will equate the present value of a projected stream of cash flows with *any positive* initial cash investment. This rate is known as the *internal rate of return*. It has also been called *actual yield* on investment. *Yield*, however, is an ambiguous term which often is used in other contexts. *Internal rate of return*, the more precisely definiable and more generally used term, is therefore preferable. The equation for the internal rate of return (IRR) is

$$\text{Cost} = \sum_{t=1}^{n} (CF)_t \frac{1}{(1 + k)^t}$$

where *CF* is the cash flow projected for year *t*, *cost* is defined as the initial cash outlay, and *k* is the discount rate (internal rate of return) which makes the present value of the expected future cash flows exactly equal to the initial cash outlay. All the terms in the equation are taken as known except *k*, for which the appropriate value is determined to satisfy the equation.

Consider a project which is expected to yield a cash–flow stream, CF_1, $CF_2, \ldots, CF_n$ over *n* future periods. The internal rate of return is simply a rate *k* such that if we put our initial cash outlay into a fund actually earning the rate of return *k* for each period, we could withdraw from the fund the amount CF_1 at the end of period 1, CF_2 at the end of period 2, and so on through CF_n at the end of period *n*, and exactly exhaust the fund at the end of the *n*th period.

If the internal rate of return is equal to or greater than the required rate of return, a project is considered further. If the internal rate of return is less than the minimum acceptable rate of return, the project is rejected (see example 9–1).

In example 9–1, the internal rate of return is approximately 14.8 percent. This is determined by trial and error, using successive approximations of the appropriate discount rate. The process is illustrated in figure 9–1, which shows the expected cash flows for each year of the projection period and the present value at various discount rates. Annual cash-flow projections for years 1 through 7 are simply the $10,000 after-tax cash from example 9–1. In year 8 there is expected $10,000 from operations plus $45,000 from sale of the property, for a total cash-flow estimate of $55,000.

Example 9–1: The expected after-tax cash flow from a proposed investment is $10,000 per year for 8 years, with after-tax cash proceeds from sale of the property at the end of the eighth year forecasted to be $45,000. The required cash outlay to acquire the asset is $60,000. The minimum acceptable rate of return is 10 percent.

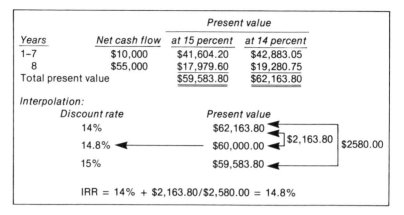

Figure 9–1. Estimating Internal Rate of Return by Successive
Approximations.

Cash flow for years 1 through 7 are discounted using factors from appendix C, since these cash flows represent a level annuity. Appendix B is employed to calculate the present value of the single sum expected in year 8. Discounting at 15 percent, the present value of all expected cash flows equals $59,583.80. This being somewhat less than the initial cash outlay required, the internal rate of return must be slightly less than 15 percent. Discounting again at the next lower rate for which the tables provide factors, the present value at 14 percent is seen to be $62,163.80. Interpolating between 14 and 15 percent, as described in chapter 8, reveals that the rate which equates the present value of expected future cash flows with the required initial outlay is approximately 14.8 percent (some error is introduced in the interpolation process).

Having calculated the internal rate of return based on expected cash flows in example 9–1, the investor compares the result with his required rate of return. Since the internal rate of return exceeds the required rate (14.8 versus 10 percent), the project is considered further. Ultimate acceptance or rejection depends on estimates of relative riskiness, and on the relative attractiveness of alternative investment opportunities.

Popularity of the Internal Rate of Return

That the IRR approach has wide appeal is unequivocally evident from the literature. A case in point is a volume of readings compiled by the American Institute of Real Estate Appraisers and the National Association of Realtors which contains no less than five articles recommending or commenting favorably on IRR as a measure of investment worth.[1] Interestingly, more than half the articles attempt to modify the basic technique to overcome generally acknowledged weaknesses.

Persistent support of a flawed technique might be admirable were there no substitutes that possess equal power to discriminate between acceptable and unacceptable opportunities. Such is not the case with respect to the IRR approach, however, and its continued advocacy is, therefore, somewhat curious.

The major distinction between the IRR approach and the net-present-value approach is that the latter requires a predetermined discount rate to be introduced early in the analysis. But this difference is more illusory than substantive as an argument for one method over the other. There still remains the necessity for users of the IRR technique to specify some minimal "threshold rate" against which the IRR can be measured to determine its acceptability. IRR users therefore only delay, but do not escape, the obligation to determine an investor's required rate of return. Decision criteria based on IRR analysis can easily be expressed in present-value, net-present-value, or profitability-index terms. IRR thus appears to have little to recommend it over alternative techniques based on the same discounting concept, other than perhaps familiarity on the part of practicing analysts, availability of computer programs based on the technique, and avoidance of the need to consider unfamiliar alternatives.

Weaknesses of Internal-Rate-of-Return (IRR) Analysis

While the IRR has little substantive advantage over alternative methods of applying discount rates to projected cash flows, it does have serious weaknesses not found in the alternatives. Problems associated with the IRR can result in conflicting decision signals from this and other discounted cash-flow approaches. Generally, when there is such a conflict, it is because the IRR signal is distorted and, if heeded, might result in serious investment error. The source of potential conflict lies in peculiarities of the IRR equation such that there may be more than one solution, and in problems associated with the reinvestment assumption built into present-value tables.

The Reinvestment-Rate Assumption. Present-value tables incorporate an implicit assumption that funds released from a project are reinvested at the discount rate. Consequently, IRR computation implies that funds are reinvested at the internal rate of return. Thus the IRR method generates reliable investment signals only if there are available other acceptable opportunities expected to yield the internal rate of return. This is, of course, an unlikely prospect when the indicated IRR is considerably above the opportunity cost of capital.

One analytical model which modifies the reinvestment assumption is called the *financial manager's rate of return* (FMRR). The FMRR model specifies a reinvestment rate prior to generating a rate of return which equilibrates the expected cash flows with initial cash outlay. This eliminates a serious problem with the IRR, but also destroys a major source of its appeal—simplicity of application and the existence of readily available computer programs. Moreover, a realistic reinvestment rate for most projects is *not* the risk-free rate, but rather the opportunity cost of capital. Having specified such an opportunity cost, why not proceed to discount at that rate?

The Multiple-Solutions Problem. Generally, the present value of a project is a decreasing function of the discount rate employed. Thus with successively higher discount rates a point is reached where the net present value is zero. This is the internal rate of return, and any discount rate greater than the IRR will result in a negative net present value. When the discounting equation is well behaved in this fashion, there is but one internal rate of return equating all cash inflows with all cash outflows.

Unfortunately, not all cash-flow forecasts are this well behaved, and investment proposals may have any number of internal rates of return, depending on the cash-flow pattern. Depending on the relative magnitude of cash-flow projections, it is possible to have multiple internal rates of return equal to the number of reversals in sign of the cash-flow stream. And reversals of sign are a common characteristic of cash-flow streams from real estate projects. There is often secondary financing associated with projects, whereby the second mortgage note "balloons" in a specific number of years (that is, the remaining balance of the note becomes due and payable). In the year the second mortgage note matures, negative net cash flow is a frequent consequence.

Reversal of sign of the cash-flow pattern is a necessary, but not sufficient, condition for multiple solutions to the internal-rate-of-return equation. Whether multiple solutions will occur depends as well on the magnitude of the cash flows. For many cases of sign reversal there will nonetheless be only one solution to the equation, which is an nth-degree polynomial. For most projects, all but one of the roots are imaginary, and there is but one internal rate of return.

Proposals for adjusting IRR calculations to eliminate the possibility of multiple solutions generally involve "borrowing" funds during years in which the sign is negative, to eliminate the change in sign. Whether the added complication is justified, in view of other weaknesses of the approach, is highly debatable. There remains the problem of the reinvestment-rate assumption. And adjusting for both these problems eliminates the greatest virtue of the approach—simplicity of interpretation and ease of understanding by users.

Review of Net Present Value

Net present value (NPV) is the net benefit that is expected to accrue to investors. A positive net present value means a project is expected to yield a rate of return in excess of the discount rate employed. Assuming the discount rate to be the minimum acceptable rate of return, a positive net present value implies the project is worthy of further consideration, while a negative net present value results in automatic rejection.

To use this approach, discount all anticipated future cash flows at the minimum acceptable rate of return. The result is the present value of expected cash flows. From this value, subtract the required initial cash outlay. The equation is

$$NPV = \frac{CF_1}{(1 + i)} + \frac{CF_2}{(1 + i)^2} + \cdots + \frac{CF_n}{(1 + i)^n} - C$$

$$= \sum_{t=1}^{n} CF_t \frac{1}{(1 + i)^t} - C$$

where i is the minimum acceptable rate of return, C is the required initial cash outlay, n is the number of years in the projection period, and CF_1 is the cash flow expected in the first year, CF_2 that for the second year, and so on through the cash-flow expectation for year n.

The present value of anticipated cash flows from the investment opportunity described in example 9-1 is $74,342, when discounted at 10 percent. Subtracting the required initial cash outlay of $60,000 results in a net present value of $14,342. Since the net present value is greater than zero, the expected rate of return exceeds the minimum acceptable rate of 10 percent, and the project merits further consideration.

**Comparison of Net Present Value and
Internal Rate of Return**

Under most circumstances the internal-rate-of-return (IRR) and net-present-value (NPV) approaches will give the same decision signals. When this occurs there is little significance in the choice of one over the other. There are, however, some conditions under which contradictory signals emerge. These two techniques may rank alternatives in different order, for example. Moreover, the methods are not equally adaptable to incorporation of risk-analysis techniques introduced in Part III.

As noted earlier, the two methods will usually give the same accept/reject signal. The rules are

1. When using IRR, reject all projects having an IRR less than the minimum required rate of return. Projects with an IRR equal to or greater than the minimum required rate of return (the "hurdle rate") are considered further.
2. When using NPV, discount at the minimum required rate of return (the "hurdle rate") and reject all projects with a net present value of less than zero. Projects with a net present value of zero or greater are considered further.

The essential similarity of these decision criteria is reflected in their mathematical formulation. The only structural difference is the discount rate. All other values are exactly the same. Remembering that the discount rate employed in the IRR is the effective yield, the net present value will be exactly zero when the internal rate of return equals the minimum required rate of return.

While the two methods therefore generally give the same basic accept or reject signals, they are susceptible to variances in the order with which they rank alternatives. Since investors are often faced with choosing between alternative opportunities rather than with a simple accept/reject choice, this can be a serious problem. Limited equity funds generally force investors to choose from among several opportunities, all of which meet minimum acceptance criteria.

Most of the time, investment rankings under the IRR and NPV methods will also be identical. Under special circumstances, however, the methods will rank projects differently. This can happen where projects differ in size, where timing of cash flows differs, or where projects have different expected lives.

Discrepancies with Mutually Exclusive Projects of Different Size

Consider two mutually exclusive projects of greatly different size (say, the use of a given site for a hotel or a service station). The initial cash outlays and the cash flows upon completion and sale are as follows:

	Cash Flows	
Year	*Project A*	*Project B*
0	($100,000)	($1,500,000)
1	$150,000	$1,900,000

Project A, requiring an initial outlay of $100,000 and returning $150,000 after 1 year, has an internal rate of return of 50 percent, while project B, with an initial cost of $1,500,000 and a return of $1,900,000 after 1 year, has an internal rate of return of only 25 percent. The internal rate of return criterion, therefore, ranks project A ahead of project B.

But consider the net present value of the two projects, assuming a 12 percent minimum acceptable rate of return. Project A has a net present value of approximately $34,000, compared with project B's net present value of approximately $340,000. This criterion thus ranks project B ahead of project A.

Discrepencies Due to Differences in the Timing of Cash Flows

Consider two projects having the following projected cash flows:

	Cash Flows	
Year	Project C	Project D
0	$(100,000)	$(100,000)
1	35,000	0
2	35,000	0
3	35,000	0
4	35,000	0
5	35,000	250,000

The internal rate of return on project C is 22 percent, whereas that on project D is 20 percent. Project C therefore ranks superior to project D using this criterion. But discounting at a minimum acceptable rate of return of 12 percent, project D, with a net present value of $41,857, ranks superior to project C, whose net present value is only $26,167. If, because of limited available investment capital, only one of the projects can be accepted, there is an obvious conflict in signals creating a serious decision problem.

General Superiority of Net-Present-Value Criterion

In situations where the internal-rate-of-return and net-present-value methods give different decision signals, the question arises as to which provides the best guide for evaluating investment opportunities. The answer depends on the appropriate assumption regarding the reinvestment rate.

With a high internal rate of return, an equally high reinvestment rate is implied. With a low internal rate of return, an equally low reinvestment rate is implied. Since each investment opportunity is unique in many respects, either of these implications is likely to misguide decision makers. The method can be adjusted to account for this problem, but doing so involves additional computations and increases difficulty of comprehension. For these reasons and others previously discussed, the net–present–value approach is generally considered superior to the internal rate of return method.[2]

Extending the Usefulness of Net Present Value

Having argued for the general superiority of net present value, there remains the problem of overcoming weaknesses associated with the chosen criterion. The major problems concern choosing an appropriate discount rate, choosing between alternatives requiring different levels of initial cash outlay, and adjusting for risk of variance from expected future cash flows. This section addresses each of these issues in turn. It then illustrates use of the net–present–value criterion with an extensive example.

Choosing a Discount Rate

An argument often advanced by advocates of the internal rate of return is that the method avoids the need to choose a discount rate. While this argument is specious, it does dramatize the issue of appropriate selection of the rate of discount to be factored into the net–present–value equation.[3]

The choice of a discount rate is critical to selection between alternative opportunities, as well as to deciding what opportunities merit additional consideration. Minor adjustments in the discount rate can result in rather dramatic changes in net present value. The further into the future the cash-flow projections are made, the greater is the influence of discount–rate variations. Moreover, relative ranking of opportunities can be changed by altering the discount rate, when opportunities differ in the timing of antici-pated cash flows (see example 9–2).

Example 9–2: Two projects are available, each requiring an immediate outlay of $100,000 of equity funds. But the projects differ in amount and timing of expected net cash inflows. Project A offers the prospect of receipt of $25,000 per annum for 10 years, with no receipts or disbursements thereafter. Project B is expected to generate a total of $500,000 of net cash inflow, all of which is to be received at the end of the tenth year. The investor has sufficient equity funds to invest in only one project and wishes to rank them in the order of their desirability.

Relative desirability of the projects in example 9-2 depends on the choice of a discount rate. At a rate of 15 percent, project A is preferable to project B, with respective net present values of $25,469 and $23,592. But at a rate of 14 percent, the relative rankings are switched, with project B's revised net present value of $34,872 being preferable to project A's new net present value of $30,403. Thus with a discount rate of 14 percent or less, project B appears more desirable, while project A is more desirable with discount rates of 15 percent or more.

Discussions concerning the appropriate discount rate for deriving net present value generally center about three alternatives. These are a risk-free rate, a risk-adjusted rate, and the cost of capital.

Risk-Free Rate. Advocates of the risk-free rate seek to isolate differences in present value attributable solely to variances in timing of anticipated cash flows. The risk-free rate is assumed to be the reward solely for waiting, with no premium for associated risk. The idea is to take the time value of money into account by the discounting process, and then as a separate operation to incorporate considerations associated with existence of risk.

Reference to a *risk-free rate* generally means a rate devoid of risk of default. To understand the distinction, consider a loan made to the federal government. Such loans are generally considered the safest possible use of funds, but investors recognize that even here there are risks involved. While the risk of default is virtually zero, there remains the risk of loss of purchasing power because of inflation. There remains also the risk that an unfavorable change in the current market rate of interest will either reduce the value of the investment or cost the investor the opportunity to earn a return at the new, higher rate.

The default-free rate, then, is the rate an investor could earn from an alternative use of his funds without appreciably increasing his exposure to default or to "business risk." Since a publicly held firm always has the option of buying back its own stock or retiring outstanding debt, the default-free rate will generally be the same as its marginal cost of capital.

Risk-Adjusted Rate. Possibly the most commonly employed rate—certainly the most common among real estate analysts—is comprised of a risk-free rate plus a "risk premium." This *risk-adjusted discount rate* is taken as the minimum acceptable rate of return on the class of asset to which the risk premium is applicable.

The risk premium differs with the analyst's conception of risk inherent in a project being analyzed. The riskier the project, the higher the discount rate employed. Thus the discount rate is composed of two elements: a time adjustment and a risk adjustment.

In spite of its widespread popularity, the risk-adjusted rate has few defenders among theoreticians. The approach is flawed in both theory and practice. There appears to be no easy way to eliminate the two major difficulties.

The first problem relates to determining the appropriate adjustment. In the absence of some "risk index," the adjustment must reflect the analyst's subjective "feel" concerning the degree of risk inherent in a project and his attitude toward risk. Yet it is the investor's attitude, and not the analyst's, which should be reflected in a risk premium. Risk is borne by the investor, whose attitude toward risk might be drastically different than that of the analyst.

Then there is the problem of constructing an index of risk adjustments. If risk is doubled, should the risk premium be doubled also? Or should the premium more than double? Economic theory suggests the premium should increase at an increasing rate, that is, that it should more than double when perceived risk doubles. This reflects the concept of diminishing marginal utility of wealth and the increasing aversion to risk exhibited by most people when large sums are at stake.

There appears to be no practical way to determine just how large a risk premium should be, even if the investor's perception of, and attitude toward, risk is known. But there is an even more fundamental flaw in the risk-adjusted-discount idea. Because discounting is designed to adjust for the time one must wait for future benefits, any given rate discounts by an increasing amount as one waits longer for an event to occur. Therefore, a risk-adjusted rate discounts longer-term risk more heavily than shorter-term risk purely because of the time interval, without reference to the absolute amount of risk involved.

Since it is demonstrably *not* the case that long-term ventures are inherently more risky than short-term ventures, this is a fatal flaw in the risk-adjusted-discount scheme. As a case in point, most analysts will agree that the construction and rent-up phase is the most risky part of a development project. Yet the risk-adjusted rate discounts these near-term risks much less heavily than those associated with operation of a seasoned project.

Marginal Cost of Capital. Textbooks in corporate finance generally advocate use of a firm's marginal cost of capital as the appropriate discount rate.[4] Bierman and Smidt recommend using several different rates, depending on the circumstances surrounding the decision-making situation.[5]

Because of peculiarities associated with financing most real estate projects, marginal cost of capital necessarily relates to the cost of capital other than mortgage financing. For most investing entities, this means equity financing. And for privately held corporations or noncorporate investors, marginal cost of capital is a difficult concept to apply. This is so because there is no convenient way to determine the cost of equity funds other than simply applying the opportunity cost of capital.

Opportunity Cost of Capital. The question facing an analyst is: What alternative use of funds is available which does not appreciably increase the investor's business risk? That is, how can equity funds which must be expended if a project is to proceed be used without changing the risk attendant to the project under consideration? The highest rate which could be earned by such alternative employment of equity funds can be used as the discount rate.

Opportunity cost of equity funds is a logical candidate for the discount rate and is easily understood by clients. It serves admirably as a minimum acceptable rate of return, or hurdle rate, since investors are unlikely to accept any project promising a rate of return below that available elsewhere with the same degree of risk. And this is exactly what opportunity cost implies; it is the rate of return available on the next best opportunity which embodies the same degree of risk.

Using opportunity cost as a common discount rate permits a direct comparison between projects of the same general risk category. This eliminates comparison problems which might otherwise arise when cash flows differ drastically in amount or timing. In combination with the *profitability index* (explained later), it facilitates comparison of projects requiring significantly different amounts of initial cash investment.

Finally, a common discount rate for all competing projects greatly facilitates risk analysis of the type discussed in Part III. It permits risk analysis to be incorporated into policy guidelines, which enables screening of investment opportunities by subordinates or analysts to be extended far beyond the preliminary point of simply comparing expected returns with the minimum acceptable rates.

Comparing Projects of Different Size

Net present value does not give an unambiguous decision signal when projects require different levels of initial cash outlay. But the measure can be converted to a cost/benefit ratio which does this task admirably. The ratio, called a *profitability index,* is calculated by dividing the present value of expected future cash flows by the amount of the initial cash outlay. The quotient represents present value *per dollar* of initial cash expenditure. The general decision rule, then, becomes accept the project with the greatest profitability index (assuming, of course, that there is no difference in the risk profile of competing opportunities).

Applying the profitability index technique to example 9-1 results in a decision to tentatively accept the project since there is $1.24 of present value for every $1 of initial cash investment. The calculation is

$$PI = \text{present value/cost}$$
$$= \$74,342.09/\$60,000$$
$$= \$1.24$$

When using the profitability index as an initial screening device, reject all projects with an index of less than 1. Projects with a profitability index equal to or greater than unity are then subjected to additional analysis. This is, of course, a simple variant of the rule of rejecting any project whose net present value is less than zero.

The profitability index is simply an alternate way of expressing net-present-value data, since instead of subtracting initial cash outlay from present value, we divide by that amount. Therefore, when

$$\text{Present value} - \text{cost} = 0$$

it is also the case that

$$\text{Present value/cost} = 1$$

It follows that when

$$\text{Present value} - \text{cost} < 0 \quad \text{then} \quad \text{Present value/cost} < 1$$

and when

$$\text{Present value} - \text{cost} > 0 \quad \text{then} \quad \text{Present value/cost} > 1$$

Applying the Net-Present-Value Criterion

This final section applies previously discussed procedures for developing after-tax cash-flow projections, and discounts them at the minimum acceptable rate of return. Limitations of the print medium require that several assumptions be made about key variables which, in a realistic situation, would be subject to debate and judgmental variation. We make these assumptions to expedite illustration of the mechanical process of developing net-present-value estimates. Now examine example 9-3.

Example 9-3: An investor has ordered analysis of a 5-year-old apartment complex known as Altamese Villa Apartments. The following information applies:

Current Market Price

Improvements	$280,000
Land	70,000
Total market value, land and improvements [a]	$350,000

Available Financing

First mortgage at 9½ percent for 25 years	$262,500
Second mortgage at 11 percent for 15 years	50,000
Total mortgage financing	$312,500
Add: Equity required	37,500
Total (market value)	$350,000

Income Tax Information

The investor is married and files a joint return with his wife. During each year of the investment period, the owner's taxable income from sources other than the proposed investment, after all exemptions and deductions, is expected to exceed $200,000. The owner has no other investments or income sources anticipated to generate preference income during the projected period. [b]

Other Relevant Information and Assumptions

1. Both revenue and expenses are expected to increase at about the same rate as the general cost of living, which is assumed to average approximately 6 percent per annum over the projection period.

2. The remaining useful economic life of improvements to the property under analysis is assumed to be 35 years, with salvage value at that time estimated to be negligible.

3. If the investor accepts this opportunity, he expects to liquidate his position after 6 years, at which time he will be eligible for retirement and intends to leave the state.

4. The property is expected to sell after 6 years at approximately the gross rent multiple reflected in its current market price.

5. The investor requires a minimum expected rate of return of not less than 10 percent on equity, having found he can expect to net this amount by putting all his funds into second mortgages.

---

[a] Includes proration of relevant transactions costs.

[b] See Chapter 6 for a discussion of minimum tax on preference items.

The first step in analyzing the opportunity in example 9-3 is to forecast revenue and expenses for the property over the expected holding period. The analyst notes that the area is fully developed, with no land available for significant new, competing buildings, and that the area evidences no discernible trend of either rapid growth or decline. He concludes that both rents and expenses should be fairly stable over the next few years, moving approximately with the general movement in consumer prices. He expects the consumer price index to increase at about 6 percent per annum (compounded) over the next few years, so he takes this as the expected rate of increase in both rents and operating expenses.

Starting with the owner's operating statement, adjusting as explained in chapter 3, results in a forecast of first-year operating figures shown in table 9-1.

Having determined the most likely change in operating results over the holding period to be an average 6 percent per annum increase in both revenue and expense, the forecast becomes a mechanical projection at that rate. The forecast must be made on an after-tax cash-flow basis, however. This requires the investor's income tax position to also be forecast for each year of the prospective holding period. To calculate interest expense for this purpose, an amortization table for available financing must be developed. This information is shown in table 9-2.

The investor's expected taxable income for each year consists of the expected "income from other sources" plus-or-minus the gain or loss from operation of Altamese Villa Apartments. The gain or loss from the apartment will be the forecast net operating income minus depreciation allowance and interest expense for each year. These calculations are presented in table 9-3.

While depreciation allowances reduce taxable income, they do not affect before-tax cash flow from an investment. Conversely, reduction of the principal amount of mortgage indebtedness reduces cash flow without affecting taxable income. The lower half of table 9-3 contains after-tax cash-flow forecasts, which start with net operating income and are adjusted for debt-service and income tax effects. Discounting forecast cash flows at the minimum acceptable rate of return (10 percent) by use of the table in appendix B yields the present value of each year's net cash-flow forecast.

The final step in forecasting cash flow is to estimate the after-tax cash flow from disposal of the property at the end of the proposed holding period. If the Altamese Villa Apartment Complex's current Gross Rent Multiplier continues to apply, it will have a market value of $468,000 when sold at the end of the sixth year of ownership. Subtracting estimated transactions cost of 7 percent results in a net-sales-price forecast of $435,240.

Table 9-4 converts the expected selling price into after-tax cash flow from disposal. (Income tax computations are illustrated in table 9-5.) This

Table 9–1

Adjusted Operating Statement for Altamese Villa Apartments

Potential gross revenue		$76,800
Less: Vacancy and rent loss		2,000
Effective gross income		$74,800
Less: Operating expenses:		
Real estate taxes	$14,600	
Insurance	1,500	
Wages	8,000	
Fuel	5,800	
Water	1,200	
Electricity	900	
Scavenger	850	
Painting and redecorating	500	
Repairs and maintenance	800	
Supplies	400	
Management	3,000	
Miscellaneous	700	
Reserves for replacement	1,000	
Total expenses		$39,250
Net operating income		$35,550

Table 9–2

Mortgage Amortization Schedule for Financing Altamese Villa Apartments

	First Mortgage[a]			Second Mortgage[b]		
Year	Interest	Principal	Remaining Balance	Interest	Principal	Remaining Balance
0		0	$262,500	0	0	$50,000
1	$24,821	$2,700	259,800	$5,432	$1,388	48,612
2	24,554	2,967	256,833	5,271	1,549	47,063
3	24,263	3,258	253,575	5,092	1,728	45,335
4	23,931	3,590	249,985	4,892	1,928	43,407
5	23,580	3,941	246,044	4,669	2,151	41,256
6	23,188	4,333	241,711	4,420	2,400	38,856

[a]Nine and one-half percent, 25 years, monthly payments of $2,293.45

[b]Eleven percent, 15 years, monthly payments of $568.30.

involves determining the remaining balance of mortgage indebtedness and the estimated tax on gain from disposal. Subtracting these amounts from the expected net selling price gives forecast after-tax cash flow from disposal, which is then discounted at the minimum required rate of 10 percent by reference to appendix B.

Table 9–3
Cash–Flow Forecast for Altamese Villa Apartments

	Year of Operation					
	1	2	3	4	5	6
Effective gross [a]	$74,800	$79,500	$84,000	$89,000	$94,500	$100,000
Operating expense [a]	39,250	41,500	44,000	46,500	50,000	52,000
Net operating income	$35,550	$38,000	$40,000	$42,500	$44,500	$ 48,000
Less: Interest [b]	30,253	29,825	29,355	28,823	28,249	27,608
Deprecia- tion [c]	8,000	8,000	8,000	8,000	8,000	8,000
Taxable gain (loss)	($ 2,703)	$ 175	$ 2,645	$ 5,677	$ 8,251	$ 12,392
Net operaing income	$35,550	$38,000	$40,000	$42,500	$44,500	$48,000
Less:						
Debt service [b]	34,341	34,341	34,341	34,341	34,341	34,341
Income tax [d]	(1,892)	123	1,852	3,974	5,776	8,675
After–tax cash flow	$ 3,101	$ 3,536	3,807	$ 4,185	$ 4,383	$ 4,984
Present–value factor	0.90909	0.82645	0.75131	068301	0.62092	0.56447
Present value	$ 2,819	$ 2,922	$ 2,860	$ 2,858	$ 2,721	$ 2,813

[a] First-year figures taken from table 9–1. Subsequent numbers represent an annual compound rate of 6 percent, rounded to nearest $500.

[b] From table 9–2. Combined amount from both mortgages.

[c] Assumes straight–line depreciation: cost/useful life = $280,000/35.

[d] Assumes investor is in 70 percent income tax bracket.

Table 9–4.
Forecast of After–Tax Cash Flow from Disposal of Altamese Villa Apartments

Expected sales price [a]		$468,000
Less: Selling costs		32,760
Expected net selling price		$435,240
Less: Remaining balance on mortgages [b]	$280,567	
Income tax on gain [c]	37,307	$317,874
Expected net cash flow		$117,366
Times present–value factor at 10 percent		.56447
Present value of expected net cash flow		$ 66,250

[a] Rounded to nearest $1,000.

[b] From table 9–2. Sum of balances of first and second mortgages.

[c] From table 9–5.

Table 9-5

Income Tax Consequences from Disposal of Altamese Villa Apartments

Expected gain on disposal:		
Net selling price (from table 9-4)		$435,240
Less: Adjusted basis:		
Initial basis (cost)	$350,000	
Minus accumulated depreciation	48,000	302,000
Expected gain		$133,240
Less: Portion exempt from taxation (60 percent)		79,944
Portion included in taxable income		$ 53,296
Income tax, at 70 percent [a]		$ 37,307

[a] This amount is compared with the *alternative minimum tax* as explained in chapter 6, with the taxpayer paying the greater of the normal tax or the alternative minimum. For simplicity, we assume no *excess itemized deductions*. Under these circumstances the taxpayer will incur no liability for the alternative minimum tax in the year of sale.

There remains only to sum the present value of the expected after-tax cash flow from operation with that from disposal of the property, and to compare the total present-value forecast with the required initial cash outlay of $37,500. If the present value exceeds the required initial cash outlay, then the net present value is greater than zero and the expected rate of return exceeds the 10 percent minimum acceptable rate. The final calculations are

Present value:	
From operations (from table 9-3)	$16,993
From disposal (from table 9-4)	66,250
Total	$83,243
Less: Initial cash outlay	$37,500
Net present value	$45,743

Justified Investment Price

An alternative presentation of the data from example 9-3 involves estimating the maximum purchase price to yield the minimum acceptable rate of return. This approach is a particularly valuable source of intelligence for improved negotiating. With the mortgage financing assumed to be available for the property in the example, an investor can pay the present value of cash flow to the equity position plus the amount of the available mortgage and still expect to receive a 10 percent return on equity funds. The *justified investment price* is therefore equal to the $83,243 present value plus the $312,500 mortgage, for a total of $395,743.

Of course, an element of error is introduced when the justified investment price differs significantly from the purchase price assumed in initial calculations, because assumed financing will then differ from that actually available. Recomputation with revised mortgage–financing assumptions incorporating the debt–service costs likely to be incurred when purchasing under the first approximation of the justified investment price yields a refined estimate of this measure with very little error attributable to this particular cause.

The effect of mortgage–financing assumptions on the justified investment price serves to emphasize the most valuable use of this computation—its contribution to negotiating position. Since present value differs with the amount and cost of available financing, the justified investment price will vary also. There is, therefore, a different justified investment price for every alternative set of financing arrangements. When a seller finds the justified investment price of a would–be buyer unacceptably low, there is the possibility of a tradeoff between price and credit terms.

Preparatory to negotiating price and terms, an investor should compute the justified investment price under a variety of potential prices with attendant terms for partial seller financing. These alternatives form a basis for counteroffers by the buyer, as well as for quick evalutation of proposals made by the other side.

Summary

Modern investment–evaluation techniques generally involve some variation of a discounted cash–flow model, expressing the present value of all anticipated future cash flows. Most common are the internal–rate–of–return and the present–value/net–present–value methods. The internal–rate–of–return method is conceptually appealing to many, but it contains flaws which make it less desirable than the present–value/net–present–value approach.

Present value can be expressed as an index of present value per dollar invested. This presentation, called a *profitability index,* permits comparisons between ventures which differ significantly in size. The index is also useful in applying the risk–adjustment techniques introduced in Part III.

Justified investment price is the present value of all anticipated future net cash flows to the equity position plus available mortgage financing. If an investor pays the justified investment price, he expects to receive a yield on his investment exactly equal to the discount rate employed in the analysis. The justified investment price is a valuable aid in negotiating tradeoffs between price and seller financing.

Notes

1. American Institute of Real Estate Appraisers and National Association of Realtors, *Readings in Real Estate Investment* Analysis (Cambridge, Mass.: Ballinger, 1977).

2. Doubters are referred to an extensive discussion of the relative merits of these approaches by authors generally acknowledged as eminent authorities as well as pioneers in the theoretical aspects of capital budgeting methodology. See, for example, Harold Bierman, Jr. and Seymour Smidt, *The Capital Budgeting Decision* (New York: Macmillan, 1971), pp. 38-54.

3. Having solved for the internal rate of return, analysts still face the problem of comparing this rate with some benchmark to determine acceptability. This predetermined minimum acceptable rate, often called a *hurdle rate,* could have been used to derive a net present value in the first place. Thus nothing is gained by choosing the internal-rate-of-return over the net-present-value criterion.

4. See, for example, James C. van Horne, *Financial Management and Policy,* 3rd ed. (Englewood Cliffs, N.J.: Prentice-Hall, 1974), pp. 101-128.

5. Bierman and Smidt, *The Capital Budgeting Decision,* 3rd ed. (New York: Macmillan, 1971) p. v.

Part III
The Problem of Risk

Real estate investment decision making progresses in distinct sequential steps. The first of these is specification of investor objectives. Objectives are then related to estimates of the most likely outcome of proposed investment projects. The final step involves measuring and quantifying risk in some objective and consistent manner. Only then can a rational investment decision be made.

Traditional real estate investment literature does a good job developing all but the final phase of the decision process. Analysts have generally not performed well in the area of risk analysis, however. They have fallen behind the level of sophistication in cognate fields such as corporate finance with respect to quantification and systematic incorporation of risk into the general analytical framework.

Part III reviews traditional approaches to the problem of risk in real estate analysis, toward the end of demonstrating the basic weaknesses of these techniques. It then introduces more advanced approaches which have been tested and are not a matter of serious controversy in corporate financial and capital budgeting literature. These techniques can be profitably applied to a variety of real estate investment problems.

Greater demands are placed on the reader's intellect in this final part of the book. Mastery requires a basic understanding of probability analysis and statistical inference. Because many practitioners are not well versed in these areas, some space is devoted to explanation of the fundamentals necessary for mastery of the material.

Readers unfamiliar with the tools of statistical analysis will be tempted to dismiss Part III. That is a most unfortunate reaction, because this is in fact the heart of the entire presentation. Parts I and II contain nothing new to reasonably apt appraisers or analysts. The primary benefit to be derived from this book lies in learning to use modern risk–analysis techniques.

10 The Risk Element in Investment Analysis

Earlier chapters discuss evaluation of investments based on a single best estimate of net cash flows over the projection period. Crucial steps are shown to include (1) isolation of significant factors affecting probable future cash flow, and (2) determination of the appropriate discount rate. Having forecasted cash flows and derived the discount rate, calculation of the present worth of an opportunity becomes a mechanical process.

Unsophisticated investors are often seduced by the illusion of precision inherent in point estimates of future cash flows. They frequently misunderstand the significance of forecasting errors in estimating the investment value of projects.

The future being inherently unknowable, the only certainty in financial forecasting is that actual outcomes will differ from expectations. Keep constantly in mind the probabilistic nature of all forecasts, and automatically reject the implication of precision found in forecast statements with values rounded to the nearest whole dollar. Actual outcomes will almost certainly differ from forecasts; the only uncertainty is the extent of the variance.

Moreover, not all forecasting errors are created equal. Very large percentage errors in certain income and expense items have relatively insignificant impact on investment outcomes, but even small forecasting errors in other areas can be fatal to project profitability. Sensitivity of projected outcomes to error in the various elements of a forecast is thus as crucial an issue as is the accuracy of forecasts themselves.

Uncertainty and risk surrounding expected outcomes of proposed investment projects pose both a threat and an opportunity to investors properly armed to deal with them. This chapter discusses the nature of investment risk and explains how the issue has traditionally been treated in the literature and by practicing investors. Further, this chapter treats the issues of avoidable and unavoidable risk and the relationship between investor attitude and the expected risk premium. It then considers the relative merits of traditional methods of adjusting the investment analysis for unavoidable risk.

Major Risk Factors

Some risks may be eliminated by transference to another party. These *transferable,* or insurable, *risks* become highly predictable for firms specializing in them. Such firms accept transference of risk for a fee, based on the probability of sustaining a loss and the probable amount of such loss. Other risks are a function not of the decision to invest, but rather of the decision to utilize financial leverage. These risks can be avoided by the simple expedient of foregoing the expected benefits of financial leverage, or their degree can be managed by judicious use of financial leverage. Finally, there are certain risks which are an integral part of the investment process and cannot be transferred or avoided without foregoing the expected benefits of investment.

Insurable Risk

Loss due to fire, flood, and other natural hazards is highly unpredictable with respect to any one particular building or property. It is, of course, possible to calculate statistical odds of such a loss based on generally accepted sampling techniques. But what is the significance to an investor who has just been wiped out by a major fire or flood that the likelihood of such an occurrence was, say, 1 in 10,000?

However, for investors or firms whose holdings are sufficiently diversified geographically, actual losses will approximate the probability determined by use of sampling techniques. That is, if a certain class of building included in a large sample experienced fire losses of 1 per 1,000 buildings, then a widely diversified portfolio of such buildings can expect approximately this same loss ratio so long as the same causal factors are operating. For such investors, therefore, the actual dollar amount of annual losses to these events becomes highly predictable.

Investors lacking the portfolio size necessary for such geographical diversification can transfer these risks to firms which specialize in bearing statistically predictable risk. Predictability based on large samples is, of course, the basis of the insurance industry. Because their dollar losses are relatively predictable, insurers can develop fee schedules which compensate them for all projected losses, plus a premium for expenses, profits, and a reserve for the unexpected. For large firms, the degree of uncertainty involved in the insurance function is very small.

Financial Risk

Recall from chapter 5 that use of financial leverage increases the volatility of possible returns to an investment. Mortgage lenders have a prior claim on net operating income, with the investor's before-tax cash flow (cash throw-off) being a residual. The higher the dollar amount of borrowed funds, and thus the greater the debt service relative to net operating income, the greater the probability that income will be insufficient to meet the debt-service obligation.

Inept or misguided scheduling of debt-service obligations also increases financial risk. Financial risk, therefore, is a function of both the amount of borrowed funds employed and the associated scheduling of debt-service payments. It is a phenomenon specific to the financial arrangements surrounding an individual investment decision. The amount of financial risk associated with a particular investment venture is in this sense controlled by the investor himself.

Investment Risk

Even the most precisely calibrated operating projections are subject to gross error. The likelihood that actual operating results will vary from expectations is sometimes called *business risk*. As a matter of terminological convenience, we will call it *investment risk*.

Investment risk stems both from factors internal to the investment equation and from circumstances attributable to the economic environment surrounding a project. Management inefficiencies may cause operating expenses to exceed expectations, for example, or result in an inordinately high vacancy rate. Credit-investigation and rent-collection practices may result in an unexpectedly high level of credit losses. Any of these events, all internal to the investment equation, will cause net operating income to fall below the forecast.

The economic environment may be less propitious than anticipated, with consequences which include an unexpectedly low level of demand for the space-time produced by a project. This means either a higher-than-expected vacancy rate or reduced rental rates. In either event, the unfortunate consequence of the variation from expected economic climate will be gross rental revenue below that anticipated at the time an investment commitment was made. This, in turn, means that net operating income will fall below expectations.

Investment risk associated with failure of anticipated demand to materialize can be reduced by careful management with respect to the type of tenants to which a property caters. Properly incorporated facilities for a variety of tenants whose demand for space-time is not highly correlated reduces the overall risk of a major variation between anticipated and actual gross rental revenues.

Investors involved in several simultaneous ventures may be able to reduce aggregate risk associated with their portfolio by judicious diversification. Including in the portfolio a variety of properties differing in size, type, and location reduces the risk that a significant portion will perform diametrically counter to expectations. Investors of limited means can achieve the same result by taking a position in limited-partnership ventures or real estate investment trusts.

Other techniques for minimizing investment risk include the use of options instead of outright purchase commitments and the use of exculpatory clauses in financing documents. For a price it is often possible to acquire an option to purchase property; this results in extremely limited financial exposure until events prove or disprove the investor's short-term expectations. Exculpatory clauses are legal provisions which limit personal liability in connection with large mortgages, so that if an investment proves to have been ill-advised, potential loss is limited to the investor's initial equity position.

Having exhausted these techniques, however, there remains a core of investment risk either which cannot be avoided or which an investor may wish to bear because the potential reward for doing so justifies the exposure. Attitudes toward this remaining risk will vary with the basic personalities of investors, their capacity to absorb financial reverses, and their personal investment objectives.

Investor Objectives and Risk

Any attempt to discuss investor objectives quickly runs afoul of the nebulous term *investor*. Like Humpty Dumpty, we choose to let the expression mean just what we choose it to mean, and we mean it to include any person or entity who takes an equity position in real estate. This is sufficiently broad to encompass individuals, corporations, partnerships, trusts, pension funds, and so forth. *Investor* could mean something entirely different—and frequently does when used elsewhere. Our definition is not to be universally applied, nor is it intended to be taken as exclusive. It is rather an operational definition which enables us to use *investor* as a convenient shorthand term.

Given the diverse entities included in this definition, there can be no doubt that investors will have a variety of different objectives. Some (for example, real estate investment trusts, pension funds, commercial banks), are constrained by law and regulatory agencies. Others, because of their relatively high income tax obligations, seek tax-shelter situations. Others seek fixed income. Some look for speculative situations to yield spectacular capital appreciation, while others might consider real estate their inventory in a basic merchandising sense.

There are, however, certain basic traits which most investors hold in common, regardless of their motivations or personal objectives. All rational investors seek financial return as a reward for committing resourses and as compensation for bearing risk. The amount of expected compensation and the degree of risk borne depend on the investor's attitude toward risk and his investment objectives.

Attitude toward Risk

Emotional temperament plays a large role in an investor's attitude toward risk. Some people are risk takers by nature; they not only accept it, but go out of their way to incur it. These are people who gamble even when they know the game favors the house. They seem to revel in defying the odds. The "long shot" is worth courting almost certain failure.

Other people avoid risk at almost any price. They sacrifice expected return to "hedge their bet," even where the cost of "hedging" is disproportionate to the relatively small associated risk. As investments, these people favor fixed-income securities carrying a high degree of safety of principal, such as government bonds or certificates of deposits at large commercial banks.

Most investors probably fall somewhere between these extremes. They tend to minimize risk exposure, preferring the relatively low-return certainty to the higher-return longshot. Moreover, they tend to become progressively more risk-averse as total perceived risk exposure increases and increasingly less risk-averse as their total wealth increases. These propositions about investor behavior have been explored at length in the economic and financial literature and are not generally a matter of serious dispute.

Authorities generally agree that to the extent motivated by rational financial considerations, most investors have the attitude toward risk and expected return depicted in figure 10-1. They prefer a higher to a lower return for a given perceived risk; they prefer less to more risk for a given expected return; and they accept additional perceived risk only if accompanied by additional expected return.

An additional investor characteristic demonstrated in figure 10-1 is the tendency to become increasingly averse to additional risk as total perceived risk increases. Thus the investor whose attitude is depicted in figure 10-1 can be induced to accept the additional risk indicated by the distance r_1 to r_2 by the promise of an increase in total reward indicated by the distance p_1 to p_2. But to be induced to accept an identical additional risk increment (from r_3 to r_4), he must be able to anticipate a substantially greater reward increment (from p_3 to p_4). In addition, as indicated in the illustration, there is some level of perceived risk (r_5) beyond which the investor cannot be induced to venture regardless of the possible benefits attached thereto.

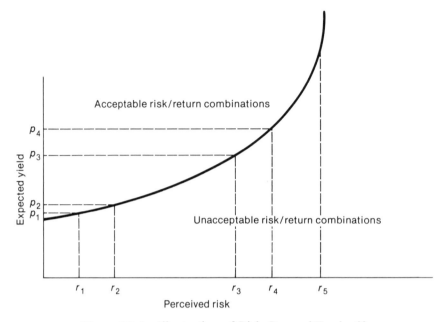

Figure 10-1. Illustration of Risk–Reward Tradeoff.

Of course, the exact shape and location of the curve depicted in figure 10-1 depends on an investor's personal attitude toward risk. A more risk-averse attitude would be depicted by a much more steeply inclined curve, while a less risk-aversive attitude would be depicted by one less steeply inclined. A "risk lover" would actually trade expected return for additional risk. These attitudes are depicted by the various "indifference curves" in figure 10-2.

Rational Risk Taking

Rational risk taking is epitomized by successful insurance firms. This industry turns a handsome and highly predictable profit by allowing insured parties to substitute the certainty of a small loss (the insurance premium) for the uncertainty of a larger, possibly catastrophic loss, such as a fire, flood, or major illness. Insurance companies can do this successfully by astute risk management. They carefully calculate the odds involved in loss, against which they issue insurance policies, and always ascertain that the premium is sufficient to compensate for the chance of loss.

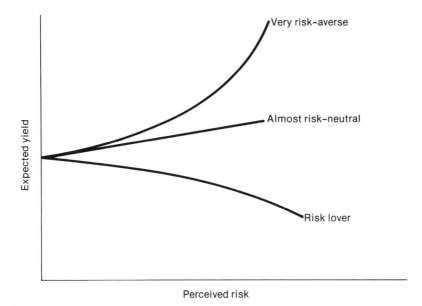

Figure 10-2. Variations in Attitude toward Risk.

Insurance firms might be characterized as *risk takers by design*—so might rational investors in real estate. Such an investor will, before committing substantial resources,

1. Carefully specify investment objectives concerning return on investment, timing of return, and acceptable risk levels.
2. Identify the major risks involved, and quantify them as completely as possible.
3. Eliminate some risks, transfer others via insurance or other techniques, and "constrain" the remaining risks to acceptable levels.
4. Make an accept/reject decision based on whether expected returns justify bearing the remaining risks in view of the contribution the venture makes toward overall investment objectives.

Of course, not all real estate investment ventures represent examples of rational risk taking. Emotional risk takers are likely to adopt an entirely different approach. Characteristic of the latter are investments made on a "hot tip" or a "hunch." Emotional risk takers are seemingly rendered blind to risk by the glare of expected return. Successful investors who have adopted an emotional attitude toward risk are prone to use their personal experience as vindication for the approach ("If investment analysts are so smart, why aren't they rich like me?"). Those driven into bankruptcy by this approach are not generally considered newsworthy.

Managing Risk

Rational investors are willing to shoulder a certain degree of risk in anticipation of financial rewards for so doing, but they will not take unnecessary chances, nor will they accept risk not justified by attendant expectation of financial gain. The difficulty arises in determining the amount of risk associated with an investment opportunity and arriving at a reasonable incremental return to justify the incremental risk. Before a price can be set on the risk-bearing function, risk must somehow be measured or ranked. Measuring levels of investment risk is no small order, nor is it a matter of mere casual concern.

Real estate analysts and investors have traditionally declined to attempt quantification of perceived risk. They simply developed a subjective impression of the risk embodied in a proposal and attached a return premium in addition to that required in the absence of "above normal" risk.

Risk premiums employed in traditional real estate analysis take the form of a shorter payback period, a larger discount rate, a higher required rate of return, or an adjustment to projected cash flows. All these approaches result in a smaller justified investment price—the amount the investor is willing to put into the project.

Traditional risk-adjustment techniques share a serious shortcoming: they are not conducive to use of explicit measures of risk or quantification thereof. This makes risk comparison between projects somewhat difficult, even for the analyst doing the risk estimation. It renders completely impossible the task of communicating risk perception to a second party.

This inability of traditional risk-management techniques to be communicated to second parties is a particularly serious problem for analysts working with client investors. Even if the analyst has accurately perceived the risk level, what is the value of the perception if it is not communicable? The common argument that the risk-premium recommendations of analysts communicate risk by implication is invalid. The risk-premium recommendation embodies not only perceived risk, but also the analyst's personal attitude toward risk. And these two elements are inseparable unless some method is devised to quantify the risk in isolation.

The difficulty lies in the subjective nature of attitudes toward risk. It will be purely coincidental if the attitude of the analyst coincides with that of his client. Moreover, the attitude of the analyst himself will most likely be different with someone else's wealth at stake than were he putting his own money at risk.

Fortunately, techniques are available for dealing with this serious problem of communicating risk assessment to a client unadulterated by the analyst's personal attitude. These techniques are discussed in subsequent chapters. They are offered as alternatives to traditional methods, which are explored more fully in chapter 11.

Summary

Risk is a problem that has been skirted in earlier chapters. It is a ubiquitous aspect of real estate analysis, however, and must be faced by rational investors. Some risks can be shifted to other parties or minimized through astute investment-management techniques. But risk avoidance has a price, and many risks are consciously shouldered by investors because the expected rewards for so doing outweigh the potential costs.

Risk must be amenable to measure and quantification before it can be properly incorporated into real estate investment analysis. Only then can trained analysts communicate their perception to clients, enabling the latter to make more fully informed investment decisions.

Traditional means of adjusting for risk inextricably intertwine the analyst's risk perception with his personal risk preference. Traditional risk-adjustment techniques are therefore appropriate only on those rare occasions when analysts and their clients share a common attitude toward risk. Because risk preference is influenced not only by wealth and preexisting risk exposure, but also by subtle psychological factors, common attitudes toward risk are about as likely as commonality of fingerprint patterns.

11

Traditional Risk–Adjustment Techniques

Both professional and academic literature reflects a deep vein of dissatisfaction with traditional approaches to the problem of risk in real estate investment analysis. A veritable flood of articles have appeared in recent years seeking to introduce techniques which have long been commonplace in other fields. Unfortunately, little of this path–breaking work has found its way into practice or into introductory textbooks or courses.

Each generation of real estate analysts educates its own successor. Training and professional certification are largely controlled by trade groups, which in turn are governed by successful practitioners who were educated by their professional predecessors. As a consequence of this "intellectual inbreeding," real estate analysts employ methods and techniques which represent the state of the art in other fields a generation ago. Old, less–effective tools of analysis tend to be perpetuated in spite of the ready availability of something better.

This explains, but does not excuse, the prevalence of outmoded technology in real estate analysis. Intellectual cross–fertilization from corporate finance and the decision sciences in general can enable real estate analysts to cast off the stigma of obsolescence and compete more effectively with professionals from such other fields as public accounting and management consulting who are experiencing increasing success in invading the traditional turf of appraisers and feasibility analysts.

Preparatory to introducing modern risk–analysis methods, this chapter reviews current practice with a view toward demonstrating the major shortcomings of the tools now employed by many practitioners. This chapter discusses adjustments to the payback period, adjustments to the discount rate, and adjustments to projected cash flow, demonstrating in each case both theoretical and practical objections. Sensitivity analysis is introduced as the final subject of the chapter because it is a useful tool of analysis with which most practitioners are at least passingly familiar.

The Payback–Period Approach

Recall from chapter 7 that the *payback period* is simply the period of time required for cash flow from an investment to equal the original outlay. If, for example, an investment requiring a down payment of $5,000 is expected to yield $2,000 per annum for several years, the payback period is 2½ years, determined by dividing the down payment by the annual net cash flow:

$$\$5,000/\$2,000 = 2.5$$

Where annual net cash-flow projections vary from year to year, as is almost always the case in after-tax analysis, the payback period is determined by cumulating the annual expected net cash flows until they equal the amount of the initial outlay. Limitations of the payback period as a method for comparative evaluation of investment opportunities is treated at length in chapter 7.

Proponents of payback-period analysis adjust for the riskiness of an investment by varying the minimum acceptable period. More-risky investments are expected to have a shorter payback period than are the less-risky ones. The precise amount of the adjustment is necessarily subjective, since risk itself is not generally measured. Analysts simply state how much shorter than the "normal" acceptable payback period a particular investment should have, based on their "feel" for inherent risk.

There is a compelling simplicity to payback-period adjustments for risk. No quantitative skills are required. This method shares with all widely used rules of thumb the attractiveness of ease of application and amenability to being stated as a policy directive.

An analyst might be instructed, for example, to further investigate investment opportunities in "declining neighborhoods" only if the payback period is less than (say) 3 years, while analyzing in depth all opportunities in designated "growth areas" where the payback period does not exceed (say) 6 years.

Payback-period analysis is not a rational method of evaluation, even in the absence of risk, and addition of the risk problem renders it even less applicable.

In a great many cases, payback-period analysis excludes a major element of risk: the likelihood that the sale price will differ significantly from expectations. The desirability of many real estate opportunities depends heavily on expected gain on disposal. In such cases, risk is primarily a function of the certainty associated with the anticipated sale price. But if the disposal point extends beyond the payback period, neither anticipated benefit nor attendant risk will be included in the analysis (see example 11-1).

In example 11-1 the payback period of 4 years is accompanied by virtual certainty that the annual cash flow from operations will in fact be realized. But how does one adjust the required payback for the uncertainty of the anticipated cash flow from sale of the property after 5 years?

Example 11-1: A warehouse, available for a down payment of $8,000, is almost certain to yield a net annual cash flow of $2,000 for the next five years, after which it is expected to have a market value such that the net cash flow from disposal will be $10,000. The annual cash flow during the holding period is secured by a tenant with an impeccable credit rating, who has 5 years remaining on his lease. The forecast selling price after 5 years is predicated upon the tenant renewing his lease—an eventuality which is far from certain. If the tenant does not renew, then the selling price will depend on the investor's ability to find a comparable tenant at the same rental rate.

At best, payback-period adjustments for perceived risk will be useful when the bulk of the risk is experienced during the payback period itself. The approach is not well suited to actual adjustments of the required anticipated rate of return over the total holding period. Neither does it lend itself to comparison of incremental risk and return from alternative investment opportunities.

Risk-Adjusted Discount Rate

Chapter 9 discusses the discounted cash-flow approach to investment analysis, using an "assumed" appropriate discount rate. Given the appropriate rate, discounting anticipated cash flows to arrive at the present value of an opportunity is a mere arithmetical exercise. Chapter 9 also demonstrates that calculating net present value by including initial cash outlay in the equation is a minor variant of the technique. An opportunity is assumed to be desirable if the net present value equals or exceeds zero.

Left unanswered in the discussion of discounted cash flows and net present value is the question of the appropriate discount rate. This deliberate omission is necessary because the question of the appropriate rate depends on how an analyst approaches the problem of adjusting for risk.

A risk-adjusted discount rate is traditionally used with the discounted cash-flow model. A risk-free rate is proposed as representative of the pure time-value of money. To this is added a premium for risk associated with a particular venture. The risk-free rate is (presumably) the same regardless of the nature of the proposal under consideration, changing only to reflect variances in the disutility of waiting. Risk premiums, on the other hand, vary with each proposal, depending on attendant risk and the attitude toward risk taking.

Specialists in corporate finance and capital budgeting have developed elaborate techniques for determining the appropriate risk premium.[1] In almost every instance, these techniques are either impractical or inappropriate for use in real estate investment analysis. Consequently, this approach can be defended neither on theoretical nor practical grounds. For real estate analysis, it simply does not well serve its intended function.

The Risk-Free Discount Rate

Choosing an appropriate risk-free discount rate is more a theoretical than a practical problem. In practice, most analysts simply select a risk-adjusted rate without bothering to stipulate the riskless return with a separate risk adjustment.

Analysts who, for reasons of procedural elegance or to satisfy custodians of professional standards, wish to demonstrate derivation of their risk adjustment do, of course, have this problem. Their difficulty is rooted in the inaccuracy of the term *risk-free*. Financial commitments always carry certain risks which can be neither eliminated nor transferred. In the context of security analysis, *risk-free* is intended to imply not absolute absence of all risk, but virtual absence of default risk. The risk-free rate is taken as that which would apply if lenders viewed a borrower's credit and collateral so favorably that they were absolutely certain of repayment at the scheduled time.

But lenders face other risks as well. One is the risk that the general level of prices will move up during a loan period, so that lenders will be repaid in dollars of substantially less value than those loaned. A second is that the market rate of interest will increase after a loan is tendered. This causes market values of existing securities to decline, and even if held to maturity, they yield less than a lender could have earned had he waited until after the movement in market interest rates before making the loan.

Facing such difficulties in specifying a riskless rate of discount, most analysts simply accept the rate available on short-term federal securities as a proxy. Federal securities are as default-free as any on the market. Using short-term rates reduces the interest-rate risk associated with such securities.

The Risk Premium

To the risk-free discount rate is added an additional discount the size of which depends on perceived risk. The risk adjustment should be based on an investor's tradeoff function between risk and return. Suppose, for

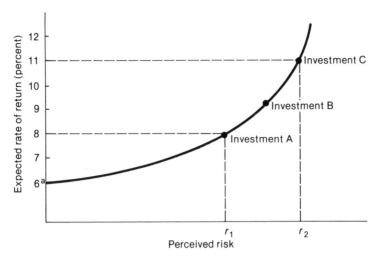

^aRiskless rate of return.

Figure 11-1. Risk/Return Tradeoff Function.

example, that the line in figure 11-1 is representative of this attitude for a particular investor. The line represents the relationship between risk and return such that the investor would be indifferent between any risk/return combination falling along the line. For lack of a better term, we call this the investor's *risk/return tradeoff function.* In figure 11-1 the riskless rate is assumed to be 6 percent. A 2 percent risk premium is required to compensate for risk level r_1, and a 5 percent premium is required to compensate for risk level r_2. The investor will be indifferent between a riskless return of 6 percent or any of the risky investments A, B, or C.

Determining the appropriate risk premium presents a seemingly insurmountable hurdle to making this approach operational. Traditionally, no such measure has been used, so the risk premium could not be stated as a specific quantity. Absent a measure of risk, there is no method of determining an investor's risk/return tradeoff function. In practice, therefore, real estate analysts using this approach simply state a risk premium embodying their perception of the risk and their *personal* risk/return tradeoff function. But since the tradeoff function reflects personal attitude toward risk, as well as the level of perceived risk, the analyst's function will be appropriate only if his attitude corresponds exactly with that of his client-investor.

Since attitude toward risk is a matter of personal psychological preference, financial ability to sustain loss, and the extent of existing risk exposure, there is no reason to suppose that the attitude of an analyst will ever exactly match that of his client. Indeed, even the analyst's attitude will likely differ when applied to an investment analyzed for a client than when he himself is placing money at risk.

Before the risk-adjusted discount rate can be effectively used for analyzing an investment on behalf of a client, therefore, some method must be devised to quantify perceived risk. Such a measure is available and is being increasingly used in other contexts. The most common measure of risk is standard deviation. This measure, which is explored more fully in the next chapter, does solve the particular problem associated with the risk-adjusted discount rate.

But there remains a fatal weakness in using a risk-adjusted discount rate that has yet to be explored. Before doing so, we should observe that having determined standard deviation of returns as a measure of risk associated with an investment opportunity, there is a much better way to use that information in connection with the discounted cash-flow approach. This alternataive is also explored in the next chapter.

Practical and Theoretical Problems

The risk-adjusted discount-rate approach is flawed, both theoretically and practically. These faults would be sufficient to discredit the approach even if there were a method to quantify risk which did not in the process present an opportunity to use a more sophisticated approach.

In spite of its weaknesses, the risk-adjusted discount rate is probably the most commonly used approach among analysts. This is likely because most analysts enter their trade by first learning real estate appraisal. And the technique of adding a risk premium to the discount rate has been a standard appraisal practice for generations. It "works" because appraisers do not really do what they claim. What they actually calculate is a ratio between anticipated future cash flows and observed selling prices of comparable cash-flow claims recently traded in the marketplace. This ratio is applied to cash-flow projections of the property being appraised to arrive at a most-probable selling price.

Widespread use notwithstanding, the approach is fatally flawed. In separating risk-free and risky portions of the discount rate, the riskless rate is intended to represent the time value of money invested. This is pure time value, without any associated risk. The only other compensation will therefore be for risk assumed. But when an additional discount factor is introduced for risk, it too takes time into account.

The consequence of this double accounting for the time value of money is that future risk is discounted more heavily than is near-term risk. This would be appropriate only if there were some systematic relationship between time and risk. But this is not the case. In point of fact, near-term risk is often greater than far-distant risk. An example would be an apartment building to be constructed and "rented up." The risk of construction-cost overruns and of misestimating the market during the rent-up period is generally far greater than that of estimating errors during the subsequent operating period. Yet the risk premium on the latter is far greater than that on the former. Each subsequent year of operation is discounted more heavily than the preceding, in spite of the fact that as neighborhoods mature, operating forecasts become more precise.

By way of illustration, consider a 10-year project for which the appropriate risk premium is taken to be 6 percent and the riskless rate is estimated to be 4 percent. The overall discount rate, the sum of the risk-free and the risk premium, is therefore 10 percent. Discounting involves dividing each year's cash-flow projection by a number derived by raising 1 + discount rate to a power equaling the number of years before the cash is expected to be received. In this illustration, therefore, the discount factors for the first 3 years are, respectively 1.10, 1.10^2, and 1.10^3.

Were there no risk involved, the discount rate would be simply 1 + riskless rate, or 1.04. The factors for the first 3 years would therefore be 1.04, 1.04^2, and 1.04^3. The factor by which the anticipated cash flows are divided to account for perceived risk is the difference between the preceding quantities. For the first 3 years, the risk adjustments are

Year	Risk-Adjusted Discount Factor	−	Riskless Discount Factor	=	Risk Factor
1	1.100		1.040		1.060
2	1.210		1.082		1.128
3	1.331		1.125		1.206

Thus the further into the future anticipated risk lies, the greater is its impact on the present value of an investment, in spite of the fact that a time adjustment has already been made by applying the riskless discount rate. This is clearly double accounting for time.

Far more serious than the theoretical weakness just discussed is the impracticality of using risk-adjusted discount rates as policy tools. Investors need a device for screening out obviously unacceptable investment projects. This requires a policy statement of minimum risk/return combinations which are to be passed for review by a final decision maker. Because risk premiums embody the attitude of the person making the adjustment, combined with his personal perception of risk, they are not suited to this type of policy orientation.

The Certainty-Equivalent Method

Some of the difficulties associated with risk-adjusted discount rates can be solved by adjusting projected cash flows instead and then discounting at the risk-free rate. This eliminates the problem of double accounting for the time value of money and neatly sidesteps the need for specific quantification of perceived risk. Practical problems with this alternative include the cost of determining the appropriate certainty-equivalent adjustment and increased risk of client alienation. As we shall see, these problems become almost insurmountable when final accept/reject decisions are made by a committee instead of by an individual.

How It Works

Analysts using this method substitute for their "best estimate" of future cash flows an amount such that the client is indifferent between expected receipt of the best estimate (with the associated risk of variation from expectations) and absolute certainty of receiving the substitute amount. This substitute amount, or *certainty equivalent,* is then discounted at the risk-free rate to adjust for the time value of money to arrive at the present worth of an opportunity (see example 11-2).

An early step in determining certainty equivalents for the cash-flow forecast in example 11-2 is to carefully explain to the investor the nature of the expected environment in which projections will materialize. After acquainting him with the risk elements, the analyst attempts to determine his reaction by asking him to indicate a preference for forecasted cash flows or various specified riskless cash-flow alternatives. Varying riskless alternatives are postulated until an amount is determined such that the investor is indifferent between the risky and the riskless flows.

Assuming that the preceding procedure has been carried out, there might result a set of certainty equivalents for the projections in example 11-2 such as those in table 11-1.

Example 11-2: A project offers an anticipated net cash flow of $5,000 per annum for 5 years, followed at the end of the fifth year by an anticipated net cash receipt of $65,000 from sale of the project. Receipt of the cash from disposal is contingent upon approval by government agencies of complementary construction proposed for adjacent property, and if approval is not granted, then the proceeds will be much less.

Table 11-1
Certainty-Equivalent Cash-Flow Factors

Time Period	Expected Cash Flow (1)	Riskless Amount Equivalent to Risky Cash Flow (2)	Certainty-Equivalent Factor[a] (3)
Year 1	$ 5,000	$ 4,700	0.940
Year 2	5,000	4,700	0.940
Year 3	5,000	4,700	0.940
Year 3	65,000	54,990	0.846

[a] Riskless amount (column 2) divided by expected amount (column 1).

Column 3 of table 11-1 is derived by dividing column 2, the risk–free equivalent, by column 1, the expected cash flow. The resultant *certainty-equivalent factor* is the amount of money receivable *with certainty*, which is just as satisfactory to the investor as the risky expectation of receiving $1 of expected return that year. Thus the investor in example 11-2 indicates in table 11-1 that he is currently indifferent between $0.94 received for certain in years 1 through 3 and the risky expectation of receiving $1 in each of those years.

The riskier an expected cash flow is perceived to be, the smaller will be the certainty-equivalent factor. In example 11-2, expected sales proceeds at the end of the projection period are assumed to be more problematic than are annual cash flows from operations. Hence a smaller certainty equivalent is associated with the $65,000 expected cash flow at the end of the third year.

Implied in the preceding discussion is that the present value (V_0) of an anticipated series of annual cash flows (CF_t) can be expressed as

$$V_0 = \sum_{t=1}^{n} \frac{CF_t}{(1 + k)^t} = \sum_{t=1}^{n} \frac{a_t CF_t}{(1 + i)^t}$$

where k is a risk–adjusted discount rate, i is the risk–free rate, and a_t represents a certainty-equivalent factor such as illustrated in table 11-1.

Using the certainty-equivalent factors from table 11-1 and assuming a riskless discount rate of 6 percent, the present value of the opportunity in example 11-2 is $58,733.82, determined as follows:

$$V_0 = \sum_{t=1}^{3} \frac{a_t CF_t}{(1 + i)^t}$$

$$= \frac{(0.94)\$5,000}{1.06} + \frac{(0.94)\$5,000}{1.06^2} + \frac{(0.94)\$5,000}{1.06^3} + \frac{(0.846)\$65,000}{1.06^3}$$

$$= \$4433.96 + \$4182.98 + \$3946.21 + \$46,170.67$$

$$= \$58,733.82$$

Problems with the Certainty-Equivalent Approach

Certainty equivalents, in effect, translate the risk-preference function from figure 11-1 into a risk-indifference function. This is accomplished by changing the horizontal scale from perceived risk to riskless rates of return. The line then traces points of indifference between risky and riskless rates of return. The slope of the line (or the slope of a straight line drawn tangent to the indifference function at the appropriate point) indicates the value for a certainty-equivalent factor a_t.

Determining the numerical value of this certainty-equivalent factor is the principal difficulty associated with applying the approach. This can be accomplished by presenting the investor with a series of combinations of risky and risk-free cash flows and asking him to state a preference between each set of alternatives. An extended series of such experiments will result in a preference map representing the investor's attitude toward risk. From this map, certainty-equivalent factors can be extracted.

Getting an investor to state his preferences in this fashion, however, is a difficult and time-consuming task. The time required, and the attendant cost, might well cause the investor to rebel. Success depends on the analyst's powers of persuasion. These powers will be sorely taxed as the necessity of making ever finer distinctions between risky and risk-free cash flows becomes increasingly frustrating to a client who is both paying for the exercise and doing the bulk of the mental work.

Where preliminary but not final investment decisions are delegated, this method is particularly unsatisfactory. Because a new preference map must be drawn for each investment opportunity (reflecting the risk elements peculiar to that venture) and for each decision maker (reflecting his personal attitude toward risk), the certainty-equivalent method cannot be crafted into a policy instrument without major modification in the way certainty-equivalent factors are generated.

One such modification is to first quantify the risk element by using standard deviation as a risk measure. Cash-flow estimates are then reduced by a number of standard deviations to ensure virtual certainty that actual cash flow will prove to be equal to or more than the certain equivalent cash flow. This eliminates the subjective attitude toward risk associated with an individual decision maker and permits discounting at the risk-free discount rate. This promising modification requires an understanding of standard deviation as a measure of risk, and its full development is deferred until a later chapter after discussion of statistical inference.

Sensitivity Analysis

Real estate analysts and investors have long wrestled with the problem of adjusting for risk. Not satisfied with the simplistic notion that adjustments can be made by merely increasing the discount rate, many have groped for alternatives. Risk-adjusted discount rates serve the needs of appraisers seeking to determine the extent to which market price reflects inherent risk, but investors need a technique for assessing the *extent* of the risk, so they can evaluate it in terms of their personal risk-preference functions.

Sensitivity analysis has been used for this purpose for a number of years. It is not, strictly speaking, a technique for making risk adjustments. It is rather a means for investors to judge the extent to which error in key forecasting variables will affect the outcome of an investment.

For example, an analyst contemplating the projected cash flow in table 9-3 might wish to know the impact on the outcome if the vacancy rate varies by, say, 50 percent. Sensitivity analysis will pretest the model to give some indication of what the effect of this variation might be.

If, in table 9-3, the vacancy rate in fact increases by 50 percent in each year, this reduces after-tax cash flow by (0.5 × vacancy loss estimate) × (1 − marginal tax rate). Discounting this variation at the required rate of return of 10 percent reveals that the effect is to reduce the net present value of the investment by about $1,500.

In a similar vein, the analyst might wish to estimate the effect of variance in financing terms. If, in example 9-3, a second mortgage for $50,000 is available at 11 percent for 15 years in addition to the indicated first mortgage financing, this reduces the down payment by the amount of the second mortgage (assuming no front-end fee) and reduces the present value of the future cash flows by the amount of the second mortgage debt service discounted at the required rate of return. In this case, the use of a second mortgage proves to be favorable. It could just as well have proved unfavorable or insignificant in impact on investment outcome.

Summary

A number of techniques have traditionally been employed to adjust for perceived risk associated with real estate investment. Though perpetuated by generations of intellectual inbreeding within the industry, these techniques generally have proven inadequate. They fail to produce a risk measure separate from the analyst's personal attitude toward risk and thus are not amenable to precise communication of risk perception. In addition, they do not lend themselves to incorporation into a policy statement enabling delegation of preliminary decision-making tasks.

The payback-period method of analysis is not, strictly speaking, a risk-adjustment technique. But risk perception, interfaced with attitude toward risk, can be expressed in terms of the maximum acceptable payback period for a particular venture.

A technique which does explicitly consider risk, and which is in wide use among analysts, is the risk-adjusted discount rate. Users add to the risk-free rate of return a premium based on their perception of attendant risk. Thus the appropriate discount rate increases directly with perceived risk. The technique fails, however, to divorce risk perception from the analyst's personal attitude toward risk. It also contains a technical flaw in that it discounts risk more heavily, the further into the future the risk lies.

Whereas the risk-adjusted discount rate adjusts for increased risk by increasing the size of the divisor in the discounting equation, the certainty-equivalent technique accomplishes the same goal by decreasing the size of the dividend. Both approaches result in a lower present value for a given expected future cash flow as perceived risk increases.

The certainty-equivalent technique avoids some of the objections associated with the risk-adjusted discount rate but introduces new problems. Principal among these are difficulty in determining the appropriate adjustment factor and need to remake the determination for each project and each decision maker. Time and expense make this approach generally impractical as a continuing risk-adjustment technique.

Sensitivity analysis, although not a method of adjusting for risk, is a useful means of sharpening risk perception. It does this by illustrating how varying degrees of error in different elements of a forecast result in discrepancies between estimated and actual cash flows. Sensitivity analysis takes a "what if" approach by postulating variances at different points in the analysis and recomputing outcomes with revised estimates.

Note

1. See, for example, Lawrence D. Schall and Charles W. Haley, *Introduction to Financial Management* (New York: McGraw-Hill, 1977), pp. 317-320.

12 Contemporary Risk-Analysis Techniques

Apologists for the status quo often argue the imprudence of rejecting traditional methodology, however flawed, in the absence of substitutes of proven superiority. Imperfection alone being scant cause for condemnation in an imperfect world, the position of apologists is not unreasonable. Lacking more-effective substitutes *capable of practical application*, only saints and fools would abandon long-established practices that impose some order on the chaotic investment problem.

But more-effective methods are available. Developed by specialists in corporate finance and capital budgeting more than a decade ago, they have become commonplace analytical tools of business and financial analysis and decision making. Their usefulness is not a matter of conjecture. They work.

Contemporary analytical techniques require risk to be expressed in quantifiable terms. Dissenters object that real estate risk is not susceptible to measure and quantification in the same manner as, for example, that associated with investment in stocks and bonds. They have a point.

Real estate investors do not have a Moody's or a Standard and Poor's to provide quality ratings for each investment opportunity. Nor do they have data from which to construct "beta coefficients" as measures of volitility, as stock market analysts have been doing for years.

Inefficient, localized markets, spotty statistical data, and high information costs make real estate risk analysis a difficult and frustrating task. But comparisons with security analysis are inappropriate. Remember that real estate is a business producing and selling space-time. A more-appropriate comparison, therefore, is with corporate capital budgeting decisions. Real property is the capital equipment with which purveyors of space-time produce their product.

Identifying the appropriate analytical model does not simplify the task of risk quantification, but it does put it in proper perspective. Difficulties notwithstanding, modern risk analysis is an integral part of the capital-budgeting process in most corporations. Techniques employed there are directly applicable to real estate investment decisions.

Real estate analysts do in fact develop some subjective "feel" for the risk inherent in investment opportunities. This is the basis for traditional risk adjustments discussed in chapter 11. All that is needed to accommodate modern risk analysis is a language permitting expression of this perception in numerical form and a set of decision criteria against which to weigh the outcome of analysis.

Expressing Risk as Probability

Intending this as a practical rather than a theoretical exposition, established elements of modern risk analysis are emphasized. The untried and controversial are left to professional journals. Several contemporary approaches are successfully employed, all sharing the common technique of expressing risk in terms of probability that forecast outcomes will or will not occur.

Uncertainty and Projected Outcomes

Decision situations can be divided into three types: certainty, risk, and uncertainty. With certainty there can be only one possible outcome, and decisions are based solely on the decision maker's preference between the certain alternatives. But certainty is not the normal state of affairs concerning future events. Most decision problems involve choosing between events whose outcomes incorporate elements of risk, elements of uncertainty, or both.

Uncertainty implies an unknown number of possible outcomes, with no significant information about their relative chances of occurrence. Under such conditions, almost anything can happen. Since it is by definition unmeasurable, there is no way to communicate degrees of uncertainty. The distinction between risk and uncertainty is that with uncertainty probabilities are neither known nor estimable, whereas with risk the probabilities associated with various possible outcomes are either known or estimable.

Some authorities gloss over the distinction between risk and uncertainty, while others clearly and carefully distinguish between them.[1] The distinction has operational significance when some probability distributions of possible outcomes can be estimated with a useful degree of precision, while others cannot.

For our purposes, *uncertainty* refers to possible occurrences which have unknown and essentially *unestimable* associated probabilities. Where uncertain events are an important aspect of the analysis, we simply state assumptions about the uncertain factors and note the significance of error in the assumptions.

Uncertainty is often a factor of time or economics. With either additional research or the passage of time, much uncertainty may be resolved. As better information becomes available, many uncertain elements can be converted to risk factors by incorporating into the analysis their associated probability distributions.

Risk in Investment Analysis

Risky events also have a number of possible outcomes, but the analyst is able to generate information upon which to estimate the probability of occurrence of each. Some risk elements are susceptible to more or less precise measure, based on sampling techniques and statistical inference. Others are subject only to educated guesses about the range of possible outcomes from one extreme possibility to the other. Formal risk analysis shapes these measures, estimates, and guesses into a concrete, standardized format incorporating probability as the measure of risk. This permits an analyst's perception of both expected outcomes and risk to be precisely communicated to decision makers in readily understood form.

Risk and Probability

Analysis such as that described in chapters 3 and 4 results in a forecast representing a best estimate of the *most probable* level and pattern of cash flow. Actual outcomes will almost certainly differ from these expectations. Our concern is with the direction and degree of variation. Probability of variation between actual and expected outcomes forms an operational definition of risk. More formally, *risk* is defined as the measurable likelihood of variance from the most probable outcome.

Probability, the most commonly employed measure of risk, is the chance of occurrence associated with any possible outcome. It is usually expressed as a percentage of the total possible outcomes. For example, if a six-sided die is tossed on a flat surface, there is an equal chance that any side might face up when the die comes to rest. The probability of any given side facing up is, therefore, 1 in 6, or 1/6. Expressed as a percentage, this is 16.67 percent.

In our die-tossing example, one of the six sides must certainly face up. Together, the associated probabilities must therefore account for 100 percent of all possible outcomes. Formally, this is expressed as

$$\sum_{i=1}^{n} P_i = 100 \text{ percent}$$

where P_i is the probability of occurrence of outcome X_i, and the i range from 1 through *n*. When the possible outcomes are arrayed over their associated probabilities, the result is a *probability distribution.*

Deriving Probability Estimates

When the influence of all factors bearing on an outcome can be held relatively constant, past experience provides a reliable indication of future events. In such circumstances, an experiment or observation of sample data permits reliable inferences about future outcomes.

This is illustrated by the earlier example of a (presumed fair) six-sided die. The intuitive deduction that each side has an equal chance of facing up can be verified by observing the outcome of repeated tosses. While one side may initially face up several times running and some sides may not at first be equally represented in the "face-up sweepstakes," if the die is fair, these are mere chance variations. A large number of tosses will manifest the tendency for each side to be equally represented. Moreover, the larger the number of tosses, the smaller will be the role played by chance, and so the more evenly will each side be represented in the tally of face-up occurrences.

Should a corner be shaved from the die, the sides will no longer have equal probability of facing up. A new set of probabilities can be quickly estimated by recording the outcome of repeated tosses of the "unfair" die. A sizable sample of trial tosses yields a highly reliable indication of the probable outcome of any future series of tosses, so long as major determinants of the outcome (such as the playing surface and the degree to which the corner of the die is shaved) remain constant. Varying any determinant, however, produces a whole new set of probabilities.

Investment analysts are not blessed with such reliable probability-estimating techniques. Making educated guesses about possible market outcomes and associated probabilities is an inexact undertaking that might be described as part art and part science. It involves isolating and understanding significant factors influencing outcomes, making estimates of or assumptions about the level of each factor, and relating these estimates or assumptions to a specific investment forecast and its associated probability.

Cash-flow forecasts such as those discussed in Part I necessarily assume some specific economic environment in which they will be generated. Were the analyst to anticipate a different economic environment, he might then forecast a revised stream of future cash flows. There might result a whole spectrum of net cash-flow forecasts, each reflecting a slightly modified set of assumptions about economic and social conditions during the projection period.

While the analyst does not know which alternative cash-flow forecast will actually materialize, he does have a feel for which is most likely, based on the data from which he makes his projections, and on the "distilled wisdom" of past study and experience. His relative confidence in each of the forecast values can be expressed as a set of probability estimates. These probabilities are not of the highly reliable and predictable type involved in repeated throws of a die. They are, rather, subjective in nature. They represent a quantification of the analyst's impression of the risky nature of anticipated cash flows.

Those accustomed to working with reliable statistical data may be seduced by the impression of precision associated with probabilistic measures of possible outcomes. They can avoid this error by keeping constantly in mind that the numbers usually represent not sample data, but rather the quantified perception of a trained analyst. As such, they are only as reliable as the judgment of the analyst whose opinion they reflect. Subjective probability measures do not simplify the analyst's task in any way; they do contribute massively to accurate communication of his conclusions.

Communicating an analyst's opinion in precise, readily understandable terms permits investment decisions consistent with his assessment of the situation, while incorporating the decision maker's investment philosophy and personal risk–preference function. This is the special virtue of using subjective probability distributions to reflect perceived risk. The adjective *subjective* is appended to indicate that the probability estimates are statements of opinion or beliefs held by an individual analyst (see example 12-1).

Multiple cash–flow projections in example 12-1 reflect the analyst's estimate of the influence of general business conditions and of the presence

---

Example 12-1: Analysis of a shopping center subject to a percentage lease yields six separate present–value estimates of possible cash flows for year n, depending on the general economic environment and whether a competing center is built in the near future.[a] The estimates are presented below:

Competitive Center Built?	General Business Conditions		
	Good	Average	Poor
No	$325,000	$275,000	$225,000
Yes	$300,000	$250,000	$200,000

[a] A *percentage lease* is one in which a percentage of the tenant's gross business receipts constitutes the rent. Thus, the rent receipts will vary with the level of general business activity and with the presence or absence of close competitors. Most percentage leases contain a provision for a minimum rent amount, but not for a maximum.

or absence of a competing shopping center. The better the general economic environment during the lease period, the greater will be the cash generated from the net lease. Regardless of general business conditions, however, construction of a competing center will have an adverse impact on cash flows and thus on profitability of the investment.

A great number of additional possibilities could be factored into the matrix of possible outcomes in example 12-1. A different set of forecast cash flows might be shown to reflect the impact of labor strife or major change in the general level of employment. Another set of possibilities might be shown depending on what happens to tax laws, whether a proposed highway interchange is actually built, and so on. The possibilities are virtually endless. The analyst's task is to identify those possible events which have a significant likelihood of actually transpiring and which will have a significant impact on investment outcome. He then makes separate forecasts based on the possible outcome of all particularly crucial eventualities.

The final product of this analytical exercise is an estimate of the most likely outcome for year n, and a measure of possible variation from the expected. This latter information, along with associated probability measures, forms a measure of risk associated with an investment venture.

Before further pursuing the concept of risk measurement, it is worthwhile to review the distinction between risk and uncertainty. Additional possible variables are mentioned which will have an impact on the outcome of the venture in example 12-1. The possible influence of these other factors, such as labor strife, major economic recession, tax-law revisions, and the like, have been excluded from the analysis. Since no effort has been made to assess their probability of occurrence, they become elements of uncertainty with respect to this particular analysis.

Should time and resources be made available, some of the uncertainty could be resolved by additional research. These elements would then be factored into the analysis and would result in additional probabilistic measures of possible outcomes. The factors would thereby have been transformed from uncertainty to risk elements. This interchangeable nature of risk and uncertainty, and the important difference in treatment, is a crucial issue which must be constantly borne in mind by analysts and decision makers alike.

Conventional Probability Rules

General agreement on the meaning of probabilistic expressions is what makes them so useful. By convention, the probability assigned to each possible event must be a positive number between 0 and 1, where 0 represents impossibility of occurrence and 1 represents absolute certainty of occurrence. If a set of eventualities are mutually exclusive (only one of them can occur) and exhaustive (includes all possible outcomes); then the sum of the probabilities associated with the events in the set must be 1. To illustrate the point, on any given day it will either rain or will not rain. Therefore, the sum of the probabilities associated with these two possibilities must be 1. If the probability of rain is 0.4 (4 chances out of 10), then the probability that it will not rain must be 0.6 (6 chances out of 10).

A very important probability rule is sometimes called the *multiplicative law of probability.* It is used to determine the probability of occurrence of an event whose outcome depends in turn on the outcome of some prior event. If we call these events *A* and *B*, then the probability of *B* is the product of the probability of occurrence of *A* times the probability of occurrence of *B*, given that *A* occurs. This is an example of *joint probabilities.*

Application of Joint Probabilities

To apply the preceding concept to real estate investment, consider again the illustration in example 12-1. The analyst assigns subjective probabilities to the likelihood of each specific eventuality (accept, for the present, the convenient fiction that these are the only possible outcomes).

Assessing the economic environment, the analyst arrives at the probabilistic estimates of most likely general economic conditions during the forecast period indicated in table 12-1. He also estimates the probability of construction of a competing shopping center in the immediate market area as being related to general economic conditions. The probabilities attached to each possible general economic state is presented in table 12-2. Note that the probabilities are *conditional,* depending on the state of the local economy. But for each conditional economic state, there either *will* or *will not* be competition. Thus the sum of these *mutually exclusive* probabilities for each economic state must equal 1.

Table 12-1
Probability of Various General Economic Conditions

Forecast Economic Conditions	Probability of Occurrence
Good	0.25
Fair	0.50
Poor	0.25
Sum of all possibilities	1.00

Table 12-3 indicates the various probabilities of competition, *given* the level of general economic activity. The factors in this table are the product of those in tables 12-1 and 12-2. For example, the probability that general economic conditions will be good *and* that there will be competition is given in table 12-3 as 0.1875, or 18.75 percent. This is calculated by multiplying the probability of good general economic conditions from table 12-1 (0.25) by the probability from table 12-2 that a competing center will be built *if* general economic conditions are good (0.75).

Since table 12-3 exhausts all the possible combinations of general economic conditions and competitive environments, the sum of all probabilities on the table must equal 1. Moreover, the probability of various general economic conditions can be determined by summing the factors in table 12-3 vertically. Comparing the footings from table 12-3 with the probabilities in table 12-1 confirms that the probability of good economic conditions is 0.25; of fair conditions, 0.50; and of poor conditions, 0.25. Summing table 12-3 horizontally gives the probability of competition. Finally, since there either will or will not be competition and *some* general economic condition will prevail, both vertical and horizontal cross-footings in table 12-3 must sum to 1.

Interpreting Risk

Probabilistic estimates of possible investment outcomes provide valuable intelligence about relative risk associated with investment proposals. Projections can be made even more useful with additional manipulation of data to provide estimates of *most likely* outcomes and associated *probability distributions* of all possible alternatives.

Probability Distributions

An array of all possible outcomes and related probabilities of occurrence is called a *probability distribution.* Data from tables 12-1 and 12-3 are combined in table 12-4 to illustrate the concept. The net cash flow resulting from each possible combination of economic environments and competitive states is related to the probability of that combination occuring. These data can also be shown in graphic form. Such a graph is presented in figure 12-1.

Distributions such as that in table 12-4 and figure 12-1 are called *discrete-probability distributions,* reflecting the fact that there are a finite number of possible outcomes. The assumption that six cash-flow alternatives exhaust all the possibilities associated with example 12-1 is, of course, a convenient fiction. Since the cash flows are a function of gross sales of the tenant, the actual distribution includes all intermediate values. This is descriptive of a *continuous-probability distribution.*

Table 12–2
Probability of Competition under Various Economic Environments

	Economic Conditions		
Competition	Good	Fair	Poor
Yes	0.75	0.50	0.25
No	0.25	0.50	0.75
Sum of probability	1.00	1.00	1.00

Table 12–3
Subjective Probability Estimates of General Economic Conditions and Related Competitive Environment

	General Economic Conditions			
Competition	Good	Fair	Poor	Summation
Yes	0.1875	0.2500	0.0625	0.5000
No	0.0625	0.2500	0.1875	0.5000
Summation	0.2500	0.5000	0.2500	1.0000

Table 12–4
Probability Distribution of Possible Cash Flows during Year n from Percentage Lease on Shopping Center

Net Cash Flow	Probability of Occurrence
$200,000	0.0625
225,000	0.1875
250,000	0.2500
275,000	0.2500
300,000	0.1875
325,000	0.0625
Sum of probabilities	1.0000

The discrete–probability distribution of figure 12–1 can be converted to a continuous distribution by explicit recognition of values between and beyond the point estimates of table 12–4 as being in the realm of probabilities. This is illustrated in figure 12–1 by the solid line tracing the outer range of the discrete estimates of possible outcomes.

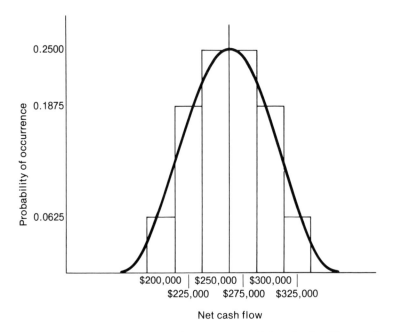

Figure 12-1. Probability Distribution of Possible Cash Flows from Percentage Lease.

Having made the transition from discrete to continuous functions, the appropriate mode of expression of possible outcome moves also from specific point estimates to ranges of possible results. We might, for example, express the probability that the cash flow from example 12-2 will prove to be between $275,000 and $300,000.

Expected Value

The expected value of a probability distribution is the weighted average of the values making up the distribution, with each value weighted by its attendant probability of occurrence. The relationship can be expressed as

$$\overline{CF} = \sum_{i=1}^{n} CF_i P_i$$

where $\overline{CF}$ is the expected value of the distribution, CF_i is the value associated with the ith probability, and P_i is the probability associated with that value. To illustrate this, return to table 12–4, which presents possible cash flows with associated probabilities of occurrence. The expected value of that distribution is $262,500, determined as follows:

Possible Cash Flow	×	Probability of Occurrence	=	Weighted Average
$200,000		0.0625		$12,500.00
225,000		0.1875		42,187.50
250,000		0.2500		62,500.00
275,000		0.2500		68,750.00
300,000		0.1875		56,250.00
325,000		0.0625		20,312.50
Expected outcome			$\overline{CF} =$	$262,500

Measuring Dispersion

When expected outcome is taken to be the probability-weighted average of all possible outcomes associated with a project, risk is generally measured as the dispersion of possible outcomes about the expected value. The most common measures of dispersion are *variance* and *standard deviation.*

Variance is the weighted average of the squared differences between each possible outcome and the expected outcome. Expressed algebraically, this relationship is,

$$V = \sum_{i=1}^{n} (CF_i - \overline{CF})^2 P_i$$

where V is the variance, CF_i is the ith possible outcome, $\overline{CF}$ is the expected value, and P_i is the related probability of the outcome. Applying this formula to the possible nth-year cash flow in example 12–1, and combining the previously calculated expected value of $262,500 with the probability measures from table 12–4, the variance is $1,093,750, computed as follows:

(× $1,000) CF_i	P_i	(× $1,000) (CF_i − $\overline{CF}$)^2 P_i
200	0.0625	244.141
225	0.1875	263,672
250	0.2500	39.062
275	0.2500	39.062
300	0.1875	263.672
325	0.0625	244.141
		$\sum = $1,093.75

Variance = $1,000 × 1093.75 = $1,093,750

Since variance measures dispersion of possible outcomes from the mean, it increases as the degree of dispersion increases. But because it employs squared differences between observed values and the mean of the distribution (to eliminate distortions introduced by negative differences), the relationship is nonlinear. The square root of the variance provides a much more usable measure of dispersion, particularly when it is used to compare alternative investment opportunities which have significantly different expected values.

Standardizing the Dispersion

The square root of the variance is called *standard deviation.* It eliminates the distorting effect of squaring differences which vary greatly in magnitude. Standard deviation also has other mathematical properties which make it particularly useful as a measure of risk.

When the probability distribution of possible values is symmetrically distributed about its midpoint, it is said to be a *normal distribution.* Fifty percent of the actual outcomes from such a distribution will fall to the right of the expected value and fifty percent to the left. The probability is 50 percent, therefore, that the actual outcome will be equal to or greater than the expected value. The probability is likewise 50 percent that the actual value will be equal to or less than expected. This, of course, exhausts the spectrum of all possible outcomes.

Earlier mention was made of "useful mathematical properties" of standard deviation. One of these properties relates to the character of the area under the probability distribution. So long as the distribution is approximately normal, 68.3 percent of all possible values of the distribution will lie within one standard deviation of the expected value. Two standard deviations encompasses approximately 95 percent of all possible outcomes, while three standard deviations to either side of the expected value includes virtually all possible outcomes. Figure 12-2 illustrates this relationship.

Having calculated the standard deviation of a probability distribution, we can determine what percent of the area under the curve lies within any interval by reference to a table of standardized values expressing the relationship. Such a table, sometimes called a table of *Z* values, or simply a *Z* table, is presented in appendix G. It gives the portion of the area under the normal distribution which lies to the left or right of some specified value. The *Z* value from the table is simply the number of standard deviations from the mean to the value of *X*. Thus,

$$Z = \frac{X - \overline{X}}{\sigma}$$

where X is some specified value under the normal curve, $\overline{X}$ is the midpoint

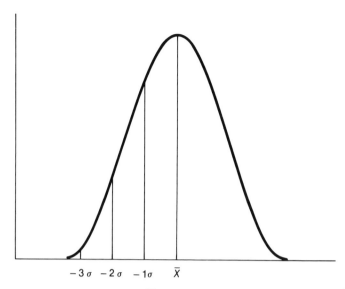

Figure 12–2. Distance Between $\overline{X}$ and X Standard Deviations from $\overline{X}$ under the Normal Curve

of the curve (the expected value), and σ is the value of one standard deviation (that is, the square root of the variance of the distribution).

Continuing example 12-1, we determined that the variance of the distribution is $1,093,750. The standard deviation is simply the square root of this amount, or $1,045.83. We also previously determined the expected value to be $262,500. These two parameters, the expected value and the standard deviation, effectively determine the entire distribution of a normally distributed variable.

Figure 12-3 illustrates the relationship calculated for example 12-1. The expected value of $262,500 is the midpoint of the distribution. One standard deviation is plus or minus $1,045.86, which we know (from the earlier discussion) to encompass approximately 68.2 percent of all possible values. The probability of the actual value falling within any range corresponds to the percent of the total area under the curve which falls within that range. Therefore, the probability is approximately 68.2 percent that the actual present value of this investment will prove to be between $262,500 ± $1,045.86, which is to say between $261,453 and $262,547 (rounded to the nearest whole dollar).

To determine this by reference to the table in appendix G, first calculate the percent of the total area *not* falling within one standard deviation of the midpoint (the unshaded area in figure 12-3). Since this is a symmetrical distribution, we need solve the problem for only one side of the curve. The

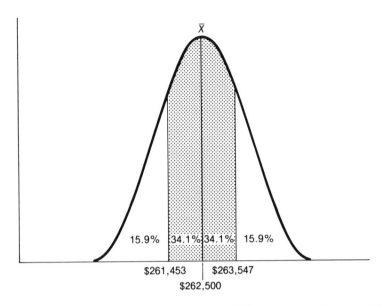

Figure 12–3. Probability that Present Value Will Be between Plus or Minus One Standard Deviation from the Mean.

same value will also apply to the other side. Solving for the unshaded area to the left of the midpoint, we get

$$Z = \frac{X - \bar{X}}{\sigma}$$

$$= \frac{\$261{,}453 - \$262{,}500}{\$1{,}046}$$

$$= -1$$

Having determined the value for Z, the number of standard deviations from the midpoint of the distribution to point Y, refer to the Z table in appendix G to find the percent of the total area under the curve to the left of point X. The area is 0.1587 or 15.9 percent. Now since 50 percent of the total area under the curve lies to the left of the midpoint, it follows that the area from point X to the midpoint must be 50 percent minus 15.9 percent, or 34.1 percent. The same portion, of course, lies between the midpoint and one standard deviation to the right. The total portion of the area under the curve which lies between one standard deviation to either side of the midpoint, therefore, is 2(34.1 percent), or approximately 68.2 percent.

Now use the table of Z values to determine the probability that the cash flow in example 12–1 will actually prove to be equal to or more than

$265,000. The first step is to determine how many standard deviations this variable (X) lies from the mean ($\overline{X}$):

$$Z = \frac{X - \overline{X}}{\sigma}$$

$$= \frac{\$265,000 - \$262,500}{\$1,046}$$

$$= 2.39$$

From the table in appendix G, find that approximately 0.0082 of the total area lies to the right of the point associated with 2.4 standard deviations from the midpoint. We can therefore be 0.50 - 0.0082 = 0.4918, or 49.2 percent confident that the cash flow will actually be between $262,500 and $265,000, providing we have correctly specified the parameters of the problem. Moreover, we know that 50 percent of the possible outcomes are below $262,500. It follows that the probability of cash flow equal to or more than $265,000 is 100 percent minus (50 + 49.2 percent), or 8/10 percent.

Incorporating Risk into the Investment Decision

There remains the problem of how best to incorporate the risk measure into the investment equation. Several acceptable methods have been utilized, the most appropriate being in part determined by the nature of the analysis and the need for a policy guideline permitting delegation of decision–making authority.

Mean/Standard Deviation Approach

This is perhaps the simplest approach to incorporating risk into an investment decision when the discounted cash–flow model is used. It involves developing both an expected cash flow and a standard–deviation measure for each year of the projection period. The present value of the expected cash flows is then determined as discussed in chapter 9, by using the formula

$$PV = \sum_{t=1}^{n} \frac{\overline{CF_t}}{(1 + i)^t}$$

where PV is the present value of the expected cash flows from the project, $\overline{CF_t}$ is the mean value of the probability distribution of possible cash flows (the expected value) for year t, and i is the opportunity cost of equity funds.[2]

The model includes a measure of possible variance of the present value of actual cash flows from the expected outcome. To derive this measure, which we call the standard deviation of the present value σ_{PV}, we use the following formula:[3]

$$\sigma_{PV} = \sqrt{\sum_{t=1}^{n} \frac{\sigma_t^2}{(1 + i)^{2t}}}$$

where σ_t is the standard deviation of the probability distribution of possible cash flows in year t.

The above formula assumes each year's cash flows are independent of those for all other years. Where annual cash flow outcomes are interrelated, the formula for the standard deviation of the present value is more complicated. That problem is addressed later in this chapter.

Notice the differences between this formulation of the risk/return problem and that formulated with respect to example 12-1, which demonstrated the concept of a probability distribution of possible investment outcomes by using a single measure of possible variability of results. The mean/standard deviation model includes a probability distribution of possible outcomes for *each year* of the projection period.

To understand the concept and the application of the mean/standard deviation approach, consider the situation presented in example 12-2.

Assuming the appropriate discount rate (the opportunity cost of equity capital) in example 12-2 to be 12 percent, the present value of the project (rounded to the nearest whole dollar) is $102,644, calculated as follows:

$$PV = \sum_{t=1}^{3} \frac{\overline{CF_t}}{1.12^t}$$

$$= \frac{\$20,000}{1.12} + \frac{\$26,000}{1.12^2} + \frac{\$90,000}{1.12^3}$$

$$= \$102,644$$

The solution is simplified by reference to appendix B. Simply multiply each year's expected cash flow by the value factor from the table for the appropriate number of years at 12 percent.

Example 12-2: An analyst considers a 3-year project which requires an initial cash outlay of $95,000. He develops a probability distribution of net cash flows for each year of the project. His client's minimum acceptable rate of return is 12 percent. The outcome for each year is considered completely independent of that for other years. The mean value of each year's projected cash flow, with the associated standard deviation, is as follows:

Year	Mean of Cash Flow Distribution	Standard Deviation
1	$20,000	$5,400
2	$26,000	$4,500
3	$90,000	$7,500

The standard deviation of the present values is

$$\sigma_{PV} = \sqrt{\sum_{t=1}^{3} \frac{\sigma_t^{\,2}}{(1+i)^{2t}}}$$

$$= \sqrt{\frac{(\$5,400)^2}{1.12^2} + \frac{(\$4,500)^2}{1.12^4} + \frac{(\$7,500)^2}{1.12^6}}$$

$$= \quad \$8038$$

Again, the solution is simplified by reference to appendix B. Use the value for $(1+i)^n$ for the number of years indicated by the power to which $(1+i)$ is to be raised. In the present case, this includes factors from the 12 percent table for 2, 4, and 6 years, respectively.

Having computed a measure of both expected reward and perceived risk for the opportunity in example 12-2, decision makers are in a position to decide whether potential gain justifies the risk. This explicit consideration of risk may be further incorporated into the decision model in several different ways, the most useful of which are described next.

Probability of Acceptance Error Approach

Risk tolerance can be expressed in a policy statement capable of implementation by subordinates. Specifying both the minimum acceptable expected rate of return and the maximum acceptable probability of accepting a project that ultimately yields less than the minimum acceptable rate creates a filter mechanism which eliminates many unacceptable opportunities without need for actual review by final decision makers. Top management is thereby left free to concentrate on choosing between alternative opportunities which do meet minimum acceptance criteria.

When applied to the mean/standard deviation model, the objective of this approach is to determine the probability that actual present value will prove to be less than the initial cash outlay required to accommodate the project. Should this occur, the actual rate of return will have been less than the required rate, and the project will have been accepted in error.

Applying the method to example 12-2 reveals that the project will yield an actual rate of return of less than the required 12 percent if the actual present value proves to be less than the initial cash outlay of $95,000. This is illustrated in figure 12-4. All the possible outcomes that lie to the left of PV = $95,000 imply that the project should not be accepted. Thus the portion of the area lying left of PV = $95,000 corresponds with the probability that the actual PV will in fact be less than $95,000 and that acceptance will have proven to be an error.

Since the shaded area in figure 12-4 is the probability that project profitability will be less than the minimum acceptable rate, the project will be rejected if that area exceeds the maximum acceptable risk of such error.

Assuming the probability distribution to be approximately normally distributed (that is, assuming the curve to be symmetrical in shape, with 50 percent of the area lying on either side of the mean), we can determine the area under the curve to the left of PV = $95,000 by reference to the standard deviation procedure discussed earlier in the chapter:

$$Z = \frac{X - \overline{X}}{\sigma_{PV}}$$

where Z = the standardized value from appendix G
         X = the minimum acceptable present value
         $\overline{X}$ = the expected (that is, arithmetic mean) present value
         σ_{PV} = the standard deviation of the present value

In example 12-2, the mean present value of the expected cash flows is $102,644, and its standard deviation is $8,038. The initial cash outlay, and thus the minimum acceptable present value of project cash flows, is $95,000. Substituting these values into the equation, the Z value becomes

$$Z = \frac{95,000 - \$102,644}{8,038}$$

$$= -0.951$$

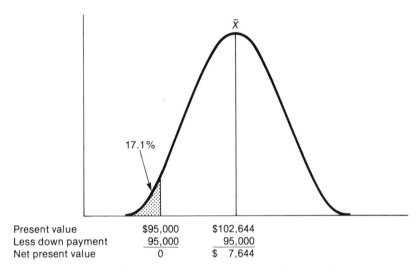

Present value	$95,000	$102,644
Less down payment	95,000	95,000
Net present value	0	$ 7,644

Figure 12–4. Probability of Acceptance Error (Probability that Actual Rate of Return Will Be Less than Minimum Acceptable Rate).

Reading this factor from the table of area under the normal curve in appendix G reveals that approximately 17.1 percent of the area lies to the left of $PV = $95,000$. This implies that should the project be accepted, there is a 17.1 percent chance that the decision maker will have erred and that the present value of actual cash flows will be less than the initial cash outlay. It remains for the investor to decide whether this degree of risk is justified by the expected present value of $102,644.

Establishing Acceptable Risk Profiles

Having specified an absolute maximum probability of acceptance error beyond which no investment opportunity will be accepted, there remains the problem of discriminating between acceptable and unacceptable risk/reward combinations lying within the range of provisional acceptability. Certainly not all opportunities falling within such an acceptability threshold are equally desirable. Within the range of tolerable probability of acceptance error there are gradients of risk. Investors expect compensation for all incremental risk assumed.

To facilitate choice between risky opportunities, and to ensure consistency over time, investors may specify the maximum acceptable dispersion associated with various levels of present values per dollar of invested cash. Reference to these *risk profiles* permits more refined preliminary screening by subordinates, further reducing the time spent by final decision makers on projects destined for ultimate rejection.

Before risk profiles can be constructed, expected outcomes must be expressed in terms permitting interproject comparison of costs and benefits. Profitability indices (discussed in chapter 9) have this characteristic, inasmuch as they represent the ratio of present value to initial cash outlay. They thereby convert absolute levels to a measure of relative present value per dollar of required initial cash expenditure. To illustrate, consider again the investment in example 12-2. The expected value or the distribution of possible outcomes, expressed in terms of present value, is $102,644, and the initial cash outlay is $95,000. The expected value of the resultant distribution of profitability indices is

$$\overline{PI} = \$102,644/\$95,000$$

$$= 1.08$$

By way of review, recall from chapter 9 that when present value just equals initial cash outlay, the profitability index is exactly 1 and the net present value is 0. Also recall that this means the internal rate of return exactly equals the discount rate used to determine present value. Present value, net present value, and the profitability index therefore all measure the same relationship. An advantage of the profitability index is that it permits comparison of projects of different magnitudes.

Figure 12-5 replicates figure 12-4, with a second scale measured in terms of profitability index. Note that at the point where the present value of future net cash flows equals the initial cash outlay of $95,000, the profitability index is 1, indicating that this corresponds to an internal rate of return just equal to the 12 percent minimum acceptable rate.

If investment decision makers specify maximum risk profiles for various values of profitability indices, project proposals can simply be compared with the risk profile for an expected profitability index of the level computed for that proposal. If the dispersion of possible indices exceeds that of the risk profile, the proposal is automatically rejected. If not, it is passed to the investor for a final accept/reject decision. All projects passing this risk-profile filter are considered, and final decisions are made according to portfolio risk/return considerations, with available cash acting as a constraint.

A risk-profile tabulation will reflect a positive relationship between expected profitability index and dispersion of possible indices. The exact tradeoff between dispersion and expected profitability incorporates the decision maker's personal attitude toward risk. This permits interface between investor risk preference and the analyst's informed opinion of risk implicit in a particular project.

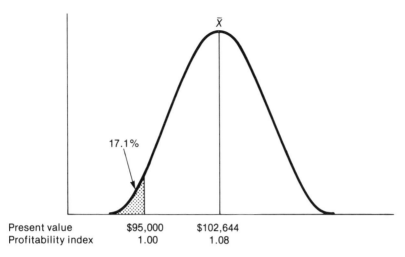

| Present value | $95,000 | $102,644 |
| Profitability index | 1.00 | 1.08 |

Figure 12–5. Probability of Acceptance Error (Probability that Actual Profitability Index Will Be Less than Minimum Acceptable Rate).

Certainty Equivalent Method

This technique, discussed in chapter 11, involves multiplying the anticipated annual cash–flow projection by a factor (less than 1, but greater than 0) such that the product of the calculation will be a "certainty equivalent." The investor is presumed to be indifferent between the possibility of receiving the actual projected cash flow, with attendant risk of variation from expectations, and the certain promise of receiving its certainty equivalent.

The approach was criticized in chapter 11 because of the time and client vexation associated with conventional efforts to develop equivalence factors. The technique becomes more practical when combined with standard deviation as a risk measure.

After expressing anticipated annual cash flows in terms of a probability distribution of possible occurrences, standard deviation permits adjustment of expected values from the annual distributions to virtual certainty, before discounting. The present value of the certainty–equivalent cash flow for a single year is

$$PV = \frac{\alpha \, \overline{CF}_n}{(1 + i)^n}$$

where PV is the present value of an anticipated future cash receipt, $\overline{CF}$ is the cash flow anticipated in period n, α is the adjustment for certainty equivalence, and i is the discount rate.

To make the formula operational, simply adjust the anticipated cash flow by three standard deviations. From the table in appendix G, note that virtually 100 percent of the area under a normal distribution lies between the mean and three standard deviations to either side. Thus adjusting by the factor for three standard deviations results in a cash-flow projection with virtually 100 percent probability that the actual cash flow will be equal to or greater than projected.

The procedure can be illustrated by applying this formulation to the data from example 12-2, which presents expected annual cash flows and attendant estimates of standard deviation. The present value of certainty-equivalent cash flows is determined by solving for

$$PV = \sum_{t=1}^{3} \frac{\alpha \overline{CF_t}}{(1 + i)^t}$$

Solving the equation obviously requires calculation of the certainty-equivalent factors α for each year. As described earlier, these factors are determined as follows:

$$= \frac{\text{Certainty-equivalent cash flow}}{\text{risky cash-flow projection}}$$

Using the risky cash-flow projections and attendant standard deviations from example 12-2, the factors are determined as follows:

Year	Certainty-Equivalent Factor
1	[$20,000 − (3 × $5,400)]/$20,000 = 0.190
2	[$26,000 − (3 × $4,500)]/$26,000 = 0.481
3	[$90,000 − (3 ×$7,500)]/$90,000 = 0.750

These annual certainty-equivalent factors are combined with expected cash-flow projections from example 12-2 to determine the present value of the opportunity. Discounted at a (presumed) 6 percent risk-free rate of return, the present value is

$$PV = \frac{\alpha_1 \overline{CF_1}}{(1 + i)} + \frac{\alpha_2 \overline{CF_2}}{(1 + i)^2} + \frac{\alpha_3 \overline{CF_3}}{(1 + i)^3}$$

$$= \frac{0.19(\$20,000)}{1.06} + \frac{0.481(\$26,000)}{1.06^2} + \frac{0.75(\$90,000)}{1.06^3}$$

$$= \$3,800 \left(\frac{1}{1.06}\right) + \$12,506 \left(\frac{1}{1.06^2}\right) + \$67,500 \left(\frac{1}{1.06^3}\right)$$

Referring to appendix B for interest factors to replace the bracketed terms, the solution to the equation becomes

$$PV = \$3,800\,(0.94349) + \$12,506\,(0.89000) + \$67,500\,(0.83962)$$

$$= \$71,396$$

This is less than the required initial cash outlay assumed in example 12-2. The investor expects a rate of return in excess of 12 percent, but he cannot be absolutely certain of earning even the rate available from relatively riskless sources. This is, or course, not surprising, since our earlier discussion makes the point that additional risk must (usually) be assumed in order to gain a greater expected return. With the expectation of return exceeding that from alternative opportunities comes the possibility of a return considerably below that rate.

Dealing with More Complex Cash–Flow Patterns

To avoid premature complications, all previous probabilistic cash–flow discussions have assumed that cash flows in each period were independent of those in all other periods. This simplifies the dialogue, but it is highly unrealistic with respect to most investment proposals. For most projects the cash flow in subsequent periods will depend at least in part on what happened in prior periods. If projections proved overly optimistic in earlier years, the chances are that the same will hold for the entire life of the project. Likewise, if cash flows in early years are much greater than anticipated, favorable deviations should also occur in future years so long as the same causal influences are present. Moreover, total deviation over the life of a project may become quite large as a result of the cumulative effect of annual variances.

Expected present value does not change when the possibility of serially dependent (correlated) cash flows is introduced, but the standard deviation of the present-value distribution may be rather drastically altered. In general, the greater the degree of correlation of annual cash flows, the greater will be the dispersion, and thus the greater the standard deviation of the probability distribution of possible present values.

Significance of Independent Cash Flows

To reiterate, the expected outcome of an investment project is *not* affected by the degree of correlation or independence of the cash flows if the distribution is symmetrical about the mean. But the standard deviation increases when cash flows are serially correlated. Before studying a model designed to deal with this problem, consider the nature of the issue of dependent or independent cash flows.

Perfectly Correlated Cash Flows

When cash flows are perfectly correlated, deviation from the expected outcome in one period will result in deviations in all future periods in the same relative manner. If actual cash flows in one period are exactly (say) one-half standard deviation to the right or left of the mean value of the probability distribution of possible cash flows for the period, then the actual cash flows for all future periods will be exactly one-half standard deviation to the right or left of these probability distributions of possible cash flows.

The degree of dependence of the cash flows through time is measured by the *coefficient of correlation,* which can go from 0 to ± 1. When the correlation coefficient equals 0, cash flows are completely independent of each other. A coefficient of ± 1 indicates perfect serial correlation of the cash flows. The standard deviation of the present value (or of the internal rate of return) of a perfectly correlated stream of cash flows is

$$\sigma_{PV} = \sum_{t=0}^{n} \frac{\sigma_t}{(1 + i)^t}$$

Returning to the project in example 12-2, the impact of the assumption of perfect correlation is determined by recomputing the standard deviation of the present value under this revised assumption. Substituting the cash-flow projections and the discount rate from example 12-2 into the preceding equation, the revised standard deviation of present value is[3]

$$\sigma_{PV} = \frac{5,400}{1.12} + \frac{4,500}{1.12^2} + \frac{7,500}{1.12^3}$$

$$= \$13,747$$

Now compare this with the earlier computation under the assumption of serial independence of cash flows. Changing the assumption to perfect correlation raises the standard deviation from $8,038 to $13,747. This illustrates that risk, as measured by standard deviation, is significantly higher for serially correlated cash–flow streams than for those which are mutually independent. With perfectly correlated flows, in the words of Steven E. Bolton, "Once you start downhill, you gather momentum and continue into the pit at the bottom.[4]

Partially Correlated Cash Flows

Moving from an assumption of serial independence over time to one of perfect correlation changes the computation of standard deviation and thus the shape of the probability distribution of possible outcomes from an investment, but it does not significantly complicate the solution. Problems do arise, however, with the possibility of *partial* correlation.

In situations involving less–than–perfect correlation, some of the expected cash flows may be highly correlated over time, while others may be more nearly independent. This, of course, is more illustrative of real–world circumstances. When this occurs, solving the standard deviation problem becomes difficult and complex.

Frederick S. Hillier has developed a model to deal with this issue which is particularly applicable to real estate investment situations.[5] His model groups annual cash flows on the basis of whether they are more nearly independent or serially correlated over time. The two groups are then treated as if they were completely independent and perfectly correlated, respectively.

The present value of these segmented income streams are unaffected by the treatment afforded in Hillier's model. The formula for the revised standard deviation of the present value, however, becomes

$$\sigma_{PV} = \sqrt{\sum_{t=0}^{n} \frac{\sigma^2_{yt}}{(1+i)^{2t}} + \left[\sum_{t=0}^{n} \frac{\sigma_{xt}}{(1+i)^t} \right]^2}$$

where σ_y is the standard deviation for the cash flows assumed to be serially independent, and σ_x is the standard deviation for the stream of net cash flows assumed to be perfectly correlated. The formula can be adjusted to handle situations involving several separate perfectly correlated cash–flow streams.

To illustrate the use of the model, consider the data in example 12-3, which represents a breakdown of supporting data from example 12-2.

Example 12-3: Attempting to get a better grip on the risk element associated with the investment in example 12-2, the analyst separates net cash-flow projections into revenue and expense categories and develops separate standard deviation estimates for each.

Because rental revenues are so dependent on locational factors, the revenue stream is considered to be highly correlated over time. If the location is less desirable than anticipated, resulting in a less-than-expected gross rental revenue in the first year, the same factors should cause equally disappointing outcomes in the final 2 years of the holding period as well. The same factors will affect the selling price of the property at the end of period 3, which is included in expected cash flow for that period.

Operating expenses, on the other hand, are largely independent of locational influences. They are considered to be serially independent over time and are expected to vary from projected values only as a result of random factors.

The annual projections of revenue and expense, and their associated standard deviation estimates, are as follows:

	Rental Revenue Projections		Expense Projections	
Year	Projected Revenue	Standard Deviation	Projected Expenditures	Standard Deviation
1	$ 42,000	$5,670	$22,000	$5,940
2	50,000	4,327	24,000	4,153
3	116,000	4,833	26,000	2,167

The expected present value of the venture remains unchanged from that of example 12-2:

$$PV = \frac{(\$42,000 - \$22,000)}{1.12} + \frac{(\$50,000 - \$24,000)}{1.12^2} + \frac{(\$116,000 - \$26,000)}{1.12^3}$$

$$= \$102,644$$

The standard deviation of the expected present value, however, is drastically altered by the assumption of serial correlation of gross revenues. Substituting standard deviation measures from example 12-3 into the formula developed by Hillier gives

$$\sqrt{\left(\frac{\$5,940^2}{1.12^2} + \frac{\$4,153^2}{1.12^4} + \frac{\$2,167^2}{1.12^6}\right) + \left(\frac{\$5,670}{1.12} + \frac{\$4,327}{1.12^2} + \frac{\$4,833}{1.12^3}\right)^2}$$

$$= \$13,576$$

Summary

Modern risk-analysis techniques have been developed in the fields of corporate finance and capital budgeting. The techniques allow risk to be expressed in terms of probability of variance from expectations. Because data are not available for statistical sampling of the type employed in the physical and biological sciences, probabilities in investment analysis are frequently subjective, reflecting the informed opinion of an analyst rather than being generated from obejctive information sources.

Techniques for expressing risk in probabilistic terms involve developing probability distributions of possible outcomes and estimating related standard deviations. This in turn permits expression of likely investment consequences as ranges of possible outcomes and accompanying levels of confidence. Probability distributions of possible outcomes may be expressed as present values, net present values, profitability indices, or any number of other measures, as desired by the analyst or his client.

Notes

1. Contrast, for example, the distinction made by Steven E. Bolton, *Managerial Finance* (Boston: Houghton Mifflin, 1976), pp. 222-223, with that of J. Fred Weston and Eugene F. Brigham, *Managerial Finance*, 5th ed. (Hindsdale, Ill.: Dryden Press, 1975), p. 313.

2. This assumes annual cash flows are mutually independent. Authorities disagree whether the discount rate should be the cost of capital or the risk-free rate. Contrast, for example, Steven E. Bolton, *Managerial Finance*, p. 235, with James C. Van Horne, *Financial Management and Policy*, 2d ed., (Englewood Cliffs, N.J.: Prentice Hall, 1971), p. 132. For our purposes, the appropriate rate is the opportunity cost of capital, defined as the minimum acceptable rate of return to the investor.

Cost of capital, as used by the preceding authors, includes the cost of both debt and equity funds. But as we have constructed the discounting equation, cost of debt has already been eliminated. Therefore, the discount rate should include only the cost of equity funds. This difference is due to the unique nature of financing arrangements in most real estate transactions, where lenders look only to the value of mortgaged property as security for a loan.

3. The equation for the standard deviation of present value can be solved quickly by reference to appendix B, which gives values for $1/(1 + i)^n$ for various interest rates and number of years. To use the table, simply multiply the standard deviation measure for each year by the appropriate factor from the table and sum the products.

4. Steven E. Bolton, *Managerial Finance*, p. 265.

5. Frederick S. Hillier, "The derivation of Probabilistic Information for the Evaluation of Risky Investments," *Management Science* 9 (April 1963): 443–457.

13 Using the Mean/ Standard Deviation Model: A Case Example

This chapter presents an analytical framework for developing probability distributions of possible present values associated with cash-flow forecasts. Since each annual estimate represents the midpoint of a probability distribution of possible cash flows for that year, the present value of each year's expected outcome is just one of a corresponding set of possible actual present values for that year. An alternative present-value operator exists for each of the possible actual cash-flow outcomes for the year in question. There is, of course, a similar set of possible present-value outcomes for every year in the projection period.

Summing the present values of expected outcomes for each year yields the expected value of the probability distribution of possible present values for the entire series of expected cash flows. As with any probability distribution, there is a standard deviation associated with this distribution of possible present values.

Determining the present value of the series of expected annual cash flows is relatively straightforward. Calculating the standard deviation of the present-value distribution is somewhat more complicated. The exact procedure (and the outcome of the calculations) differs depending on the degree of serial correlation existing between the annual cash-flow estimates. A useful analytical model must provide for a variety of assumptions concerning serial correlation.

A method for dealing with partial correlation of cash flows through time was introduced in chapter 12. This technique, called Hillier's model, involves separating expected cash flows into categories depending on whether they are assumed to exhibit high or low serial correlation. Those assumed to be highly correlated are treated by the model as if perfectly correlated, while those in the low-correlation category are treated as if serially independent. There results a manageable risk-analysis framework which minimizes error introduced by serial correlation.

Hillier's model provides a powerful tool for analyzing real estate projects, because the pattern of expected cash flows conforms so obligingly to that of the model.

Gross rental revenue, depending as it does on major causal factors likely to continue in effect over a number of years, tends to be very highly correlated through time. A factor such as location or design which affects the first year's rental revenue is likely to have roughly the same impact on rental revenue for all subsequent years.

Operating expenses, in contrast, are not greatly influenced by a property's design or precise location. They are much more likely to be affected by random factors which do not continue systematically over a number of years.

Thus it is that for many projects, little damage is done to reality by assuming perfect serial correlation of gross rents and complete independence of operating expenses. The potential for applying Hillier's model to real estate investment analysis problems ought therefore to be pursued at greater length.

Toward this end, the present chapter revisits the apartment project employed to illustrate the discounted cash–flow model in chapter 9. Cash–flow estimates from that project (example 9-3) are categorized according to the assumed degree of serial correlation and discounted by those categories. The outcome of the reformulated model is compared with the calculations in chapter 9 to demonstrate that the expected outcome is not changed by reformulation.

Standard deviation estimates are then generated for annual cash–flow estimates in each category. These are discounted, as explained in chapter 12, to derive the standard deviation of the present–value distribution.

Use of the model for assessing expected return and perceived risk is then demonstrated by applying standard risk–analysis techniques to the expected present value and standard deviation of the present value for the project.

The chapter concludes with a presentation of how the usefulness of the model can be extended. Of particular significance is the explanation of how data from the model can be interfaced with predetermined levels of risk–expected return to screen out obviously unacceptable projects. Those passing preliminary screening are considered further. This additional analysis includes comparison of a project's risk–return pattern with that of alternative projects.

Some Preliminaries: An Assumption and a Decision

Basic to the applicability of the model is an assumption that probabilities are distributed symmetrically about a central value. Given the validity of this assumption, analyst and client must agree on an appropriate discount rate to be applied to both anticipated cash flows and standard deviation estimates.

Symmetrical and Nonsymmetrical Distributions

Most variables observed in the physical and biological sciences exhibit scaler measurements that are symmetrically distributed about their mean value, as illustrated in chapter 12. This "normal" distribution has attributes which make it particularly convenient as a representation of the universe of phenomena from which observations are drawn. Specifically, the distribution is completely defined in terms of just two measurements: the arithmetic mean and the standard deviation.

Though emphasized in chapter 12, the importance of this point warrants repetition. While this particular shape emcompasses most distributions found in the world of natural phenomena, nonsymmetrical distributions are often encountered in financial and managerial data. Where the underlying distribution varies significantly from the symmetrical, use of the technique presented here will lead to conclusions not warranted by facts.

So long as the underlying data are approximately symmetrically distributed, however, it is appropriate to proceed under the assumption of symmetry, recognizing that the error thereby introduced is minor and justified by the powerful decision tool rendered usable by that assumption.

Choosing a Discount Rate

Corporate financial theorists wage a running battle concerning whether the appropriate discount rate is the risk-free rate or the cost of capital. Fortunately, we can avoid participation in this particular fight because neither of these precise definitions are appropriate for most real estate investors. The cost of capital would be appropriate, were it possible to calculate such a figure. But this not being practical for noncorporate investors or for closely held corporations, a more useful approach is to simply specify the minimum acceptable rate of return to equity capital.

If every real estate investment has an expected return equal to or greater than this minimum acceptable rate, then the average rate over a large number of ventures will equal or exceed the minimum. Moreover, the model permits minimum acceptable levels of confidence to be specified for any desired rate of return.

Choices between alternatives can be made by comparing data derived from the model with parameters set down by policy fiat. Expected-value and standard deviation patterns of the alternatives can be compared, and choices can be made on the basis of highest expected reward consistent with predetermined acceptable levels of risk.

Advantages of the Model

Economists and other theoreticians refer to their analytical schemes as *models* because they purport to be simplified representations of reality. Thus it is with the mean/standard deviation model. It is a formalization of how rational investors analyze risks and opportunities perceived in a venture.

While academicians might bask in the descriptive elegance of the model, practitioners are more concerned with operational utility. From an operational perspective, the crucial test of any theory is whether it aids in making better investment decisions. The mean/standard deviation model contributes to this end in four ways: (1) it goads analysts to look more closely at the risk element; (2) it facilitates communication of analysts' risk perception to investment decision makers; (3) it aids in establishing accountability for persistent error in investment decisions; and (4) it permits specification of risk–reward parameters as policy goals in readily understandabale terms.

Analysts Become More Diligent

Analysts who are not expected to quantify risk have little incentive to refine their assessments. Under such circumstances there is a tendency to use some simplified rule of thumb or conventional risk adjustment which might not be related even remotely to the reality of the proposed project. Such an approach might be considered the safest course if it replicates "what everybody else is doing," without particular regard to its specific applicability.

But when an analyst knows that his risk assessment will be precisely understood by clients, and that it will be a matter of record to be compared with future eventualities, he has a powerful incentive to be as exact as possible in his predictions and to delve as deeply into the risk question as time and budget allocations permit.

Communication Becomes More Precise

Even the most sophisticated analysis is fruitless if results cannot be communicated to prospective users of the information. An analyst's perception of the hazards and potential rewards of a venture are a product of complex interaction of specific project data with the distilled wisdom of his formal knowledge and prior field experience. With diligence and good fortune he may achieve an accurate grasp of the risk and reward potential attendant to a proposal. But before this understanding can be incorporated into an investment decision, it must be fully and accurately communicated to the investor.

Client communication requires a vocabulary common to all parties, and this vocabulary must be capable of expressing relatively small increments of risk differential as well as the probabilistic nature of expected returns. Just as dollars serve as a commonly understood unit of potential profitability, so does the mean/standard deviation model provide a common unit for expressing risk.

Accountability is Facilitated

With risk assessments properly quantified, an analyst's performance can be evaluated in terms of the extent to which the difference between his projections and actual outcomes exceeds that attributable to chance. Systematic error, as revealed by comparing a series of forecasts with actual outcomes, can be further investigated, and corrective action can be taken where indicated. The mean/standard deviation model thereby arms management with a powerful quality-control tool.

Span of Management Control is Broadened

Need for frequent interaction reduces the number of subordinates a manager can effectively supervise. Any technique permitting delegation of decision-making authority reduces the need for such interaction and releases top management for attention to more pressing duties.

A valuable byproduct of using the mean/standard deviation model is that it facilitates development of policy guidelines which permit decision making to be pushed further down the managerial hierarchy. With risk measures that mean precisely the same thing to all parties, it becomes possible to delegate many preliminary investment decisions with confidence that results will not differ significantly from outcomes desired by those at the top of the organizational pyramid.

Company policy might stipulate, for example, the minimum acceptable expected return on equity and the minimum acceptable risk of acceptance error. Proposals not meeting these minimum criteria are rejected by lower-level management, and only those which survive preliminary screening are passed upward for further study and review.

Illustrating the Mean/Standard Deviation Technique

Model building is an interesting, sometimes even fascinating, intellectual exercise, but it has little practical significance unless the models can be applied to real-life problems. To demonstrate the practicality of the mean/standard deviation model, and to provide a guide for its application in other circumstances, an extended example is illustrated using the apartment house problem introduced in chapter 9. The exercise, previously presented as example 9-3, is repeated here as example 13-1. The reproduced example includes certain related information from other illustrations in chapter 9, reorganized in example 13-1 for analytical convenience.

Careful comparison of example 13-1 with the information developed from example 9-3 reveals that nothing has been altered. The information has simply been summarized, and the format has been restructured to facilitate analysis on a probabilistic basis.

Before developing probability distributions associated with expected outcomes from the restructured example, projections are categorized according to the most plausible assumption concerning the degree of serial correlation between projection periods. Standard deviation estimates are then developed for the expected outcome in each subcategory for each year of the projection period. Both expected annual outcomes and associated standard deviation measures are then discounted at the required rate of return to arrive at the expected present value of the venture and the standard deviation of present value.

Classifying the Cash Flows

As an analytical convenience, all probabilistic cash-flows projections are developed on an after-tax basis. The outcome is a net after-tax cash-flow projection. The investor is assumed to be in the 70 percent income tax bracket for each year of the projection period. This assumption has been chosen to minimize complicating factors, so that attention will be focused on the central issue of the analysis. Were the investor in a lower tax bracket, the optimal approach would involve use of his marginal tax bracket for each year, but this introduces an element of error at extreme ranges of the probability distribution. The error is an increasing function of the distance actual outcomes fall from the midpoint of the probability distribution of possible outcomes.

With the investor in the 70 percent income tax bracket, it follows that 70 cents of every dollar of rental revenue is taxed away and only 30 cents flows through to the taxpayer. Likewise, each dollar of operating expense and tax-deductible interest reduces income taxes by 70 cents and cash flow to the equity position by only 30 cents. It should be evident that this approach accomplishes the same result as applying the 70 percent marginal tax rate to the net income (gross revenue less expenses).

Recall (from chapter 12) that gross revenues are generally considered to be highly correlated as a result of the consistent influence of location. If locational factors cause actual revenue to vary significantly from expectations during early years, they are likely to cause similar variations in all

Example 13-1: Analysis of the 5-year-old Altamese Villa Apartments, introduced in chapter 9, yields the following data:

Current Market Price

Improvements	$280,000
Land	70,000
Total market price, land and improvements	$350,000

Available Financing

First mortgage at 9.5 percent for 25 years	$262,500
Second mortgage at 11 percent for 15 years	50,000
Total mortgage financing	$312,500
Add: Equity required	37,500
Total (market value)	$350,000

Summary of Projected Operating Results

	Year of Operation					
	1	*2*	*3*	*4*	*5*	*6*
Effective gross rents	$74,800	$79,500	$84,000	$89,000	$94,000	$100,000
Operating expenses	39,250	41,500	44,000	46,500	50,000	52,000
Net operating income	$35,550	$38,000	$40,000	$42,500	$44,500	$ 48,000
Less:						
Debt service	34,341	34,341	34,341	34,341	34,341	34,341
Cash throw-off	$ 1,209	$ 3,659	$ 5,659	$ 8,159	$10,159	$ 13,659
Plus:						
Principal payments [a]	4,088	4,516	4,986	5,518	6,092	6,733
Less:						
Depreciation	8,000	8,000	8,000	8,000	8,000	8,000
Taxable income (loss)	($ 2,703)	$ 175	$ 2,645	$ 5,677	$ 5,677	$ 8,251
Cash throw-off	$ 1,209	$ 3,659	$ 5,659	$ 8,159	$10,159	$ 13,659
Less:						
Income tax (+ benefit)	(1,892)	123	1,852	3,974	5,776	8,675
After-tax cash flow	$ 3,101	$ 3,537	$ 3,808	$ 4,185	$ 4,383	$ 4,985
Present value of after-tax cash flow (at 10 percent)	$ 2,819	$ 2,923	$ 2,861	$ 2,858	$ 2,722	$ 2,814

Summary of Expected Benefits from Disposal

Expected sales price (rounded to nearest $1,000)		$468,000
Less: Selling costs		32,760
Expected net selling price		$435,240
Less: Remaining balance on mortgages	$280,567	
Income tax on gain	37,307	317,874
Expected net proceeds from disposal		$117,366
Present value (at 10 percent)		$ 66,250

Present Value of Expected Outcome

Present value of expected cash flow from operations	$16,997
Present value of expected cash flow from disposal	66,250
Total	$83,247
Less: Initial cash outlay	37,500
Expected net present value	$45,747

---

[a] Debt service minus interest expense equals principal payments.
[b] From table 9-4.

---

future years. Moreover, causal factors surrounding locational influence change relatively slowly and consistently over time, so that once a trend is started, it will usually continue in the same direction for a number of years. For these reasons we can generally expect rental revenues to be influenced by the same dominant causal factors from year to year and to exhibit a high degree of serial correlation.

Since the analytical model does not provide for less–than–perfect correlation, rental revenues are treated as perfectly correlated over time. This minimizes error in the model by making the simplifying assumption which does the least damage to reality.

Expenses, on the other hand, are influenced relatively little by specific locational factors. Instead, they tend to fluctuate through time with general economic conditions and as a result of chance occurrences. There are, of course, some serially correlated factors, but those which fluctuate independently through time comprise the bulk of total operating expenses. For these reasons, and again to make the model manageable while minimizing consequent error, expenses are treated as though completely independent through time.

Table 13-1
Projected After-Tax Revenue, Altamese Villa Apartments

Year	Expected Gross Revenue [a]	×	1 − Tax Rate	=	After-Tax Revenue
1	74,800		0.30		22,440
2	79,500		0.30		23,850
3	84,000		0.30		25,200
4	89,000		0.30		26,700
5	94,500		0.30		28,350
6	100,000		0.30		30,000

[a] Source: Example 13-1 and table 9-4.

The result of restating expected after-tax consequences of ownership in this fashion is illustrated in table 13-1. Expected after-tax revenue is simply expected gross revenue multiplied by 1 − tax rate. This is what the net income would be on an after-tax basis were there no expenses.

Projected expenditures for operating expenses are similarly computed on an after-tax basis for multiplying expected tax-deductible outlays by 1 − tax rate. The product is that portion of expenditures which reduces after-tax cash flow to the equity investor. These data and computations are shown in table 13-2.

Certain cash-flow items are not properly treated as probabilistic variables, since they can be exactly projected. These include after-tax debt service and income tax savings from the depreciation allowance. This set of projections can be merged with the probabilistic cash flows *after* standard deviation estimates are developed for the probabilistic projections. For the moment, they are best set aside in a separate category.

Table 13-2
Projected After-Tax Operating Expenses, Altamese Villa Apartments

Year	Expected Expenses [a]	×	1 − Tax Rate	=	After-Tax Expenses
1	39,250		0.30		11,775
2	41,500		0.30		12,450
3	44,000		0.30		13,200
4	46,500		0.30		13,950
5	50,000		0.30		15,000
6	52,000		0.30		15,600

Source: Example 13-1 and table 9-4.

Income tax savings from depreciation estimates are simply the amount of the annual depreciation allowance (given in example 13-1 as $8,000), multiplied by the tax rate of 70 percent. The product ($5,600) is the expected annual reduction in the investor's income taxes resulting from claiming the allowance. After-tax cash outflows resulting from the debt-service obligation are shown in table 13-3.

The cash-flow statement from example 13-1 can, with the foregoing information, be reconstructed in a fashion amenable to probabilistic expression. Table 13-4 shows this reconstruction, with benefits (net of income taxes) grouped into a separate category from costs (also net of income taxes). Benefits and costs are categorized separately because of the different assumptions made about their serial correlations. This rearrangement permits calculation of standard deviation estimates and construction of a probability distribution of possible net present values.

Since effective gross income is assumed to be perfectly correlated through time, while tax savings from depreciation is a constant rather than a variable, it is convenient to group these items together on the reconstructed cash-flow statement. Depreciation, as a constant, has zero standard deviation. It follows that the standard deviation of effective gross income is also the standard deviation of total benefits (gross revenue plus tax savings from depreciation).

It is equally convenient to group debt service with operating expense. Debt service is a precise amount having zero standard deviation. Therefore, the standard deviation of total costs equals the standard deviation of operating expenses.

Note carefully that expected net cash-flow estimates for each year on the reconstructed cash-flow statement (table 13-4) differs from that on the summary statement in example 13-1 by only $1. This minor difference is due solely to rounding error consequent to the reconstruction. Absent the rounding error, the outcome will be an exact replica of the original statement. Elements have simply been rearranged for computational convenience; otherwise, nothing has been changed.

Developing Probability Estimates

As risk-management tools, the concepts of probability distributions and confidence intervals are theoretically appealing. They are so useful in the physical sciences and in many areas of social science (where characteristics under study are capable of measure either in universal or in sample form) that it is tempting to compare their use in those contexts with the potential they hold for adaptation to real estate investment analysis.

Table 13-3
After-Tax Consequence of Financial Leverage, Altamese Villa Apartments

Years	Interest Payments	1 − Tax Rate	= After-Tax Interest	+ Principal Payments[a]	After-Tax Debt Service
1	$30,253	0.30	$9,076	$4,088	$13,164
2	29,825	0.30	8,948	4,516	13,464
3	29,355	0.30	8,807	4.986	13,793
4	28,823	0.30	8,647	5,518	14,165
5	28,249	0.30	8,475	6,092	14,567
6	27,608	0.30	8,282	6,733	15,015

[a] Source: Table 9-2, combined amounts for both mortgages.

Table 13-4
Reconstructed Cash-Flow Forecast, Altamese Villa Apartments

	Year of Operation					
	1	2	3	4	5	6
Benefits, net of taxes:						
Effective gross rent [a]	$22,440	$23,850	$25,200	$26,700	$28,350	$30,000
Tax savings from depreciation [b]	5,600	5,600	5,600	5,600	5,600	5,600
Total	$28,040	$29,450	$30,800	$32,300	$33,950	$35,600
Costs, net of taxes:						
Operating expenses [c]	$11,775	$12,450	$13,200	$13,950	$15,000	$15,600
Mortgage interest [d]	9,076	8,948	8.807	8,647	8,475	8,282
Amortization [d]	4,088	4,516	4,986	5,518	6.092	6,733
Total	$24,939	$25,914	$26,993	$28,115	$29,567	$30,615
Net cash flow	$ 3,102	$ 3,536	$ 3,807	$ 4,185	$ 4,383	$ 4,985

[a] Table 13-1.
[b] Annual depreciation x tax rate = $8,000 × 0.70.
[c] Table 13-2.
[d] Table 13-3.

But something is lost in the transfer. The statistical concepts are, of course, the same, but their application necessarily differs. Understanding these differences is crucial to correct interpretation of the results of applying the mean/standard deviation model.

A major difference stems from how probability estimates are derived. In the physical and biological sciences, probabilities are developed from sample data which are more or less representative of the universe from which they are drawn. This is *sometimes* the case in real estate investment applications as well. But therein lies the difference: in the former instances, assumption of representativeness is subject to testing and verification, while in real estate applications, such testing is seldom possible.

In many real estate applications, sample data will be so sparse as to preclude reliable inferences therefrom using traditional statistical techniques. Instead, analysts frequently are forced to rely on *subjective* estimates of the probabilities associated with point estimates of values they are trying to measure.

Standard Deviation of Expected Expenses. Assume that for the apartment building in example 13-1 there is sufficient sample data available to permit reliable statistical inferences. This will often be so because expenses are not inordinately affected by locational influences. A sample can therefore be collected over a rather wide geographical area and still be applicable to the project under analysis. Primary constraints over choice of observations in the sample include influences of labor cost, per unit utility costs, and materials costs. So long as these are subject to the same market influences as the project to be analyzed, sample data may be comparable.

Of course, buildings included in the sample must be of comparable age and in comparable physical condition. They must be of approximately the same material composition. Variation due to differences beyond these can generally be eliminated by use of some common unit of measure, such as cost per square foot of area or per room.

Collecting expense estimates from sample data was discussed in chapter 3. Simply assume for now that a sufficiently large sample is available. Applying generally accepted statistical computational procedures, the mean and standard deviation of the sample data are calculated, with the appropriate correction for sample size. For illustrative purposes, assume that the standard deviation of the expense estimates applicable to the apartment building example include plus or minus 20 percent of the expected (that is, the mean) value.

Having assumed the investor to be in the 70 percent tax bracket both before and after the investment, it follows that the relationship of before-tax and after-tax expenses is invariant over the relevant portion of the probability distribution. The practical significance of this is that after-tax expenses will have the same relative standard deviation as before taxes, plus or minus 20 percent of the mean.

Applying the assumed deviation estimates to the after-tax expenses in table 13-2 yields the standard deviation estimates illustrated in table 13-5.

Standard Deviation of Gross Revenues. Techniques used to estimate standard deviation of the probability distribution of possible expenses generally

Table 13-5
Annual Standard Deviation Estimates Associated with After-Tax Expenses, Altamese Villa Apartments

Year	After-Tax Expenses [a]	Standard Deviation [b]
1	11,775	2,355
2	12,450	2,490
3	13,200	2,640
4	13,950	2,790
5	15,000	3,000
6	15,600	3,120

[a] From table 13-2.
[b] Twenty percent of expense estimate.

are not applicable to the estimation of standard deviation associated with gross-revenue projections. The distinction is due to differences in locational influences. Whereas locational factors are not particularly influential determinants of expenses, they often are a dominant factor in determining gross revenues.

Since inferences from sample data are generally an inapplicable approach to estimating gross revenue, reliance must often be placed on *subjective probability estimates.* Accuracy of subjective estimates depends less on statistical expression of the relationship than on precision of the analyst's risk perception.

Having assumed the probability distribution of possible gross revenues to be symmetrically distributed around the expected value, specifying the mean (that is, expected value) and one other point on the distribution in effect defines the shape of the entire distribution. This is a consequence of the mathematical expression of the relationship and is not a subject of disagreement among mathematicians and statisticians. If an error is introduced, it lies in the assumption of symmetry, which is necessary to render the model operational. The model could be altered to deal with asymmetrical distributions, but complications introduced thereby are beyond the scope of this discussion.

If it appears that the assumption of symmetry does not introduce an unacceptable degree of error, subjective estimates of standard deviation can be developed by reference to the midpoint and one other location on the distribution of possible outcomes. In addition to specifying the most likely (that is, the expected) gross revenue for each year of the projection period, the analyst provides an estimate of the minimum gross revenue such that the minimum is *virtually certain* to be equaled or exceeded.

Figure 13-1 illustrates the relationship between expected outcome and an alternative possibility which is virtually certain to be equaled or

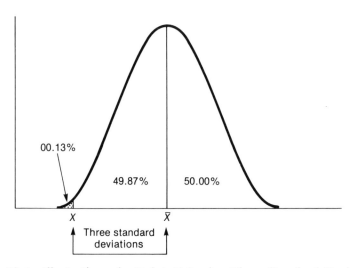

Figure 13-1. Illustration of a Point X Laying Three Standard Deviations from the Midpoint $\bar{X}$ of a Symmetrical Distribution.

exceeded. Recall from the discussion of basic probability rules in chapter 12 that the total area under the probability distribution is unity, indicating certainty that *some* value under the distribution will occur. It follows that if the value indicated by X on the far left of the distribution in figure 13-1 is virtually certain to be equaled or exceeded, the area to the left of X must be virtually zero.

The table of Z values in appendix G indicates that the area to the left of three standard deviations from the mean is only 0.0013 of the total area under the curve. Further inspection of the table reveals that the area to the left approaches zero asymptotically. This means the area never becomes absolutely zero, but that the area decreases at a decreasing rate, with zero as the limit. This and most other tables of Z values present no value below plus or minus three standard deviations, because for most practical problems the area between these points can be treated as encompassing the entire area under the curve. Values beyond three standard deviations have essentially zero probability of occurring.

Summarizing the argument, a value under a symmetrical probability distribution which lies three standard deviations or more to the left of the mean is virtually certain to be equaled or exceeded when a random selection is made from the probability distribution of possible outcomes. Translated from jargon, a gross rental estimate which the analyst states is virtually certain to be met or exceeded can be treated as a value lying approximately

Table 13-6

Annual Standard Deviation Associated with After-Tax Gross Rent Estimates for Altamese Villa Apartments

Year	Expected Gross Rent [a]	Minimum Gross Rent [b]	Standard Deviation [c]	After-Tax Standard Deviation [d]
1	74,800	37,400	12,467	3,740
2	79,500	40,250	13,083	3,925
3	84,000	42,000	14,000	4,200
4	89,000	44,500	14,833	4,450
5	94,500	47,250	15,750	4,725
6	100,000	50,000	16,667	5,000

[a] From example 13-1.

[b] Amount analyst asserts is virtually certain to be met or exceeded (three standard deviations from the mean, or expected, gross rent).

[c] One-third the difference between the expected outcome and the minimum gross (that is, one standard deviation from the expected outcome).

[d] Standard deviation multiplied by 1 − income tax rate.

three standard deviations to the left of the mean, as indicated in figure 13-1. Dividing this number by 3 yields a standard deviation estimate of gross rental revenue. Since the tax rate is assumed to remain invariant at 70 percent over the relevant range of the distribution, the standard deviation of after-tax gross revenue for the apartment building in example 13-1 is 1 − tax rate, or 30 percent of the before-tax amount. Table 13-6 presents the annual standard deviation estimates for that project.

To understand how the after-tax standard deviation estimates are computed in table 13-6, consider the first-year expected gross rent reflected thereon. Of that amount 70 percent represents an expected increase in income taxes, with the remaining 30 percent expected to flow through to the owner. The *expected* after-tax gross rental revenue for year number 1 is therefore $22,440, determined as follows:

Expected gross rental revenue	$74,800
Less: Taxes (at 70 percent)	52,360
Expected after-tax gross	$22,440

The before-tax gross rental which is assumed to be virtually certain to occur (that is, lying approximately three standard deviations from the midpoint of the distribution) in the first year of operations is $37,400. But again, only 30 percent of this will remain after taxes. Therefore, the *min-*

imum after–tax gross rental revenue (that which is virtually certain to occur) is $11,220:

Minimum gross revenue	$37,400
Less: Income taxes (at 70 percent)	26,180
Minimum after–tax gross	$11,220

Now the difference between the *expected* after–tax gross of $22,440 and the *minimum* after–tax gross of $11,220 is $22,440 − $11,220, or $11,220. This represents a movement of three standard deviations from the midpoint of the distribution. One standard deviation, on an after–tax basis, is therefore one-third this amount, or $3,740. This is the amount shown in the after–tax standard deviation column of table 13-6 for the first year of operations. The same result is achieved by multiplying the before-tax standard deviation figures by 1 – tax rate. In each instance, therefore, the after-tax standard deviation in table 13-6 is 30 percent of the before-tax amount. Figure 13-2 illustrates the relationship, using the first-year figures.

The product of all the foregoing "number crunching" is summarized in table 13-7. Expected annual benefits on an after-tax basis are shown with

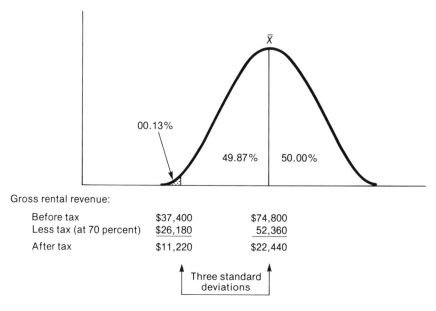

Figure 13–2. Illustration of After–Tax Standard Deviation Associated with First Year's Estimated Gross Rental Revenue, Altamese Villa Apartments.

Table 13-7

Reconstructed After-Tax Cash-Flow Forecast with Associated Standard Deviation Estimates, Altamese Villa Apartments

	Years of Operation					
	1	2	3	4	5	6
Benefits:						
Gross rental income [a]	$22,440	$23,850	$25,200	$26,700	$28,350	$30,000
Tax savings from depreciation [a]	5,600	5,600	5,600	5,600	5,600	5,600
Total	$28,040	$29,450	$30,800	$32,300	$33,950	$35,600
Standard deviation [b]	$ 3,740	$ 3,925	$ 4,200	$ 4,450	$ 4,725	$ 5,000
Costs:						
Operating expenses [a]	$11,775	$12,450	$13,200	$13,950	$15,000	$15,600
Mortgage interest [a]	9,076	8,948	8,807	8,647	8,475	8,282
Amortization [a]	4,088	4,516	4,986	5,518	6,092	6,733
Total	$24,939	$25,914	$26,993	$28,115	$29,567	$30,615
Standard deviation [c]	2,355	2,490	2,640	2,790	3,000	3,120

[a] From table 13-4.
[b] From table 13-6.
[c] From table 13-5.

associated standard deviations of the probability distributions of possible benefits. Note that benefits include tax savings from depreciation allowances, but that the standard deviation is solely that associated with after-tax gross-revenue estimates from table 13-6. This follows from the observation that tax savings from depreciation is a point estimate having no variability. Since there is no possibility of variance from the point estimate, there can be no standard deviation of the tax saving from this source.[1]

Table 13-7 also summarizes costs, net of taxes, and illustrates the associated standard deviation of the probability distribution of possible after-tax costs. As in the case of after-tax benefits from depreciation allowance, the after-tax cost of debt service is a single number rather than a distribution, and thus has zero standard deviation. Consequently, the standard deviation estimate associated with total annual after-tax costs is simply the standard deviation of the operating expenses from table 13-5.

Expected Cash Flow from Disposition

Example 9-3 assumes that the apartment project, if acquired, will be sold after 6 years, at a price representing approximately 4.68 times the effective gross rental revenue being generated at the time of sale. There is, of course, no way to be certain that the current gross multiple will continue in effect 6 years hence. It would be more appropriate to develop a probability distribution of possible multiples and to interface that distribution with the distribution of possible gross revenue outcomes for the year of sale to arrive at a distribution of possible sale prices representing a joint probability-density function.

A probability function of the type just mentioned is not amenable to incorporation in the present model, however, because the model requires all cash flows (positive and negative) to be either completely independent of previous annual outcomes or perfectly correlated with previous events. Accommodating this assumption of the model, variations in the gross rent multiplier are taken as an element of uncertainty. Using a joint function requires a more complex analytical model and is therefore more expensive and time consuming to apply.[2]

Taking the present gross–rent multiplier of 4.68 as an assumption of the model, the probability distribution of possible gross selling prices of the 28–unit apartment has a midpoint of $468,000, representing 4.68 times the midpoint of the probability distribution of possible gross rental incomes in the year the project is expected to be sold. Moreover, the actual gross sales price is assumed to vary, in a ratio of 4.68 to 1, with the actual gross rental income in the year of sale.

Since the gross rental revenue was earlier calculated to be virtually certain to equal or exceed $50,000 in the sixth year of the projection period, it follows that the gross sales price is equally certain to be 4.68 times that amount, or more. Thus three standard deviations from the expected gross sales price lies $234,000 from the midpoint of the distribution. One standard deviation is therefore $234,000/3, or $78,000.

If a broker is engaged to sell the property, selling costs will vary almost directly with the gross sales price, because brokerage fees are usually quoted as a percentage of gross sales proceeds rather than as a flat rate, and because the brokerage fee will comprise the bulk of selling costs. Assuming this rate to be 7 percent, the net sales price will be approximately 93 percent of the gross, and the standard deviation of the possible net sales prices will be 93 percent of the standard deviation of the gross sales price. Therefore, the midpoint of the distribution of possible net sales prices (that is, the expected net sales price) is $435,240, with an associated standard deviation of $72,540. These relationships are illustrated in figure 13-3.

Of course, cash proceeds from the sale will be considerably less than the net sales price, which includes the balance of outstanding mortgage indebtedness and any income tax obligation arising from the transaction. The mortgage balance remains unaffected by the actual sales price, but the income tax obligation is a direct function thereof.

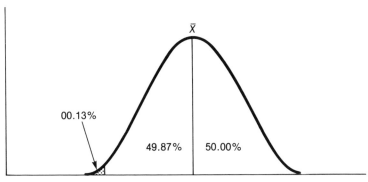

Net sales price:

Gross sales price	$234,000	$468,000
Less selling costs	16,380	32,760
Net sales price	$217,620	$435,240

$$X - \bar{X}/\sigma = -3$$
$$= 217{,}620 - 435{,}240/\sigma$$
$$\therefore \sigma = \pm 72{,}540$$

Figure 13-3. Standard Deviation of Expected Net Selling Price, Altamese Villa Apartments.

The remaining balance on the proposed mortgage will be its face amount minus all previous payments on principal. The balance after 6 years is $280,567, determined as follows:

Initial mortgage financing:	
First mortgage note	$262,500
Second mortgage note	50,000
Total	$312,500
Less: Total amortization (from table 13-3)	31,933
Remaining balance of mortgage indebtedness	$280,567

The taxable gain on disposal will be the net sales price minus the adjusted tax basis of the property. The adjusted tax basis is, of course, unaffected by the actual sales price, being simply the original cost minus all depreciation deductions claimed during the holding period. Since acquisition cost, under the proposed financing terms, is $350,000, and since $8,000 of depreciation will be claimed during each of the 6 years in the projected holding period, the adjusted basis after 6 years will be $302,000. The calculations are:

Original cost		$350,000
Less: Accumulated depreciation:		
Annual depreciation deduction	$8,000	
Times length of holding period (years)	6	
Total depreciation claimed		$ 48,000
Adjusted basis at time of projected sale		$302,000

Only 40 percent of long-term capital gains are subject to taxation. Since the investor is presumed to be in the 70 percent marginal income tax bracket, the tax rate on his long-term gain will be 40 percent times 70 percent, or 28 percent. His income tax liability resulting from the transaction will therefore be 28 percent of the difference between the net sales price and his adjusted basis of $302,000. If the actual sales price is as expected (that is, $468,000), the investor's income tax liability will be $37,307, and his net cash proceeds will be $117,366. If, on the other hand, the actual sales price is only $234,000 (the assumed minimum possible outcome), there will be a loss on disposal resulting in a tax saving of $23,626, and the net cash proceeds will be a *negative* $39,321. The underlying calculations are illustrated in table 13-8.[3]

Having calculated the net proceeds from disposal at both the expected gross sales price and the possible sales price lying three standard deviations from the midpoint, the standard deviation of the probability distribution of *net proceeds* from disposal can now be determined. Since three standard deviations moves the net cash proceeds from the expected amount of $117,366 to a possible *negative* $39,321, a single standard deviation of possible net cash proceeds is one-third of the difference between these two possible outcomes, or $52,229. The relationship is illustrated in figure 13-4.

Present-Value Calculations

After estimating expected values for the probability distributions of expected cash outflows and inflows for each year in the projected holding period, and the attendant standard deviations, there remains only to discount all expected annual outcomes to arrive at an estimated present value of the investment opportunity.

At this point the distinction between serially correlated and independent annual cash flows becomes crucial. Recall from chapter 12 that the formula for standard deviation of the present value of independent cash flows differs drastically from that of serially correlated flows. That is why cash flows were previously categorized as being either perfectly serially correlated or completely independent.

Table 13–8
Possible Net Cash Proceeds from Disposal, Altamese Villa Apartments

	Minimum Possible	Most Likely
Net cash proceeds:		
Actual gross sales price (to nearest $1,000)	$234,000	$468,000
Less: Selling costs (at 7 percent)	16,380	32,760
Net sales price	$217,620	$435,240
Less: Income tax (or plus saving)	($ 23,626)	$ 37,307
Mortgage balance	280,567	280,567
Net proceeds from disposal	($ 39,321)	$117,366
Income tax liability		
Net sales price (from above)	$217,620	$435,240
Less: Adjusted basis	302,000	302,000
Gain (or loss) on disposal	($ 84,380)	$133,240
Times marginal tax rate	.28 [a]	.28
Income tax obligation (tax benefit)	($ 23,626)	$ 37,307

[a] See footnote 3 at end of chapter.

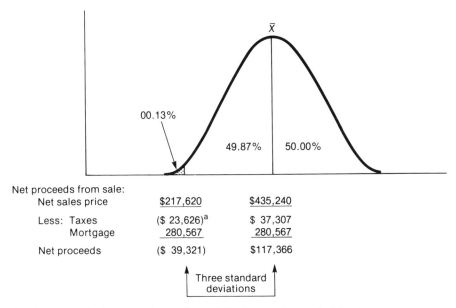

Net proceeds from sale:

Net sales price	$217,620	$435,240
Less: Taxes	($ 23,626)[a]	$ 37,307
Mortgage	280,567	280,567
Net proceeds	($ 39,321)	$117,366

Three standard deviations

[a]Indicates tax reduction due to loss on disposal. See footnote 3, at end of chapter.

Figure 13–4. Probability Distribution of Possible Net Cash Proceeds from Sale of Altamese Villa Apartments.

Present Value of Cash Receipts. Gross income from rents is assumed to be perfectly correlated through time. Likewise, variances in the after-tax cash flow from disposal are assumed to depend on exactly the same elements which determine annual gross rents. All these cash-flow elements are therefore grouped together and discounted at the appropriate discount rate. The calculations are displayed on table 13-9.

Present Value of Cash Disbursements. In contrast with receipts, cash disbursements for operating expenses are assumed to vary randomly about the expected value. Annual estimates are therefore treated as being serially independent. Since other cash disbursements (for debt service) have *no* expected variation whatsoever, it follows that the standard deviation of all disbursements equals the standard deviation associated with after-tax cash disbursements for operating expenses. The present value of expected cash disbursements and the associated standard deviation calculations are presented in table 13-10.

Present Value of All Expected Future Cash Flows. Summing the present-value calculations from table 13-9 and 13-10 yields the present value of all expected future cash flows, both receipts and disbursements. There results the expected present value of the investment venture. Since disbursements have a negative present value, the arithmetic operation is in fact subtraction. The difference ($83,245) is determined as follows:

Present value of cash inflows (from table 13-9)	$202,456
Less: Present value of disbursements (table 13-10)	119,212
Present value of all anticipated cash flows	$ 83,244

Except for rounding error accumulating to 1, this is the same present-value estimate derived in chapter 9. Identical outcomes are, of course, expected, since at this point the data have simply been rearranged for analytical convenience. The outcome, which represents a simple point estimate of present value in chapter 9, is presented here as the midpoint of a probability distribution of possible present values.

Standard Deviation of the Present Value

Having reached identical conclusions regarding present value of the investment proposal in chapters 9 and 13, what has been gained by this lengthy restatement of the problem? The reformulation enables attendant risk to be expressed in probabilistic terms. The standard deviation of the present value of expected cash disbursements (independent cash flows) is calculated in

Table 13–9
Present Value of Serially Correlated Cash Flows and Standard Deviation Calculations, Altamese Villa Apartments

Year	After-Tax Cash Benefits	Present Value at 10 Percent	Standard Deviation	$\dfrac{\sigma}{1.10^t}$
1	$ 28,040	$ 25,491	$ 3,740	$ 3,400
2	29,450	24,339	3,925	3,244
3	30,800 [a]	23,140	4,200 [a]	3,156
4	32,300	22,061	4,450	3,039
5	33,950	21,080	4,725	2,934
6	35,600	20,095	5,000	2,822
	117,366 [b]	66,250	52,229 [c]	29,482
		$\sum$ 202,456		$\sum$ 48,075

[a] Annual after-tax benefits from operations, from table 13–7.
[b] Expectd after-tax cash flow from disposal, from table 13–8.
[c] From figure 13–4:

Expected net proceeds from disposal	$117,366
Plus less lying 3 standard deviations away	39,321
Dollar amount of 3 standard deviations	156,687
One standard deviation ($156,687/3)	$ 52,229

Table 13–10
Present Value and Standard Deviation Calculations of Serially Independent Cash Flows, Altamese Villa Apartments

Years	After-Tax Cash Flows [a]	Present Value at 10 percent	Standard Deviation [a]	$\left[\dfrac{\sigma^2}{1.10^{2t}}\right]$ [b]
1	(24,939)	(22,672)	2,355	4.583×10^6
2	(25,914)	(21,417)	2,490	4.235×10^6
3	(26,993)	(20,280)	2,640	3.934×10^6
4	(28,115)	(19,203)	2,790	3.631×10^6
5	(29,567)	(18,359)	3,000	3.470×10^6
6	(30,615	(17,281)	3,120	3.102×10^6
		$\sum$ (119,212)		$\sum$ 22.955×10^6

$$\sqrt{\frac{\sigma^2}{1.10^{2t}}} = 4,791$$

[a] Annual after-tax costs and related standard deviations, from table 13–7.
[b] Column uses scientific notation due to large size of numbers ($10^6 = 10,000,000$).

table 13–10 as $4,791. The standard deviation of expected future cash inflows (serially correlated cash flows) is determined in table 13–9 to be $48,075. These estimates are combined to derive a standard deviation of the present value of *all* expected future cash flows.

Because cash flows differ with respect to the assumptions regarding serial correlation, this calculation is something more than a mere summation of the respective standard deviations. The formula for the standard deviation of this model, described in chapter 12 as Hillier's model, is presented there as

$$\sigma_{PV} = \sqrt{\left[\sum_{t=0}^{n} \frac{\sigma^2}{(1+i)^{2t}} \right] + \left[\sum_{t=0}^{n} \frac{\sigma}{(1+i)^{t}} \right]^2}$$

Applying the formula to the data in tables 13-9 and 13-10 yields an overall standard deviation of the present value of:

$$\sigma_{PV} = \sqrt{(22.955 \times 10^6) + 48,075^2}$$

$$= \$48,314$$

Analysis of Possible Outcomes

Since discounting at 10 percent yields a present value in excess of the required down payment, it follows that the expected yield exceeds the required rate of 10 percent. The exact amount of the expected yield is neither evident nor particularly significant at this juncture. The analysis is extended in chapter 14 to include, among other information, the expected rate of return. But the presentation of this chapter concludes with determining the probability that the yield will ultimately prove to be not less than the target rate of 10 percent.

Figure 13-5 illustrates the probability distribution of possible present values for the project. Remembering that the actual yield equals the discount rate when the present value of future cash flows equals the initial cash outlay (that is, when the net present value equals zero), that point on the probability distribution where the actual outcome results in a realized yield of just 10 percent can be identified.

Since the down payment required for this project, as currently structured, is $37,500, the actual yield will equal the discount rate employed in the analysis at the point where actual cash flow has a present value of exactly $37,500. This point is illustrated in figure 13-5 to the left of the midpoint of the distribution, where the net present value (present value minus down payment) is zero. Since the net present value at the midpoint of the distribution is $45,745, the number of dollars to the left of the expected value to the point where net present value is zero is exactly $45,744. And since one standard deviation is (as previously determined) $48,314, this distance equals $45,745/$48,314, or 0.95 standard deviations from the mean.

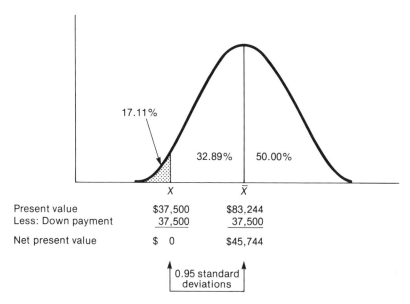

Present value	$37,500	$83,244
Less: Down payment	37,500	37,500
Net present value	$ 0	$45,744

Figure 13–5. Expected Net Present Value and Probability that Actual Net Present Value Will Be Equal to or Less than Zero, Altamese Villa Apartments.

Expressing the relationship in terms of the by now familiar equation:

$$X - \bar{X}/\sigma = \$37,500 - \$83,244/\$48,314$$

$$= \$45,744/\$48,314$$

$$= -0.95$$

The Z table in appendix G shows that the area under the curve to the left of 0.95 standard deviations from the mean is 0.1711. It follows that the area to the right is 1 - 0.1711, or 0.8289. This is the probability that the actual present value of this venture will prove to be $37,500 or more. Expressed differently, the investor can be 83 percent confident that the actual yield on the project will be 10 percent or more.

Summary

When the array of possible annual cash flows from an investment can be assumed to be distributed approximately symmetrically about the midpoint of a distribution, return and risk can be analyzed in terms of expected values and standard deviation. A model which is particularly applicable to many real estate investment analysis problems is often called Hillier's model, after the individual who first developed the analytical framework from which it is adapted.

To employ Hillier's model, cash flows are first divided into subcategories, based on whether they are more nearly perfectly correlated serially or more nearly independent through time. To avoid complications introduced by partial correlation, these categories are then treated as in fact either perfectly correlated or completely independent.

Expected cash flows and associated standard deviations are computed for each category of cash flows for every year in the projection period. All expected cash flows are discounted to the present, using a predetermined discount rate. Standard deviations are likewise discounted, and a standard deviation of the combined present values is calculated using the formula developed by Hillier.

Once the expected present value or net present value of a project has been estimated, along with the standard deviation of the present value, risk and return can be analyzed in terms of the probability of earning any specific present value, net present value, or profitability index.

Notes

1. It does not follow that expected benefits from depreciation allowances will actually be reaped. Changes in tax law, natural disaster, or other unforeseen events might result in a drastically different outcome. These eventualities represent elements of *uncertainty*, as defined in chapter 12, rather than elements of risk. They could, of course, be melded into the risk measure by sufficient research to enable assignment of probability estimates to each possible alternative outcome. It is unlikely, however, that an investor would enjoy benefits from such research sufficient to compensate him for the additional cost.

2. An example of a joint probability-density function is presented in chapter 12.

3. These calculations implicitly assume no tax obligation under the *alternative minimum tax* rules described in chapter 6. They also assume the investor has other long-term capital gains against which to offset any loss on disposal. If this latter assumption is invalid, then the model (as illustrated) will misstate the after-tax cash flow from disposal. The size of the misstatement will be directly related to the variance of actual sales price from the expected price. Adjusting to eliminate or reduce this potential distortion substantially complicates the mathematics of the model.

14

Investment Risk: An Expanded Viewpoint

Investment intelligence is a costly product. All analyses must therefore be fully exploited, with no informational content wasted. For these reasons the presentation of findings is as important as the analytical process itself. Data generated by analysts cannot be incorporated into investment decisions until it is fully comprehended and accepted by the prime decision maker.

This chapter presents methods for extending the benefits of the mean/standard deviation model by enhancing communication of findings to the ultimate user of the information. It explains how the presentation can be altered to fit the knowledge level and attitudes of investor-clients and how graphic analysis can enhance the client's understanding of the findings.

An alternative analytical model is also introduced. This model, involving simulation of probability distributions, is particularly appropriate for very large-scale projects where the interrelationship between variables renders the more simple model unwieldy. The simulation model is itself somewhat complex to administer, requiring access to computer facilities and appropriate programming knowledge on the part of the analyst or his staff. The more advanced procedure should be employed where potential benefits of additional investment intelligence justifies the magnified cost.

Because much risk can be diversified away, the chapter concludes with an explanation of the benefits to be achieved by portfolio diversification and a discussion of the means of achieving desired diversification within the confines of a budget constraint. Suggested techniques include incorporation, formation of partnerships, and fractionalizing of fee interests.

Extending the Usefulness of the Mean/Standard Deviation Model

Beyond basic advantages outlined in chapter 13, the mean/standard deviation technique can be modified and extended to enhance its usefulness as a management decision tool. Probabilities can be expressed in almost any fashion decision makers wish. They can, for example, be expressed in terms of the probability that any specified profitability index or net present value will be realized. Or an array of possible outcomes can be expressed as a probability distribution of such indices.

Alternative forms of graphic presentation can enhance understanding of the data. Perhaps the most useful alternative is to employ a cumulative probability–density function.

Using Profitability Indices

Profitability indices are explained in chapter 9. They relate the present value of future cash flows to initial cash outlay. The profitability index is simply the present value per dollar of initial cash investment and is calculated by dividing the present value of an opportunity by the total amount of required initial cash outlay. Engineers will recognize this as a cost/benefit ratio, wherein the present value of all costs is compared with the present value of all benefits.

The expected profitability index associated with the apartment project analyzed in chapter 13 is 2.22, when expected cash flows are discounted at 10 percent. This is determined by dividing the expected value of $83,245 by the required down payment of $37,500. Of course, if the actual present value proves to be different from that which is expected, then the actual profitability index will also vary. Such variation is almost certain to occur, since only coincidence would cause the actual outcome of a particular event to correspond exactly with the midpoint of the probability distribution of possible outcomes. The crucial factor is the likely direction and degree of variance from expectations.

Figure 13–5 illustrates the probability distribution of possible present values and indicates that the distribution also serves as a probability distribution of *net* present values. The latter observation is true because the relationship between present value and net present value is determined by the amount of the initial cash outlay, which in this particular example remains invariant as the present value varies.

The relationship between present value and profitability index is equally invariant. So long as the initial cash outlay remains unchanged, the profitability index will vary directly with changes in the present value. Therefore, there is a determinable profitability index associated with every point along the probability distribution of present values in figure 13–5. This relationship is illustrated in figure 14–1, which replicates the distribution of present values shown in figure 13–5.

For any present value found along the horizontal axis of figure 14–1, a profitability index can be computed by dividing the present value by the $37,500 down payment required to take advantage of the opportunity. Therefore, should the actual outcome of the venture result in a present value of only $37,500, the actual profitability index will prove to be exactly

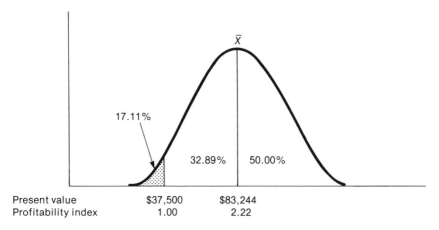

Figure 14-1. Probability Distribution of Profitability Indices, Altamese Villa Apartments.

unity. Below this point the actual profitability index (when discounting at 10 percent) will prove to be less than 1, which means the venture will have yielded less than 10 percent per annum on invested funds.

Using Risk-Profile Charts as Policy Tools

The two points illustrated in figure 14-1 have special significance. They represent the expected present value per dollar invested and the minimum acceptable present value per dollar invested, respectively. This information—the expected return and the probability of earning less than the minimum acceptable rate—can be compared with a risk-profile chart, as described in chapter 12, to determine whether a particular proposal merits further consideration.

Two representative risk-profile charts are compiled in table 14-1 and illustrated in figure 14-2. Expressing a relatively conservative investment philosophy, investor A will not accept any opportunity where the probability of experiencing a yield below the minimum acceptable rate exceeds 0.035, regardless of the attendant expected profitability. A proposal such as example 13-1, which has an expected profitability index of 2.2, would thus have to indicate a probability of not more than 0.035 that the profitability index will prove to be equal to or less than 1. Since the probability of that eventuality is in fact 0.17 (see figure 14-1), the project is perceived as far too risky by investor A.

Table 14-1

Risk–Return Profiles for Two Investors Who Express Risk in Terms of Probability of Earning less than a Specified Minimum Acceptable Rate of Return

	Maximum Acceptable Probability that Profitability Index Will Be Equal to or Less than 1	
Expected Profitability Index	Investor A	Investor B
0.0	0.0000	0.0000
1.2	0.0150	0.0150
1.4	0.0230	0.0260
1.6	0.0290	0.0345
1.8	0.0330	0.0430
2.0	0.0350	0.0460
2.2	0.0350	0.0490
2.4	0.0350	0.0500

Investor B is relatively less risk averse than investor A. He is willing to accept probabilities as high as 0.049 that the actual rate of return will prove to be less than the minimum acceptable rate. Even so, the investment is too risky to be acceptable, since the probability of 0.17 exceeds the acceptable level of any possible expected profitability index.

Cumulative Probability–Density Functions

Probability distributions of possible returns are a convenient and generally enlightening method of illustrating possible consequences of an investment venture. But clients untutored in basic concepts of probability analysis may find themselves somewhat confused. They often find data presented in a cumulative probability format more understandable.

Almost everyone is familiar with basic graphic analysis which presents numerical data on a two-dimensional plane. Figure 14-2 is an example which most investors will find intuitively comprehensible. A predetermined policy concerning acceptable risk–reward tradeoffs permits ready reference to such data for comparison with any investment proposal.

Investors with no established policy expressed in terms of acceptable risk–reward combinations can nevertheless use such graphic presentations as an aid to understanding the anticipated profitability and attendant risk associated with any particular proposal. Graphing the cumulative probability of realizing progressively more attractive returns enables an investor to visualize the potential as perceived by the analyst.

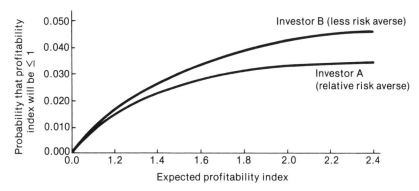

Figure 14-2. Risk–Return Profiles for Two Investors Whose Attitudes toward Risk Are Expressed in Terms of Probability of Earning Less than Minimum Acceptable Rates of Return.

Plotting a cumulative–probability distribution on regular graph paper leads to a pattern such as that shown in figure 14-3, when the underlying distribution is symmetrically distributed about the mean value. The data illustrated in figure 14-3 are derived from the apartment project analyzed in chapter 13. Using the expected outcome and associated standard deviation from that problem, the information in table 14-2 was derived. This information was then plotted on standard graph paper to yield the functional relationship illustrated in figure 14-3.

To develop the data in table 14-2, refer to the Altamese Villa Apartment project in chapter 13. Note that the project has an expected value of $83,245 and a standard deviation of the expected value of $48,314. Since the initial down payment requirement is $37,500, the expected *PI* is $83,245/ $37,500, or 2.22. And since one standard deviation is $48,314, the present value at minus one standard deviation from the mean is $83,245 − $48,314, or $34,931. At minus two standard deviations, the present value becomes $83,245 − (2 × $48,314), or minus $13,383. At minus three standard deviations, the present value is $83,245 − (3 × $48,314), or minus $61,697. At each of these points the *PI* is simply the present value divided by the $37,500 downpayment. The *PI*s are thus 0.93, − 0.36, and − 1.65, respectively.

Moving one standard deviation to the right of the midpoint yields a present value of $83,245 + $48,314, or $131,559, and a *PI* of $131,559/ $37,500, or 3.51. Two standard deviations to the right yields a present value of $83,245 + (2 × $48,314), or $179,873, and a *PI* of $179,873/$37,500. Continuing in this fashion yields as many *PI* calculations and associated probability measures as desired. The results of several such computations are displayed in table 14-2.

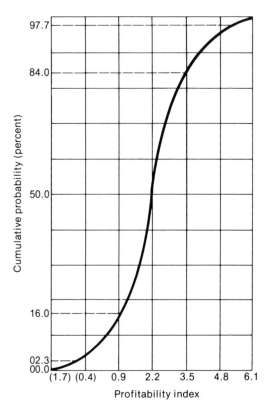

Figure 14-3. Cumulative Probability of Realizing a Profitability Index Equal to or Less than Specified Levels, Altamese Villa Apartments.

Data from table 14-2 are simply transferred to figure 14-3 to graphically display cumulative probabilities associated with profitability indices at various distances from the mean.

To emphasize specified profitability indices instead of specific distances from the mean, the graph can be redrawn so that the horizontal scale presents information in the desired format. Such a transformation is computed in table 14-3 and illustrated in figure 14-4.

Table 14-3 starts with profitability index numbers of particular concern to the investor rather than with specific distances from the mean. Probabilities are once again expressed on a cumulative basis. Graphing this informa-

Table 14–2
Cumulative Probabilities Associated with Specified Distances from the Mean, Altamese Villa Apartments

Distance from Mean to Point X	Present Value at Point X [a]	Profitability Index at X [b]	Value from Z Table	Percent of Area to Left of Point X [c]
− 3	− $ 61,698	− 1.65	− 0.0013	0.13
− 2	− $ 13,384	− 0.36	− 0.0228	2.28
− 1	$ 34,930	0.93	− 0.1577	15.77
0	$ 83,244	2.22	0.5000	50.00
+ 1	$131,558	3.51	0.1577	84.23
+ 2	$179,872	4.81	0.0228	97.72
+ 3	$228,186	6.08	0.0013	99.87

[a] X = $83,244 − $48,314 times the number of standard deviations from mean to point X.

[b] PI = (present value at point x)/$37,500.

[c] When present value at point X is less than present value at the mean, area equals (value from Z table times 100); when present value at point X is greater than present value at the mean, area equals (1 minus value from Z table times 100).

Table 14–3
Cumulative Probabilities Associated with Specified Profitability Indices, Altamese Villa Apartments

Profitability Index	Present Value at Point X [a]	Distance from Mean to Point X [b]	Value from Z Table	Percent of Area to Left of Point X [c]
Lim 0.0	0	− 1.72	0.0428	4.3
0.5	$ 18,750	− 1.33	0.0918	9.7
1.0	$ 37,500	− 0.95	0.1711	17.1
1.5	$ 56,250	− 0.56	0.2878	28.8
2.0	$ 75,000	− 0.17	0.4325	43.3
2.5	$ 93,750	+ 0.22	0.4129	58.7
3.0	$112,500	+ 0.61	0.2710	72.9

[a] Present value = PI times $37,500.

[b] Distance = (present value at mean minus present value at point X)/(standard deviation).

[c] When present value at point X is less than present value at the mean, area equals (value from Z table times 100); when present value at point X is greater than present value at the mean, area equals (1 minus value from Z table times 100).

tion (figure 14–4) results in a somewhat easier to read presentation than was the case in figure 14–3. Note, however, that exactly the same information is presented in both figures. Only the scale has been altered. Note also that

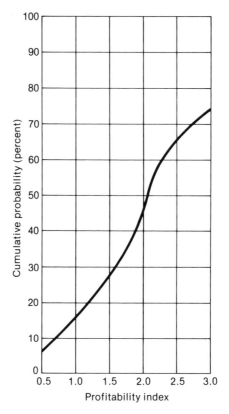

Figure 14-4. Cumulative Probability of Realizing a Profitability Index
Equal to or Less than Specified Levels, Altamese Villa
Apartments.

both graphs exhibit the characteristic shape always associated with a symmetrical distribution when displayed on a cumulative basis on arithmetical
graph paper.

More Complex Models: The Simulation Approach

When the number of probabilistic variables is large, and where the interrelationships of the variables are uncertain, developing a probability distribution of expected returns becomes a difficult task. The problem can be simplified somewhat by using a widely practiced simulation technique. The

simulation model, introduced by David B. Hertz in a pioneering article in 1964,[1] involves artificial duplication of the anticipated market process at an abstract and highly simplified level.

Imagine a large-scale land-development project with building lots to be developed and sold over a number of years. The crucial variables include market-absorption rates, cost and availability of third-party financing, payment records of purchasers who buy lots on the installment plan, cost of development work, availability and terms of equity financing where needed, and so forth.

Having identified the critical variables through a large number of projections with varying assumptions, probability values are assigned to the most likely values of the variables, and the variability is estimated. The analyst quantifies his beliefs about the future values of the variables in terms of expected values and perceived standard deviations.

The merit of expressing risk judgments in quantitative terms is argued at length in chapter 12. The subjective nature of the analyst's perception should be made explicit, but perception is expressed in the same terms as would be the case with objectively measured means and standard deviations. Contrary to the procedure explained in chapter 12, however, when simulation is employed the serial correlations of the variables must be specifically included in the equations.

These operations result in a probability distribution of possible values for each critical variable. The outcome of the overall project depends on which particular combination of possible values of the critical variables in fact occurs. A distinct possible overall outcome is associated with each possible combination of values. Considering all possible combinations results in a probability distribution of possible outcomes for the venture.

In the absence of computer facilities, establishing the parameters of the overall probability distribution is a formidable task. Computer simulation makes it possible to estimate the parameters by running a large number of cash-flow projections in which values of the critical variables are chosen randomly, with the chance of selecting each possible value corresponding to the probability of occurrence of that value.

Assume, for example, that the possible values of a particular critical variable and the associated probabilities are as follows:

Possible Values	Associated Probability
$10,000	0.10
15,000	0.25
20,000	0.30
25,000	0.25
30,000	0.10

Conceptually, the computer draws values for the variable from a box where the chances are 10 in 100 that the value drawn will be $10,000, 25 in 100 that it will be $15,000, and so on. Imagine that there are 100 tokens placed into a box, and the possible values of the variables are inscribed on the tokens. The computer draws one token from the box, includes the value from the token as the expected value of the variable for that particular trial run of the cash-flow projection and then places the token back into the box and draws again for the values to be included in the next trial run. Ten of the tokens will have $10,000 inscribed, twenty-five will be inscribed with a value of $15,000, thirty will be inscribed with $20,000, twenty-five will be inscribed with $25,000, and ten will be inscribed with $30,000.

The computer repeats this process to choose a value for each of the critical variables and completes a large number of consequent cash-flow projections. The resultant distribution of possible outcomes will approximate a symmetrical probability distribution of present values of possible future cash flows. The analysis can then proceed as developed in chapter 12.

In the July 1977 issue of *The Appraisal Journal,* Howard Stevenson and Barbara Jackson described an actual application of this type of analytical model to a large-scale real estate development problem. Analysts with access to computer facilities and an interest in the subject should refer to that article.[2]

Risk-Management Techniques

After so many years of almost embarrassing silence on the subject, it is heartening to find that risk analysis has become a popular subject in professional real estate journals. For many investors, however, the more sophisticated techniques are simply inappropriate. They represent less than optimal solutions when the additional cost of analysis more than offsets the benefit from avoiding selection error. For projects which are relatively inexpensive ventures, or where outcomes are highly predictable, less complicated or less indepth analysis might be appropriate. Moreover, risk can often be greatly reduced by relatively simple risk-management steps.

Avoid "Analysis Paralysis"

It is no easy task to decide when investment analysis should cease and a go/no-go decision should be made. Obviously, there is such a point—the problem is in deciding when it has been reached. As with so many issues, this one is conceptually simple, but neigh impossible in application.

That analysis costs increase with degree of refinement is obvious. Less obvious is that the cost is an increasing function of the degree of refinement. Much information can be gleaned at little cost. Additional information is available at modest cost. But further refinement of analytical information, past some point, becomes very costly while adding little to a decision maker's knowledge of the risk–return relationship.

A little knowledge goes a long way when the starting point is total ignorance. But as the investor becomes more informed about a proposed investment, he benefits progressively less from additional (and increasingly expensive) knowledge. Consequently, there must be a point where the incremental cost of knowledge exceeds its value to the investor.

Risk Reduction by Judicious Investment Decisions

One way to decrease risk is, of course, to select less risky projects. Recalling the earlier definitions of risk and uncertainty, it becomes obvious that this is also a way to reduce uncertainty. Choosing only those opportunities whose outcomes are fairly well ascertained in advance permits reduction of default risk to essentially zero and virtual elimination of uncertainty associated with the outcome of the investment itself (though not the uncertainty and risk of purchasing–power loss through inflation which exceeds the rate of return on investment).

An unfortunate byproduct of this strategy is the virtual elimination of opportunity for extraordinary profits. The fundamental relationship at the heart of all financial markets is the tendency for expected return to increase or decrease along with associated risk. Should opportunities for extraordinary gains without commensurate risk appear, investors will quickly enter that market and drive prices up to the point that expected returns will become not significantly greater than exists in other investment opportunities of the same general risk category.

There is, of course, a whole spectrum of risky investment opportunities in the economy. Financial markets allow investors to interact in competitive bidding so that an appropriate level of return is assigned by the market to each opportunity, commensurate with the level of risk perceived by market participants. Figure 14–5 illustrates a proportional tradeoff between risk and expected return necessary to attract potential investors into a project or projects. As the associated risk increases, investors require a higher expected return on their investment to compensate for the additional risk exposure. Keep in mind that this diagram reflects investor *expectations* only. The expected profits may never materialize—investors may in fact suffer substantial losses. But for investors to accept a project in the first place, they must be convinced that the potential reward is sufficiently high to justify bearing the perceived risk.

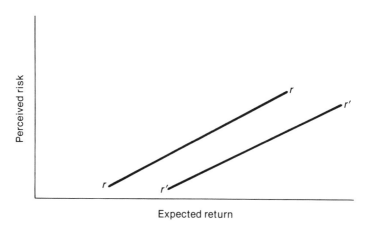

Figure 14-5. Shift in Risk–Return Tradeoff, Caused by Revised Market
Expectations.

Figure 14-5 also reflects typical investor response to increased uncertainty. When the level of uncertainty increases, they generally require a
higher rate of expected profit for every level of perceived risk. Thus an
increase in uncertainty is reflected in figure 14-5 by a shift in the risk–return
function from *rr* to *r'r'*, which associates a higher level of expected profits
with every level of perceived risk. Of course, if the general level of uncertainty decreases, then the risk–return relationship shifts to the left, reflecting a lower required rate of expected return associated with each level of
perceived risk.

Risk–Return Relationships and Market Efficiency

As observed earlier, the actual outcome of investments will almost never
correspond exactly with expectations. Thus, while figure 14-5 depicts
expectations of market participants, actual outcomes are more likely to be
as illustrated in figure 14-6. The dots in figure 14-6 depict actual outcomes
of market ventures as they relate to the expectations of participants
(depicted again by the solid line *rr*). If the market is *efficient,* then actual
outcomes will vary randomly about expected outcomes reflected by the
market line. In such an efficient market, unusually high or low gains relative to expectations will occur randomly and will tend to cancel each other
out. Since all participants have approximately the same information in an
efficient market and draw approximately the same conclusions from that
information, outcomes for individual participants will also vary randomly
in approximately the same proportion as do outcomes for the entire market.

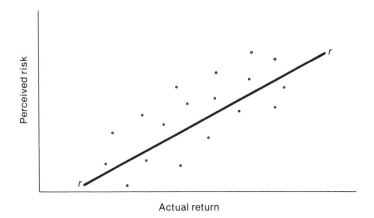

Figure 14-6. Perceived Risk and Actual Investment Returns in an Efficient Market.

The significance of all this is that in an efficient market the only way to reduce risk associated with a single-investment venture is to choose a venture with a lower expected return.

Real estate markets, however, tend to be somewhat less efficient than do organized securities markets. The practical significance of this is that investors who attain a monopoly position with respect to certain locations or with respect to significant market information can expect to consistently reap greater than ordinary gains without shouldering commensurately greater risk. They are able to consistently identify those opportunities whose outcomes lie to the right of line *rr* in figure 14-6.

Diversification as a Risk-Management Tool

Investors holding a portfolio of two or more assets can benefit by considering the relationship between investments already held and potential new acquisitions. Since causal agents affecting profitability and market value do not impact uniformly on all properties, holders of diversified portfolios of real estate assets can expect a more stable (and predictable) pattern of earnings than would result from concentrating all wealth in a single project.

Chapter 12 introduced standard deviation as a useful measure of risk. Standard deviation measures the likelihood of variation of actual outcomes from the expected. Expressing the effect of diversification in these terms, standard deviation of returns from a portfolio of assets may be less than the sum of the standard deviations of returns from individual assets in the portfolio.

To illustrate the point, consider a portfolio which includes an equal mix of apartment and office buildings. If vacancies in apartments are large when those in office buildings are small, the consequence is a combined vacancy rate which is relatively stable. The circumstances just postulated assume vacancy rates in these two components of the local real estate market are *negatively correlated:* whenever vacancies move up in one, they move down in the other. When two segments of the market have high negative correlation, including assets from both segments in a portfolio reduces overall risk.

If, on the other hand, two or more assets having a high *positive correlation* (for example, two office buildings serving the same market) are included in a single portfolio, no particular advantage is gained from diversification. If the correlation coefficient of the two assets is +1, then absolutely no risk reduction will have been achieved.[3]

Including in a portfolio two or more assets having absolutely no correlation of income and expense factors does reduce portfolio risk to some extent. The greater the number of assets whose market performance is not influenced by the same causal agents, the smaller will be the standard deviation of the expected present values of the outcomes of the total portfolio. This illustrates the principle of the *law of large numbers*. As the number of assets held increases (assuming the outcome of each venture is unaffected by the outcomes of all the others, and that they are not affected by the same causal agents), the standard deviation of returns to the entire portfolio decreases with the square root of the number of projects and included in the portfolio. The principle assumes that means and standard deviations of individual assets in the portfolio are approximately equal.

As a matter of fact, of course, most real estate projects are positively correlated to some degree, since there are certain causal influences which impact on all such projects. These include the cost of using financial leverage, the general (national) economic climate, federal income tax laws, and so forth. Other factors of less than national scope nevertheless impact on real estate on a regional basis, adding to the degree of positive correlation between projects in that region.

Projects are seldom perfectly correlated, however. The degree of correlation depends on economic and political factors, and these factors are amenable to analysis. Returns on apartment projects catering to the same socioeconomic class of renters and serving the same market will, for example, be very highly correlated. But projects serving different communities will be much less highly correlated, providing the two communities have different economic bases (that is, providing economic prosperity and employment in the two communities do not depend on the level of activity in the same, or highly related, industries).

Investing in real estate projects in different communities, different states, and even in different regions of the nation all tend to reduce the degree of positive correlation of investment outcomes and so reduce portfolio risk. Even greater risk reduction can be achieved by diversifying between types of real property as well, such as between industrial and office buildings or between resort properties and downtown apartment complexes.

Achieving Diversification within a Budget Constraint

Portfolio diversification is a relatively simple proposition for multimillion dollar real estate investment corporations. They can hold property diversified geographically between major sections of the country to reduce the impact of the regional shifts in economic activity. Likewise, they can easily acquire any desired mix of apartment complexes, office towers, suburban office parks, industrial parks, and so on.

But most investors assuredly do not hold multimillion dollar portfolios. With typically more sever budget constraints, diversification becomes somewhat more difficult. If it means sacrificing economies of scale by investing in smaller properties, it may also entail giving up some expected return. Diversification poses a problem, therefore, for investors who can control only one or two economically sized properties.

One solution is to pool equity funds with other investors facing the same dilemma. This rather popular approach to the problem is often called *syndication*. A frequent arrangement involves a promoter who organizes the syndicate and manages the venture for a fee plus a percentage ownership, while passive investors put up all or most of the equity funds.

Real estate syndication may be thought of as a procedure for fractionalizing the ownership interest in property into individual shares in much the same fashion as common stock represents fractionalized ownership interest in a corporation. Investors contribute money with no expectation of management control and under an arrangement which drastically limits their personal financial or legal liability. The promoter of the syndicate, who assumes management responsibilities, also assumes full liability for the general obligations of the syndicate.

Syndications may take any one of a number of organizational forms. The most common forms of organizational entities are general partnerships, limited partnerships, and corporations.

General Partnership

A *partnership* is created by two or more people agreeing to place their assets and/or talents into some common income–producing activity. The partners agree among themselves on how the management tasks of the venture are to be shared and also on the ratio in which they will share all profits and losses. In the absence of specific agreement, partners generally share profits and losses equally, without regard to their actual contribution to the venture.

Assuming due care is taken to ensure that the partnership is not treated by the Internal Revenue Service as a taxable entity, there are particular benefits to be derived from holding real estate in this manner. The deductibility of interest payments and depreciation allowances often results in accounting losses during the early years of a venture, coupled with significant net cash inflows. Because partnerships are not taxable entities, it is possible to distribute cash to the partners with no resultant tax liability, while allowing the partners to also use their pro rata shares of accounting losses to offset income from other sources. This tax–shelter aspect of real estate ownership can be very profitable and is often the primary motivation of those entering into such arrangements.

Against the income tax benefits of general partnerships must be weighed certain potential disadvantages. Partners may be held jointly and severally liable for any obligation contracted or incurred by any one of the partners on behalf of the partnership. This is particularly onerous for a partner who has substantial assets other than those invested in the firm. The disadvantage is compounded if one partner obviously is substantially more wealthy than the others. Because of the "joint and several" nature of liability, any legal action will be aimed primarily at the wealthy partner.

Properly orchestrating the partnership arrangement can alleviate these disadvantages to some extent. Insurance can shift the risk of civil penalties arising from lawsuits against the partnership or of losses from natural disasters. Liability for debts incurred by the partnership can be controlled by inserting exculpatory clauses in all mortgage instruments. This latter strategy may, of course, create some difficulty in borrowing.

Generally partnerships seem to work best where the partners have a sustained record of close cooperation in other business arrangements, where there are few partners, and where the affairs of the partnership are relatively uncomplicated and of limited duration. As the number of partners or the number of major business decisions multiply, general partnerships become increasingly cumbersome as ownership entities.

Limited Partnerships

Limited partnerships have attained immense popularity among real estate investors and promoters in recent years. This is the organizational entity most people mean when the refer to "syndication." Appealing features include income tax "conduit" treatment coupled with limited personal liability for passive investors. Its popularity is probably more appropriately attributable, however, to the opportunity offered promoters to gain an equity position in real estate with no personal financial commitment and, in most cases, with little or no downside risk to themselves.

Successful limited-partnership ventures bring together the interacting elements that make real estate so vital an activity: people with energy, ideas, and ambition; people with investment funds but little time and real estate investment knowledge; and real estate that is currently underutilized and ripe for redevelopment. The idea men become the general partners, the monied members become limited partners. The objective is to package (or repackage) the real estate to fulfill the needs of all participants.

The Limited Partners. Partners who supply the bulk of investment capital are usually passive investors. They are attracted to a limited partnership for the same reasons they might be attracted to any other investment opportunity: the prospect of a substantial after-tax rate of return on funds placed at risk. But limited partnerships offer an additional attraction not always available in other opportunities. By remaining passive with respect to operating decisions, money partners can usually limit their personal liability for partnership obligations to the amount of funds actually invested in the venture plus any additional assessments to which they may have voluntarily committed themselves. Thus claims against the partnership in excess of partnership assets may be collected only from the general partners.

But the limitation of personal liability associated with limited partnerships is not different from that of shareholders in a corporation and certainly does not account for the widespread popularity of this form of organization among real estate investors. The special attraction of limited partnerships is that they *combine* liability limitation with special income tax benefits not generally available to corporate shareholders. For income tax computation purposes, real estate owned by a limited partnership is treated as if it were owned directly by the individual partners.[4]

Blending the limited liability of the corporate form of organization with the tax benefits of a sole proprietorship explains much of the popularity of limited partnerships among investors who earn substantial ordinary income from their business or profession, but who are not particularly knowledgeable in the specialized field of real estate. The tax-shelter aspects reduce taxes on income from other sources, while limited liability reduces the potential for catastrophic economic loss.

But limited partnerships are not only for wealthy investors or those in high income tax brackets. The vast middle class has in fact become a major source of limited-partnership funds in recent years. While income tax benefits may be less alluring to investors of more modest means, they are by no means inconsequential.[5] Of particular benefit to such investors is the opportunity to reach for capital gains while reducing risk exposure through the diversification available only to large-scale investor groups. This procedure enables relatively small investments to enjoy the benefits of economies of scale not otherwise available.

The General Partners. Every limited partnership must have one or more general partners. The general partners conduct the affairs of the partnership. They also assume unlimited liability for general-partnership obligations (but typically seek exculpation from personal liability associated with notes secured by a mortgage on real estate). Benefits accruing to general partners depend on the specific structuring of the partnership deal and are generally spelled out in the partnership agreement.

In most states the general partner may be either an individual or a corporation. But a corporate general partner who is controlled by the limited partners may spawn legal complications with respect to both income tax conduit treatment and claims of limited liability by the controlling limited partners.

Any attempt to catalogue potential benefits to a general partner is hampered by the almost unlimited number of variations these benefits can take. They are limited only by the ingenuity of the promoter, but they are also constrained by state and federal laws governing formation of partnerships.

The Certificate of Limited Partnership. Limited partnership is not a common-law concept. It is rather a creature of statue, and each state in which it is recognized has enacted enabling legislation. Some interstate uniformity has been achieved by the Uniform Limited Partnership Act, which has been enacted (albeit in considerably modified form in many instances) by every state except Louisiana.

The Uniform Limited Partnership Act specifies that two or more people must sign a certificate of limited partnership which specifies the name under which the partnership will conduct its business affairs, the nature of the business, and the principal location. The certificate lists the name and place of residence of each member of the partnership and specifies each as either a general or a limited partner.

The certificate must state the contribution made by each partner, the profit- and loss-sharing arrangement, any additional contributions to be made or compensation to be received by any member, and any provisions for taking either property or cash out of partnership control. It must also disclose any priorities established among the partners for receiving either cash or noncash property from the partnership and any provisions for continuation of the partnership arrangement in the event of death or retirement of a general partner.

State statute designates an ''office of record'' in which the certificate is filed. Many states also have a requirement that the certificate be publicized for a minimum specified period of time in one or more general circulation newspapers to ensure public notice of the arrangement.

Failure to comply with all the technical requirements associated with filing a certificate of limited partnership does not necessarily preclude creation of the entity. The Uniform Limited Partnership Act provides that the limited partnership is formed so long as there has been "substantial compliance in good faith" with the requirements of the act. But there are numerous technical defects which might defeat the efforts of the limited partners to attain limitation of their personal liability. An early step taken by attorneys for the plaintiff in any proceedings against the partnership will be to search the record for a basis of claiming that the partnership is in fact general rather than limited in nature.

The Limited-Partnership Agreement. Whereas the certificate of limited partnership creates the partnership entity and specifies the relationship between the partners and the general public, the specific relationship between the partners themselves is set forth in the partnership agreement. Some states permit the partnership agreement to be filed and to serve as a certificate of limited partnership, but even where permitted the partners may wish to keep the specifics of the agreement private by filing only an abbreviated document to serve as a certificate.

The partnership agreement spells out the rights and obligations of all parties to the arrangement. It should include the name under which the partnership will conduct its affairs, the principal place of business, the purpose of the partnership, and the time period over which the partnership arrangement is to exist. The principal contributions and rights to share in profits and losses of the partnership need to be carefully spelled out in the agreement, as does the arrangement for distribution of residual assets upon dissolution of the partnership arrangement.

Corporations

The most prevalent form of business entity among firms of any substantial size is the *corporation*. The evolution of the corporation made it possible to pool resources from large numbers of geographically separated investors so as to accumulate the monumental capital investment without which the industrial revolution might never have occurred in a free-enterprise setting.

Though a creature of state statute, the corporation is a very old institution. Over the centuries, there has accumulated a sizable catalogue of case law which makes the legal ramifications of various corporate activities much more predictable than is the case for limited partnerships.

Corporations are chartered by the state in which corporate headquarters are to be domiciled. Activity in states other than that in which chartered generally requires registration as a foreign corporation. There is an annual tax liability in the state of incorporation, whether or not a corporation actually does any business there. Moreover, corporations must comply with a morass of regulations and regulatory bodies. This imposes a heavy record-keeping burden, particularly for relatively small business entities who may not be able to afford skilled attorneys and accountants having extensive experience in such matters.

The corporation is a legal entity separate and distinct from its stockholders and management. As a legal entity it has the right to own property, including real estate, in its own name. It is also a tax-paying entity, unfortunately, and thus liable for both state and federal income tax. This often makes the corporation an unattractive entity for real estate investment purposes.

But the corporate alternative should not be dismissed lightly. Offsetting advantages include well-established limited liability for shareholders, general familiarity with the entity among the investing public, ease of transference of shares among investors, and perpetual life.

While a corporation can sue and be sued, shareholder liability is limited so that no investor stands to lose more than his actual investment in corporate shares. Thus incorporation reduces downside risk associated with investment in large real estate ventures employing substantial financial leverage.

Because most investors are well familiar with the corporate form of ownership, they may be less hesitant to take a financial position in a venture in which the ownership entity is a corporation rather than a limited partnership.

Corporate shares may be traded at will, with no general restrictions such as may exist in association with limited-partnership shares. Moreover, the corporate entity is devoid of complications associated with provisions for succession of general partners in a limited-partnership arrangement. Death of a key management party may jeopardize the success of a particular corporate venture, but it has no impact whatsoever on the corporation's legal existence.

Most real estate promoters and investors who reject the corporate-ownership entity cite federal and state income tax considerations. But the disadvantageous income tax position of corporations may be more illusory than real. Liberal tax loss carryback and carryforward provisions, coupled with rules permitting dividends paid in the absence of accumulated earnings to be treated by the recipient shareholder as a tax-free return of capital, greatly reduce income tax problems conventionally associated with corporate ownership and investment. Moreover, there are offsetting advantages offered corporations in the federal income tax law, particularly when a real estate venture involves new construction. Liberal provisions for corporate writeoff of construction period interest and property taxes (not available to noncorporate investors), coupled with lenient treatment of corporations with respect to the minimum tax on preference items, often makes incorporation the most attractive ownership entity alternative.

Fractionalizing the Fee

Investors wishing to limit their equity investment in any one single property, but who are loath to become involved in a plan to pool equity interests with other investors, might consider an approach pioneered by William Zeckendorf, a legendary real estate speculator of the 1950s. Zeckendorf's idea was to divide the interests in real estate in much the same manner as corporate financial interests are spread among common and preferred stockholders, bondholders, and holders of convertible bonds.

It is a truism that securities markets are multifaceted. Participants in each segment of the market are interested in somewhat different combinations of risk and return characteristics. Therefore, the returns on various securities differ dramatically, as does the volatility of returns. Compare the expected returns on common and preferred stocks of the same corporation, for example, or contrast the yield on convertible and nonconvertible bonds of the same corporate borrower.

Adapting to real estate this idea of dividing property interest to appeal to a variety of investors with widely differing goals and distinctively different attitudes toward risk results in a total market value of the ownership interest greatly in excess of the worth of the entire property as a single-ownership package. The market, in effect, rewards innovative repackaging and marketing efforts.

Perhaps the best illustration is a summary of the technique as used by Zeckendorf himself in his much publicized splintering of the interest in the property at One Park Avenue in New York. The property, owned by Zeckendorf in the early 1950s, had at that time a net cash flow of approximately $1 million. Trying to imagine some way to pull profit from what seemed a losing proposition, Zeckendorf applied what he called his "Hawaiian technique" (he developed the concept while on vacation in Hawaii).

Capitalizing the $1 million of cash flow at the then market rate of 10 percent, the property at One Park Avenue had a market value of $10 million. By splitting the interests to appeal to different segments of the market, Zeckendorf increased the aggregate value to more than $15 million. Here is how it worked.

1. The ground under the building was sold and leased back at a rental

rate of $250,000 per annum. Since the owner of the ground has a prior claim on all assets and income, this is an extremely secure position comparable to that of holders of first mortgage bonds of a corporation. The market at the time enabled this interest to sell at $5 million, yielding the purchaser a five percent return on assets. The purchaser of the ground was able to leverage his position by borrowing $3 million on a land mortgage at the then-current interest rate of 4 percent. The net outcome to the purchaser was an extremely secure position with expected net cash flow before taxes of approximately 6.5 percent on an equity investment of $2 million.

2. The entire building was then leased to a tenant who would manage the building and collect rents from subtenants. The expected annual rental receipts from subtenants, net of building operating expenses, was approximately $1 million. The terms of the master lease called for annual rent to the building owner of $750,000, leaving the master tenant an expected net cash flow of $250,000 per year. Capitalized at 7 percent, this lease had a market value of $3,600,000, at which price the leasehold interest was sold.

3. The building itself was then sold to a purchaser who would pay the owner of the land an annual rental fee of $250,000 and would in turn collect $750,000 annually from the holder of the outer, or operating, lease. The building was mortgaged for $4 million, requiring annual debt service of $350,000. This left an expected $150,000 annual net cash flow to the owner of the building. Capitalizing this income stream at 6 percent, Zeckendorf was able to sell the equity position in the building for $2,500,000 above the $4 million balance on the mortgage. The low capitalization rate (and thus high market value) was possible because of the building owner's relatively secure position, and because he had the additional benefit of income tax deductions for building depreciation.

Summary

Output generated from the mean/standard deviation model is rendered more useful by enhancing its understandability in the hands of ultimate users of the information. A number of techniques are available to accomplish this. They include expressing the expected return in alternative fashion, developing risk-return measures capable of comparison with predetermined minimum acceptable risk-return profiles, and using visual displays of a form familiar to clients.

Profitability indices are a particularly useful measure of potential profitability because they eliminate distortions otherwise introduced when comparing projects of different financial magnitude. By expressing expected outcomes in terms of present value per dollar of initial cash investment, the profitability index enables direct comparison between a diverse array of opportunities.

Probability distributions of potential profitability indices extend the usefulness of the measure by permitting comparison of risk-return potential with predetermined standards. Managment can specify the maximum acceptable probability of earning less than $1 of present value for every current $1 invested, with a variable standard which moves in any desired ratio to the *expected* present value per dollar invested.

Many investors not familiar with probability analysis find the concept intuitively understandable when output is expressed in graphic form. Graphic format can be either a standard probability distribution or a cumulative distribution. The cumulative probability format is often most comprehensible to clients untutored in probability analysis.

Hillier's model, the subject of much of the discussion in chapters 13 and 14, is suitable for many real estate projects. It is less suitable for complex or large-scale projects where there are a great number of variables to be considered. These more complicated proposals lend themselves to use of a simulation model. But this model requires access to computer facilities and is somewhat more time consuming and expensive than the model featured in this book.

Risk analysis is ignored at the investor's peril. But like all good things, it can be overdone. Potential benefits must always be weighed against the cost of further analysis to determine the extent to which research should continue in an effort to subsume uncertain factors into the risk equation.

Investors can reduce risk by the simple expedient of choosing investments embodying fewer risk elements. But doing so generally entails sacrificing potential return, because of the market tradeoff between expected return and perceived risk. To the extent that an investor can exploit market inefficiencies, however, he may be able to move into less risky investments without commensurate sacrifice of potential return.

Composite risk associated with an investment portfolio can be reduced by attention to the interrelationships of investments included therein. Combinations of projects having negative covariances reduce overall portfolio risk. Reduction can also be achieved by selecting investments which are independent or in which positive covariance is less than perfect. Diversification is therefore a valuable risk-management technique.

Budget limitations place constraints on the ability of investors to achieve diversification. Several techniques are available to alleviate this problem. Most commonly employed are partnership arrangements (either general or limited partnerships) or corporate ownership. Fee ownership may also be fractionalized to accomplish the same purpose, either independent of, or in consort with, other techniques.

Notes

1. David B. Hertz, "Risk Analysis in Capital Investment," *Harvard Business Revue* (January-February 1964): 95-106.

2. Howard H. Stevenson and Barbara B. Jackson, "Large-Scale Real Estate Investments—Understanding Risks Through Modeling," *The Appraisal Journal* (July 1977): 366-382.

3. The correlation between returns of component assets may fall anywhere between plus one and minus one. A zero correlation coefficient indicates an absence of correlation. A coefficient of 1.00 indicates perfect correlation. This implies that variations in the return to one asset will be matched by variations in return to the other. A −1.00 coefficient implies that variations will occur in the same proportions, but in opposite directions.

4. For a detailed analysis of the limited partnership form of organization, see Theodore Lynn, Harry Goldberg, and Daniel Abrams, *Real Estate Limited Partnerships*. (New York: Wiley, 1977). For an extended discussion of the income tax considerations, refer to Gaylon E. Greer, *The Real Estate Investor and the Federal Income Tax*. (New York: Wiley-Interscience, 1978).

5. With recent income tax legislation, the shelter benefits associated with real estate in fact favor modest income earners over the high-rollers. Investors with a limited portfolio generally incur much less of a liability for minimum tax on items of "preference" income and thereby stand to benefit more handsomely from accelerated depreciation and capital gains.

Appendix A
How $1 Left at
Compound Interest
Will Grow

			Annual Compound Interest			
Years	1%	2%	3%	4%	5%	6%
01	1.0100	1.0200	1.0300	1.0400	1.0500	1.0600
02	1.0201	1.0404	1.0609	1.0816	1.1025	1.1236
03	1.0303	1.0612	1.0927	1.1249	1.1576	1.1910
04	1.0406	1.0824	1.1255	1.1699	1.2155	1.2625
05	1.0510	1.1041	1.1593	1.2167	1.2763	1.3382
06	1.0615	1.1261	1.1941	1.2653	1.3401	1.4185
07	1.0721	1.1487	1.2299	1.3159	1.4071	1.5036
08	1.0829	1.1717	1.2668	1.3686	1.4775	1.5939
09	1.0937	1.1951	1.3048	1.4233	1.5513	1.6895
10	1.1046	1.2190	1.3439	1.4802	1.6289	1.7909
11	1.1157	1.2434	1.3842	1.5395	1.7103	1.8983
12	1.1268	1.2682	1.4258	1.6010	1.7959	2.0122
13	1.1381	1.2936	1.4685	1.6651	1.8857	2.1329
14	1.1495	1.3195	1.5126	1.7317	1.9799	2.2609
15	1.1610	1.3459	1.5580	1.8009	2.0789	2.3966
16	1.1726	1.3728	1.6047	1.8730	2.1829	2.5404
17	1.1843	1.4002	1.6529	1.9479	2.2920	2.6928
18	1.1962	1.4283	1.7024	2.0258	2.4066	2.8543
19	1.2081	1.4568	1.7535	2.1069	2.5270	3.0256
20	1.2202	1.4860	1.8061	2.1911	2.6533	3.2071
21	1.2324	1.5157	1.8603	2.2788	2.7860	3.3996
22	1.2447	1.5460	1.9161	2.3699	2.9253	3.6035
23	1.2572	1.5769	1.9736	2.4647	3.0715	3.8198
24	1.2697	1.6084	2.0328	2.5633	3.2251	4.0489
25	1.2824	1.6406	2.0937	2.6658	3.3864	4.2919

Years	7%	8%	9%	10%	11%	12%
01	1.0700	1.0800	1.0900	1.1000	1.1100	1.1200
02	1.1449	1.1664	1.1881	1.2100	1.2321	1.2544
03	1.2250	1.2597	1.2950	1.3310	1.3676	1.4049
04	1.3108	1.3605	1.4116	1.4641	1.5181	1.5735
05	1.4026	1.4693	1.5386	1.6105	1.6851	1.7623

277

	Annual Compound Interest					
Years	7%	8%	9%	10%	11%	12%
06	1.5007	1.5869	1.6771	1.7716	1.8704	1.9738
07	1.6058	1.7138	1.8280	1.9487	2.0762	2.2107
08	1.7182	1.8509	1.9926	2.1436	2.3045	2.4760
09	1.8385	1.9990	2.1710	2.3580	2.5580	2.7731
10	1.9672	2.1589	2.3674	2.5937	2.8394	3.1059
11	2.1049	2.3316	2.5804	2.8531	3.1518	3.4786
12	2.2522	2.5182	2.8127	3.1384	3.4985	3.8960
13	2.4098	2.7196	3.0658	3.4523	3.8833	4.3635
14	2.5785	2.9372	3.3417	3.7975	4.3104	4.8871
15	2.7590	3.1722	3.6425	4.1773	4.7846	5.4736
16	2.9522	3.4259	3.9703	4.5950	5.3109	6.1304
17	3.1588	3.7000	4.3276	5.0545	5.8951	6.8660
18	3.3799	3.9960	4.7171	5.5599	6.5436	7.6900
19	3.6165	4.3157	5.1417	6.1159	7.2633	8.6128
20	3.8697	4.6610	5.6044	6.7275	8.0623	9.6463
21	4.1406	5.0338	6.1088	7.4003	8.9492	10.804
22	4.4304	5.4365	6.6586	8.1403	9.9336	12.100
23	4.7405	5.8714	7.2579	8.9543	11.026	13.552
24	5.0724	6.3412	7.9111	9.8497	12.239	15.179
25	5.4274	6.8485	8.6231	10.835	13.586	17.000

Years	13%	14%	15%	16%	17%	18%
01	1.1300	1.1400	1.1500	1.1600	1.1700	1.1800
02	1.2769	1.2996	1.3225	1.3456	1.3689	1.3924
03	1.4429	1.4815	1.5209	1.5609	1.6016	1.6430
04	1.6305	1.6890	1.7490	1.8106	1.8739	1.9388
05	1.8424	1.9254	2.0114	2.1003	2.1925	2.2878
06	2.0820	2.1950	2.3131	2.4364	2.5652	2.6996
07	2.3526	2.5023	2.6600	2.8262	3.0012	3.1855
08	2.6584	2.8526	3.0590	3.2784	3.5115	3.7589
09	3.0040	3.2520	3.5179	3.8030	4.1084	4.4355
10	3.3946	3.7072	4.0456	4.4114	4.8068	5.2338
11	3.8359	4.2262	4.6524	5.1173	5.6240	6.1759
12	4.3345	4.8179	5.3503	5.9360	6.5801	7.2876
13	4.8980	5.4924	6.1528	6.8858	7.6987	8.5994
14	5.5348	6.6216	7.0757	7.9875	9.0075	10.147
15	6.2543	7.1379	8.1371	9.2655	10.539	11.974
16	7.0673	8.1373	9.3576	10.748	12.330	14.129
17	7.9861	9.2765	10.761	12.468	14.427	16.672
18	9.0243	10.575	12.376	14.463	16.879	19.673
19	10.107	12.056	14.232	16.777	19.748	23.214
20	11.523	13.744	16.367	19.461	23.106	27.393

Years	Annual Compound Interest					
	13%	14%	15%	16%	17%	18%
21	13.021	15.668	18.822	22.575	27.034	32.324
22	14.714	17.861	21.645	26.186	31.629	38.142
23	16.627	20.362	24.892	30.376	37.006	45.008
24	18.788	23.212	28.625	35.236	43.297	53.109
25	21.231	26.462	32.919	40.874	50.658	62.669

Years	19%	20%	21%	22%	23%	24%
01	1.1900	1.2000	1.2100	1.2200	1.2300	1.2400
02	1.4161	1.4400	1.4641	1.4884	1.5129	1.5374
03	1.6852	1.7280	1.7716	1.8159	1.8609	1.9066
04	2.0053	2.0736	2.1436	2.2153	2.2889	2.3642
05	2.3864	2.4883	2.5937	2.7027	2.8153	2.9316
06	2.8398	2.9860	3.1384	3.2973	3.4628	3.6352
07	3.3793	3.5832	3.7975	4.0227	4.2593	4.5077
08	4.0214	4.2998	4.5950	4.9077	5.2389	5.5895
09	4.7855	5.1598	5.5599	5.9874	6.4439	6.9310
10	5.6947	6.1917	6.7275	7.3046	7.9260	8.5944
11	6.7767	7.4301	8.1403	8.9117	9.7489	10.657
12	8.0642	8.9161	9.8497	10.872	11.991	13.215
13	9.5965	10.699	11.918	13.264	14.749	16.386
14	11.420	12.839	14.421	16.182	18.141	21.319
15	13.590	15.407	17.449	19.742	22.314	25.196
16	16.172	18.488	21.114	24.086	27.446	31.243
17	19.244	22.186	25.548	29.384	33.759	38.741
18	22.901	26.623	30.913	35.849	41.523	48.039
19	27.252	31.948	37.404	43.736	51.074	59.568
20	32.429	38.338	45.259	53.358	62.821	73.864
21	38.591	46.005	54.764	65.096	77.269	91.592
22	45.923	55.206	66.264	79.418	95.041	113.57
23	54.649	66.247	80.180	96.889	116.90	140.83
24	65.032	79.497	97.017	118.21	143.79	174.63
25	77.388	95.396	117.39	144.21	176.86	216.54

Appendix B
Present Value of $1
Due at a Future Date

			Discount Rate			
Years	1%	2%	3%	4%	5%	6%
01	.99010	.98039	.97007	.96154	.95238	.94340
02	.98030	.96117	.94260	.92456	.90703	.89000
03	.97059	.94232	.91514	.88900	.86384	.83962
04	.96098	.92385	.88849	.85480	.82270	.79209
05	.95147	.90573	.86261	.82193	.78353	.74726
06	.94204	.88797	.83748	.79031	.74622	.70496
07	.93272	.87056	.81309	.75992	.71068	.66506
08	.92348	.85349	.78941	.73069	.67684	.62741
09	.91434	.83675	.76642	.70259	.64461	.59190
10	.90529	.82035	.74409	.67556	.61391	.55839
11	.89632	.80426	.72242	.64958	.58468	.52679
12	.88745	.78849	.70138	.62460	.55684	.49697
13	.87866	.77303	.68095	.60057	.53032	.46884
14	.86996	.75787	.66112	.57747	.50507	.44230
15	.86135	.74301	.64186	.55526	.48102	.41726
16	.85282	.72845	.62317	.53391	.45811	.39365
17	.84438	.71416	.60502	.51337	.43630	.37136
18	.83602	.70016	.58739	.49363	.41552	.35034
19	.82774	.68643	.57029	.47464	.39573	.33051
20	.81954	.67297	.55367	.45639	.37689	.31180
21	.81143	.65978	.53755	.43883	.35894	.29415
22	.80340	.64684	.52189	.42195	.34185	.27750
23	.79544	.63414	.50669	.40573	.32557	.26180
24	.78757	.62172	.49193	.39012	.31007	.24698
25	.77977	.60953	.47760	.37512	.29530	.23300

Years	7%	8%	9%	10%	11%	12%
01	.93458	.92593	.91743	.90909	.90090	.89286
02	.87344	.85734	.84168	.82645	.81162	.79719
03	.81630	.79383	.77218	.75131	.73119	.71178
04	.76290	.73503	.70843	.68301	.65873	.63552
05	.71299	.68058	.64993	.62092	.59345	.56743

281

	Discount Rate					
	7%	*8%*	*9%*	*10%*	*11%*	*12%*
06	.66634	.63017	.59627	.56447	.53464	.50663
07	.62275	.58349	.54703	.51316	.48166	.45235
08	.58201	.54027	.50187	.46651	.43393	.40388
09	.54393	.50025	.46043	.42410	.39092	.36061
10	.50835	.46319	.42241	.38554	.35218	.32197
11	.47509	.42888	.38753	.35049	.31728	.28748
12	.44401	.39711	.35553	.31683	.28584	.25667
13	.41496	.36770	.32618	.28966	.25751	.22917
14	.38782	.34046	.29925	.26333	.23199	.20462
15	.36245	.31524	.27454	.23939	.20900	.18270
16	.33873	.29189	.25187	.21763	.18829	.16312
17	.31657	.27027	.23107	.19784	.16963	.14564
18	.29586	.25025	.21199	.17986	.15282	.13004
19	.27651	.23171	.19449	.16351	.13768	.11611
20	.25842	.21455	.17843	.14864	.12403	.10367
21	.24151	.19866	.16370	.13513	.11174	.09256
22	.22571	.18394	.15018	.12285	.10067	.08264
23	.21095	.17031	.13778	.11168	.09069	.07379
24	.19715	.15770	.12640	.10153	.08170	.06588
25	.18425	.14602	.11597	.09230	.07361	.05882

Years	*13%*	*14%*	*15%*	*16%*	*17%*	*18%*
01	.88496	.87719	.86957	.86207	.85470	.84746
02	.78315	.76947	.75614	.74316	.73051	.71818
03	.69305	.67497	.65752	.64066	.62437	.60863
04	.61332	.59208	.57175	.55229	.53365	.51579
05	.54276	.51937	.49718	.47611	.45611	.43711
06	.48032	.45559	.43233	.41044	.38984	.37043
07	.42506	.39964	.37594	.35383	.33320	.31392
08	.37616	.35056	.32690	.30503	.28478	.26604
09	.33288	.30751	.28426	.26295	.24340	.22546
10	.29459	.26974	.24718	.22668	.20804	.19106
11	.26070	.23662	.21494	.19542	.17781	.16192
12	.23071	.20756	.18691	.16846	.15197	.13722
13	.20416	.18207	.16253	.14523	.12989	.11629
14	.18068	.15971	.14133	.12520	.11102	.09855
15	.15989	.14010	.12289	.10793	.09489	.08352
16	.14150	.12289	.10686	.09304	.08110	.07078
17	.12522	.10780	.90293	.08021	.06932	.05998
18	.11081	.09456	.08080	.06914	.05925	.05083
19	.09806	.08295	.07026	.05961	.05064	.04308
20	.08678	.07276	.06110	.05139	.04328	.03651

	Discount Rate					
Years	13%	14%	15%	16%	17%	18%
21	.07680	.06383	.05313	.04430	.03699	.03094
22	.06796	.05599	.04620	.03819	.03162	.02622
23	.06014	.04911	.04017	.03292	.02702	.02222
24	.05322	.04308	.03493	.02838	.02310	.01883
25	.04710	.03779	.03038	.02447	.01974	.01596

Years	19%	20%	21%	22%	23%	24%
01	.84034	.83333	.82645	.81967	.81301	.80645
02	.70616	.69444	.68301	.67186	.66098	.65036
03	.59342	.57870	.56447	.55071	.53738	.52449
04	.49867	.48225	.46651	.45140	.43690	.42297
05	.41905	.40188	.38554	.37000	.35520	.34111
06	.35214	.33490	.31863	.30328	.28878	.27509
07	.29592	.27908	.26333	.24859	.23478	.22184
08	.24867	.23257	.21763	.20376	.19088	.17891
09	.20897	.19381	.17986	.16702	.15519	.14428
10	.17560	.16151	.14864	.13690	.12617	.11635
11	.14756	.13459	.12285	.11221	.10258	.09383
12	.12400	.11216	.10153	.09198	.08339	.07567
13	.10420	.09346	.08391	.07539	.06780	.06103
14	.08757	.07789	.06934	.06180	.05512	.04921
15	.07359	.06491	.05731	.05065	.04481	.03969
16	.06184	.05409	.04736	.04152	.03643	.03201
17	.05196	.04507	.03914	.03403	.02962	.02581
18	.04367	.03756	.03235	.02789	.02408	.02082
10	.03669	.03130	.02673	.02286	.01958	.01679
20	.03084	.02608	.02209	.01874	.01592	.01354
21	.02591	.02174	.01826	.01536	.01294	.01092
22	.02178	.01811	.01509	.01259	.01052	.00880
23	.01830	.01509	.01247	.01032	.00855	.00710
24	.01538	.01258	.01031	.00846	.00695	.00573
25	.01292	.01048	.00852	.00693	.00565	.00462

Appendix C
Present Value of $1
Annuity for *n* Years

			Discount Rate			
Years	1%	2%	3%	4%	5%	6%
01	.9901	.9804	.9709	.9615	.9524	.9434
02	1.9704	1.9416	1.9135	1.8861	1.8594	1.8334
03	2.9410	2.8839	2.8286	2.7751	2.7233	2.6730
04	3.9020	3.8077	3.7171	3.6299	3.5459	3.4651
05	4.8535	4.7134	4.5797	4.4518	4.3295	4.2123
06	5.7955	5.6014	5.1172	5.2421	5.0757	4.9173
07	6.7282	6.4720	6.2302	6.0020	5.7863	5.5824
08	7.6517	7.3254	7.0196	6.7327	6.4632	6.2098
09	8.5661	8.1622	7.7861	7.4353	7.1078	6.8017
10	9.4714	8.9825	8.7302	8.1109	7.7217	7.3601
11	10.3677	9.7868	9.2526	8.7604	8.3064	7.8868
12	11.2552	10.5753	9.9539	9.3850	8.8632	8.3838
13	12.1338	11.3483	10.6349	9.9856	9.3935	8.8527
14	13.0038	12.1062	11.2960	10.5631	9.8986	9.2950
15	13.8651	12.8492	11.9379	11.1183	10.3796	9.7122
16	14.7180	13.5777	12.5610	11.6522	10.8377	10.1059
17	15.5624	14.2918	13.1660	12.1656	11.2740	10.4772
18	16.3984	14.9920	13.7534	12.6592	11.6895	10.8276
19	17.2201	15.2684	14.3237	13.1339	12.0853	11.1581
20	18.0457	16.3514	14.8774	13.5903	12.4622	11.4699
21	18.8571	17.0111	15.4149	14.0291	12.8211	11.7640
22	19.6605	17.6581	15.9368	14.4511	13.1630	12.0416
23	20.4559	18.2921	16.4435	14.8568	13.4885	12.3033
24	21.2435	18.9139	16.9355	15.2469	13.7986	12.5503
25	22.0233	19.5234	17.4131	15.6220	14.9039	12.7833

Years	7%	8%	9%	10%	11%	12%
01	.9346	.9259	.9174	.9091	.9009	.8929
02	1.8080	1.7833	1.7591	1.7355	1.7125	1.6901
03	2.6243	2.5771	2.5313	2.4868	2.4437	2.4018
04	3.3872	3.3121	3.2397	3.1699	3.1024	3.0373
05	4.1002	3.9927	3.8896	3.7908	3.6959	3.6048

Years	*Discount Rate*					
	7%	*8%*	*9%*	*10%*	*11%*	*12%*
06	4.7665	4.6229	4.4859	4.3553	4.2305	4.1114
07	5.3893	5.2064	5.0329	4.8684	4.7122	4.5638
08	5.9713	5.7466	5.5348	5.3349	5.1461	4.9676
09	6.5152	6.2469	5.9852	5.7590	5.5370	5.3282
10	7.0236	6.7101	6.4176	6.1446	5.8892	5.6502
11	7.4987	7.1389	6.8052	6.4951	6.2065	5.9377
12	7.9427	7.5361	7.1607	6.8137	6.4924	6.1944
13	8.3576	7.9038	7.4869	7.1034	6.7499	6.4235
14	8.7454	8.2442	7.7861	7.3667	6.9819	6.6282
15	9.1079	8.5595	8.0607	7.6061	7.1909	6.8109
16	9.4466	8.8514	8.3125	7.8237	7.3792	6.9740
17	9.7632	9.1216	8.5436	8.0215	7.5488	7.1196
18	10.0591	9.3719	8.7556	8.2014	7.7016	7.2497
19	10.3556	9.6036	8.9501	8.3649	7.8393	7.3650
20	10.5940	9.8181	9.1285	8.5136	7.9633	7.4694
21	10.8355	10.0168	9.2922	8.6487	8.0751	7.5620
22	11.0612	10.2007	9.4424	8.7715	8.1757	7.6446
23	11.2722	10.3710	9.5802	8.8832	8.2664	7.7184
24	11.4693	10.5287	9.7066	8.9847	8.3481	7.7843
25	11.6536	10.6748	9.8226	9.0770	8.4217	7.8431

Years	*13%*	*14%*	*15%*	*16%*	*17%*	*18%*
01	.8850	.8772	.8696	.8621	.8547	.8475
02	1.6681	1.6467	1.6257	1.6052	1.5852	1.5656
03	2.3612	2.3216	2.2832	2.2459	2.2096	2.1743
04	2.9745	2.9137	2.8550	2.7982	2.7432	2.6901
05	3.5172	3.4331	3.3522	3.2743	3.1993	3.1272
06	3.9976	3.8887	3.7845	3.6847	3.5892	3.4976
07	4.4226	4.2883	4.1604	4.0386	3.9224	3.8115
08	4.7988	4.6389	4.4873	4.3436	4.2072	4.0776
09	5.1317	4.9464	4.7716	4.6065	4.4506	4.3030
10	5.4262	5.2161	5.0188	4.8332	4.6586	4.4941
11	5.6869	5.4527	5.2337	5.0286	4.8364	4.6560
12	5.9176	5.6603	5.4206	5.1971	4.9884	4.7932
13	6.1218	5.8424	5.5831	5.3423	5.1183	4.9095
14	6.3025	6.0021	5.7245	5.4675	5.2293	5.0081
15	6.4624	6.1422	5.8474	5.5755	5.3242	5.0916
16	6.6039	6.2651	5.9542	5.6685	5.4053	5.1624
17	6.7291	6.3729	6.0472	5.7487	5.4746	5.2223
18	6.8399	6.4674	6.1280	5.8178	5.5339	5.2732
19	6.9380	6.5504	6.1982	5.8775	5.5845	5.3176
20	7.0248	6.6231	6.2593	5.9288	5.6278	5.3527

	Discount Rate					
Years	13%	14%	15%	16%	17%	18%
21	7.1016	6.6870	6.3125	5.9731	5.6648	5.3837
22	7.1695	6.7429	6.3587	6.0113	5.6964	5.4099
23	7.2297	6.7921	6.3988	6.0442	5.7234	5.4321
24	7.2829	6.8351	6.4338	6.0726	5.7465	5.4509
25	7.3300	6.8729	6.4641	6.0971	5.7662	5.4669

Years	19%	20%	21%	22%	23%	24%
01	.8403	.8333	.8264	.8197	.8130	.8065
02	1.5465	1.5278	1.5095	1.4915	1.4740	1.4568
03	2.1399	2.1065	2.0739	2.0422	2.0114	1.9813
04	2.6386	2.5887	2.5404	2.4936	2.4483	2.4043
05	3.0576	2.9906	2.9260	2.8636	2.8035	2.7454
06	3.4098	3.3255	3.2446	3.1669	3.0923	3.0205
07	3.7057	3.6046	3.5079	3.4155	3.3270	3.2423
08	3.9544	3.8372	3.7256	3.6193	3.5179	3.4212
09	4.1633	4.0310	3.9054	3.7863	3.6731	3.5655
10	4.3389	4.1925	4.0541	3.9232	3.7993	3.6819
11	4.4865	4.3271	4.1769	4.0354	3.9018	3.7757
12	4.6105	4.4392	4.2785	4.1274	3.9852	3.8514
13	4.7147	4.5327	4.3624	4.2028	4.0530	3.9124
14	4.8023	4.6106	4.4317	4.2646	4.1082	3.9616
15	4.8759	4.6755	4.4890	4.3152	4.1530	4.0013
16	4.9377	4.7296	4.5364	4.3567	4.1894	4.0333
17	4.9897	4.7746	4.5755	4.3908	4.2890	4.0591
18	5.0333	4.8122	4.6079	4.4187	4.2431	4.0799
19	5.0700	4.8435	4.6345	4.4415	4.2627	4.0967
20	5.1009	4.8696	4.6567	4.4603	4.2786	4.1103
21	5.1268	4.8913	4.6750	4.4756	4.2916	4.1212
22	5.1486	4.9094	4.6900	4.4882	4.3021	4.1300
23	5.1668	4.9245	4.7025	4.4985	4.3106	3.1371
24	5.1822	4.9371	4.7128	4.5070	4.3176	4.1428
25	5.1951	4.9476	4.7213	4.5139	4.3232	4.1474

Appendix D
Monthly Installment to
Amortize $1 Loan

Years	Annual Interest Rate					
	6.0%	6.5%	7.0%	7.5%	8.0%	8.5%
1	0.086066	0.086296	0.086527	0.086757	0.086988	0.087220
2	0.044321	0.044546	0.044773	0.045000	0.045227	0.045456
3	0.030422	0.030649	0.030887	0.031106	0.031336	0.031568
4	0.023485	0.023715	0.023946	0.024179	0.024413	0.024648
5	0.019333	0.019566	0.019801	0.020038	0.020276	0.020517
6	0.016573	0.016810	0.017049	0.017290	0.017533	0.017778
7	0.014609	0.014849	0.015093	0.015338	0.015586	0.015836
8	0.013141	0.013386	0.013634	0.013884	0.014137	0.014392
9	0.012006	0.012255	0.012506	0.012761	0.013019	0.013279
10	0.011102	0.011355	0.011611	0.011870	0.012133	0.012399
11	0.010367	0.010624	0.010884	0.011148	0.011415	0.011686
12	0.009759	0.010019	0.010284	0.010552	0.010825	0.011101
13	0.009247	0.009512	0.009781	0.010054	0.010331	0.010612
14	0.008812	0.009081	0.009354	0.009631	0.009913	0.010199
15	0.008439	0.008711	0.008988	0.009270	0.009557	0.009847
16	0.008114	0.008391	0.008672	0.008958	0.009249	0.009545
17	0.007831	0.008111	0.008397	0.008687	0.008983	0.009283
18	0.007582	0.007866	0.008155	0.008450	0.008750	0.009055
19	0.007361	0.007649	0.007942	0.008241	0.008545	0.008854
20	0.007164	0.007456	0.007753	0.008056	0.008364	0.008678
21	0.006989	0.007284	0.007585	0.007892	0.008204	0.008522
22	0.006831	0.007129	0.007434	0.007745	0.008062	0.008384
23	0.006688	0.006991	0.007299	0.007614	0.007935	0.008261
24	0.006560	0.006965	0.007178	0.007496	0.007821	0.008151
25	0.006443	0.006752	0.007068	0.007390	0.007718	0.008052
30	0.005996	0.006321	0.006653	0.006992	0.007338	0.007689
35	0.005702	0.006042	0.006389	0.006742	0.007103	0.007469
40	0.005502	0.005855	0.006214	0.006581	0.006953	0.007331

Years	9.0%	9.5%	10.0%	10.5%	11.0%	11.5%
1	0.087451	0.087684	0.087916	0.088149	0.088382	0.088615
2	0.045685	0.045914	0.046145	0.046376	0.046608	0.046840
3	0.031800	0.032033	0.032267	0.032502	0.032739	0.032976
4	0.024885	0.025123	0.025363	0.025603	0.025846	0.026840
5	0.020758	0.021002	0.021247	0.021494	0.021742	0.021993

| | Annual Interest Rate | | | | | |
Years	9.0%	9.5%	10.0%	10.5%	11.0%	11.5%
6	0.018026	0.018275	0.018526	0.018779	0.019034	0.019291
7	0.016089	0.016344	0.016601	0.016861	0.017122	0.017386
8	0.014650	0.014911	0.015174	0.015440	0.015708	0.015979
9	0.013543	0.013809	0.014079	0.014351	0.014626	0.014904
10	0.012668	0.012940	0.013215	0.013494	0.013775	0.014060
11	0.011961	0.012239	0.012520	0.012804	0.013092	0.013384
12	0.011380	0.011644	0.011951	0.012241	0.012536	0.012833
13	0.010897	0.011186	0.011478	0.011775	0.012075	0.012379
14	0.010489	0.010784	0.011082	0.011384	0.011691	0.012001
15	0.010143	0.010442	0.010746	0.011054	0.011366	0.011682
16	0.009845	0.010150	0.010459	0.010772	0.011090	0.011412
17	0.009588	0.009898	0.010212	0.010531	0.010854	0.011181
18	0.009364	0.009679	0.00998	0.010322	0.010651	0.010983
19	0.009169	0.009488	0.009813	0.010141	0.010475	0.010812
20	0.008997	0.009321	0.009650	0.009984	0.010322	0.010664
21	0.008846	0.009174	0.009508	0.009846	0.010189	0.010536
22	0.008712	0.009045	0.009382	0.009725	0.010072	0.010424
23	0.008593	0.008930	0.009272	0.009619	0.009970	0.010326
24	0.008487	0.008828	0.009174	0.009525	0.009880	0.010240
25	0.008392	0.008737	0.009087	0.009442	0.009801	0.010165
30	0.008046	0.008409	0.008776	0.009147	0.009523	0.009903
35	0.007840	0.008216	0.008597	0.008981	0.009370	0.009861
40	0.007714	0.008101	0.008491	0.008886	0.009283	0.009683

Years	12.0%	13.0%	14.0%	15.0%	16.0%	17.0%
1	0.088849	0.089317	0.089787	0.090258	0.090731	0.091205
2	0.047073	0.047542	0.048013	0.048487	0.048963	0.049442
3	0.033214	0.033694	0.034178	0.034665	0.035157	0.035653
4	0.026334	0.026828	0.027326	0.027831	0.028340	0.028855
5	0.022244	0.022753	0.023268	0.023790	0.024318	0.024853
6	0.019550	0.020074	0.020606	0.021145	0.021692	0.022246
7	0.017653	0.018192	0.018740	0.019297	0.019862	0.020436
8	0.016253	0.016807	0.017372	0.017945	0.018529	0.019121
9	0.015184	0.015754	0.016334	0.016924	0.017525	0.018136
10	0.014347	0.014931	0.015527	0.016134	0.016751	0.017280
11	0.013678	0.014276	0.014887	0.015509	0.016143	0.016788
12	0.013134	0.013746	0.014371	0.015009	0.015658	0.016319
13	0.012687	0.013312	0.013951	0.014601	0.015267	0.015923
14	0.012314	0.012953	0.013605	0.014270	0.014948	0.015638
15	0.012002	0.012652	0.013317	0.013996	0.014687	0.015390

Years	Annual Interest Rate					
	12.0%	13.0%	14.0%	15.0%	16.0%	17.0%
16	0.011737	0.012400	0.013077	0.013768	0.014471	0.015186
17	0.011512	0.012186	0.012875	0.013577	0.014292	0.015018
18	0.011320	0.012004	0.012704	0.013417	0.014142	0.014879
19	0.011154	0.011849	0.012559	0.013282	0.0140017	0.014764
20	0.011011	0.011716	0.012435	0.013168	0.013913	0.014668
21	0.010887	0.011601	0.012330	0.013071	0.013824	0.014588
22	0.010779	0.011502	0.012239	0.012989	0.013750	0.014521
23	0.010686	0.011417	0.012162	0.012919	0.013687	0.014465
24	0.010604	0.011343	0.012095	0.012859	0.013634	0.014418
25	0.010532	0.011278	0.012038	0.012808	0.013589	0.014378
30	0.010286	0.011062	0.011849	0.012644	0.013448	0.014257
35	0.010155	0.010952	0.011757	0.012568	0.013385	0.014205
40	0.010085	0.010895	0.011711	0.012532	0.013356	0.014183

Appendix E
Annual Payment to Create a $1 Sinking Fund

	Annual Compound Interest					
Years	1.0%	2.0	3.0	4.0	5.0	6.0
01	1.00000	1.00000	1.00000	1.00000	1.00000	1.00000
02	0.49751	0.49505	0.49261	0.49020	0.48780	0.48544
03	0.33002	0.32675	0.32353	0.32035	0.31721	0.31411
04	0.24628	0.24262	0.23903	0.23549	0.23201	0.22859
05	0.19604	0.19216	0.18835	0.18463	0.18097	0.17740
06	0.16255	0.15853	0.15460	0.15076	0.14702	0.14336
07	0.13863	0.13451	0.13051	0.12661	0.12282	0.11914
08	0.12069	0.11651	0.11246	0.10853	0.10472	0.10104
09	0.10674	0.10252	0.09843	0.09449	0.09069	0.08702
10	0.09558	0.09133	0.08723	0.08329	0.07950	0.07587
11	0.08645	0.08218	0.07808	0.07415	0.07039	0.06679
12	0.07885	0.07456	0.07046	0.06655	0.06283	0.05928
13	0.07241	0.06812	0.06403	0.06014	0.05646	0.05296
14	0.06690	0.06260	0.05853	0.05467	0.05102	0.04758
15	0.06212	0.05783	0.05377	0.04904	0.04634	0.04296
16	0.05794	0.05365	0.04961	0.04582	0.04227	0.03895
17	0.05426	0.04997	0.04595	0.04220	0.03870	0.03544
18	0.05098	0.04670	0.04271	0.03899	0.03555	0.03236
19	0.04805	0.04378	0.03981	0.03614	0.03275	0.02962
20	0.04544	0.04116	0.03722	0.03358	0.03024	0.02718
21	0.04303	0.03878	0.03487	0.03128	0.02800	0.02500
22	0.04086	0.03663	0.03275	0.02920	0.02597	0.02305
23	0.03889	0.03467	0.03081	0.02731	0.02414	0.02128
24	0.03707	0.03287	0.02905	0.02559	0.02247	0.01968
25	0.03541	0.03122	0.02743	0.02401	0.02095	0.01823

	7.0%	8.0	9.0	10.0	11.0	12.0
01	1.00000	1.00000	1.00000	1.00000	1.00000	1.00000
02	0.48309	0.48077	0.47847	0.47619	0.47393	0.47170
03	0.31105	0.30803	0.30505	0.30211	0.29921	0.29635
04	0.22523	0.22192	0.21867	0.21547	0.21233	0.20923
05	0.17390	0.17046	0.16709	0.16380	0.16057	0.15741

			Annual Compound Interest			
Years	7.0	8.0	9.0	10.0	11.0	12.0
06	0.13980	0.13632	0.13292	0.12961	0.12638	0.12323
07	0.11555	0.11207	0.10869	0.10541	0.10222	0.09911
08	0.09747	0.09401	0.09067	0.08744	0.08432	0.08130
09	0.08349	0.08008	0.07680	0.07364	0.07060	0.06768
10	0.07238	0.06903	0.06582	0.06275	0.05980	0.05698
11	0.06336	0.06008	0.05695	0.05396	0.05112	0.04842
12	0.05590	0.05270	0.04965	0.04676	0.04403	0.04144
13	0.04965	0.04652	0.04357	0.04078	0.03815	0.03568
14	0.04434	0.04130	0.03843	0.03575	0.03323	0.03087
15	0.03979	0.03683	0.03406	0.03147	0.02907	0.02682
16	0.03586	0.03298	0.03030	0.02782	0.02552	0.02339
17	0.03243	0.02963	0.02705	0.02466	0.02247	0.02046
18	0.02941	0.02670	0.02421	0.02193	0.01984	0.01794
19	0.02675	0.02413	0.02173	0.01955	0.01756	0.01576
20	0.02439	0.02185	0.01955	0.01746	0.01558	0.01388
21	0.02229	0.01983	0.01762	0.01562	0.01384	0.01224
22	0.02041	0.01803	0.01590	0.01401	0.01231	0.01081
23	0.01871	0.01642	0.01438	0.01257	0.01097	0.00956
24	0.01719	0.01498	0.01302	0.01130	0.00979	0.00846
25	0.01581	0.01368	0.01181	0.01017	0.00874	0.00750

Years	13.0	14.0	15.0	16.0	17.0	18.0
01	1.00000	1.00000	1.00000	1.00000	1.00000	1.00000
02	0.46948	0.46729	0.46512	0.46296	0.46083	0.45872
03	0.29352	0.29073	0.28798	0.28526	0.28257	0.27992
04	0.20619	0.20320	0.20027	0.19738	0.19453	0.19174
05	0.15431	0.15128	0.14832	0.14541	0.14256	0.13978
06	0.12015	0.11716	0.11424	0.11139	0.10861	0.10591
07	0.09611	0.09319	0.09036	0.08761	0.08495	0.08236
08	0.07839	0.07557	0.07285	0.07022	0.06769	0.06524
09	0.06487	0.06217	0.05957	0.05708	0.05469	0.05239
10	0.05429	0.05171	0.04925	0.04690	0.04466	0.04251
11	0.04584	0.04339	0.04107	0.03886	0.03676	0.03478
12	0.03899	0.03667	0.03448	0.03241	0.03047	0.02863
13	0.03335	0.03116	0.02911	0.02718	0.02538	0.02369
14	0.02867	0.02661	0.02469	0.02290	0.02123	0.01968
15	0.02474	0.02281	0.02102	0.01936	0.01782	0.01640
16	0.02143	0.01962	0.01795	0.01641	0.01500	0.01371
17	0.01861	0.01692	0.01537	0.01395	0.01266	0.01149
18	0.01620	0.01462	0.01319	0.01188	0.01071	0.00964
19	0.01413	0.01266	0.01134	0.01014	0.00907	0.00810
20	0.01235	0.01099	0.00976	0.00867	0.00769	0.00682

Years	Annual Compound Interest					
	13.0	14.0	15.0	16.0	17.0	18.0
21	0.01081	0.00954	0.0842	0.00742	0.00653	0.00575
22	0.00948	0.00830	0.00727	0.00635	0.00555	0.00485
23	0.00832	0.00723	0.00628	0.00545	0.00472	0.00409
24	0.00731	0.00630	0.00543	0.00467	0.00402	0.00345
25	0.00643	0.00550	0.00470	0.00401	0.00342	0.00292

Years	19.0	20.0	21.0	22.0	23.0	24.0
01	1.00000	1.00000	1.00000	1.00000	1.00000	1.00000
02	0.45662	0.45455	0.45249	0.45045	0.44843	0.44643
03	0.27731	0.27473	0.27218	0.26966	0.26717	0.26472
04	0.18899	0.18629	0.18363	0.18102	0.17845	0.17593
05	0.13705	0.13438	0.13177	0.12921	0.12670	0.12425
06	0.10327	0.10071	0.09820	0.09576	0.09339	0.09107
07	0.07985	0.07742	0.07507	0.07278	0.07057	0.06842
08	0.06289	0.06061	0.05841	0.05630	0.05426	0.05229
09	0.05019	0.04808	0.04605	0.04411	0.04225	0.04047
10	0.04047	0.03852	0.03667	0.03489	0.03321	0.03160
11	0.03289	0.03110	0.02941	0.02781	0.02629	0.02485
12	0.02690	0.02526	0.02373	0.02228	0.02093	0.01965
13	0.02210	0.02062	0.01923	0.01794	0.01673	0.01560
14	0.01823	0.01689	0.01565	0.01449	0.01342	0.01242
15	0.01509	0.01388	0.01277	0.01174	0.01079	0.00992
16	0.01252	0.01144	0.01044	0.00953	0.00870	0.00794
17	0.01041	0.00944	0.00855	0.00775	0.00702	0.00636
18	0.00868	0.00781	0.00702	0.00631	0.00568	0.00510
19	0.00724	0.00646	0.00577	0.00515	0.00459	0.00410
20	0.00605	0.00536	0.00474	0.00420	0.00372	0.00329
21	0.00505	0.00444	0.00391	0.00343	0.00302	0.00265
22	0.00423	0.00369	0.00322	0.00281	0.00245	0.00213
23	0.00354	0.00307	0.00265	0.00229	0.00198	0.00172
24	0.00297	0.00255	0.00219	0.00188	0.00161	0.00138
25	0.00249	0.00212	0.00180	0.00154	0.00131	0.00111

Appendix F
Future Value of $1
Deposited Annually

	Annual Compound Interest					
Years	1%	2%	3%	4%	5%	6%
01	1.0000	1.0000	1.0000	1.0000	1.0000	1.0000
02	1.0100	1.0200	1.0300	1.0400	1.0500	1.0600
03	2.0301	2.0604	2.0909	2.1216	2.1525	2.1833
04	3.0604	3.1216	3.1836	3.2464	3.3101	3.3750
05	4.1810	4.2040	4.3091	4.4163	4.5256	4.6367
06	5.1520	5.3081	5.4684	5.6330	5.8020	5.9750
07	6.2135	6.4343	6.6625	6.8983	7.1420	7.3933
08	7.2857	7.5830	7.8923	8.2142	8.5491	8.8983
09	8.3685	8.7546	9.159	9.583	10.027	10.491
10	9.462	9.950	10.464	11.006	11.578	12.181
11	10.567	11.169	11.808	12.486	13.207	13.972
12	11.683	12.412	13.192	14.026	14.917	15.870
13	12.809	13.680	14.618	15.627	16.713	17.882
14	13.947	14.974	16.086	17.292	18.599	20.051
15	15.097	16.293	17.599	19.024	20.579	22.276
16	16.258	17.639	19.157	20.825	22.657	24.673
17	17.430	19.012	20.762	22.698	24.840	27.213
18	18.615	20.412	22.414	24.645	27.132	29.906
19	19.811	21.841	24.117	25.671	29.539	32.760
20	21.019	23.297	25.870	26.778	32.066	35.786
21	22.239	24.783	27.676	30.969	34.719	38.993
22	23.472	26.299	29.537	33.248	37.505	41.392
23	24.716	27.845	31.453	35.618	40.430	45.996
24	25.973	29.422	33.426	38.083	43.502	49.816
25	27.243	31.030	35.459	40.646	46.727	53.865

Years	7%	8%	9%	10%	11%	12%
01	1.0000	1.0000	1.0000	1.0000	1.0000	1.0000
02	1.0700	1.0800	1.0900	1.1000	1.1100	1.1200
03	2.2143	2.2463	2.2778	2.3100	2.3418	2.3742
04	3.4400	3.5063	3.5733	3.6410	3.7100	3.7792
05	4.7180	4.8663	4.9844	5.1050	5.2282	5.3525

			Annual Compound Interest			
Years	*7%*	*8%*	*9%*	*10%*	*11%*	*12%*
06	6.1529	6.3363	6.5233	6.7160	6.9127	7.1150
07	7.6543	7.9225	8.2000	8.4870	8.7836	9.080
08	9.260	9.637	10.028	10.436	10.869	11.300
09	10.978	11.488	12.021	12.579	13.164	13.776
10	12.816	13.487	14.193	14.937	15.722	16.549
11	14.784	15.645	16.560	17.531	18.562	19.655
12	16.888	27.977	19.141	20.384	21.714	23.133
13	19.141	20.495	21.953	23.523	25.212	27.029
14	21.220	23.215	25.019	26.975	29.095	31.393
15	24.129	26.152	28.361	30.772	33.405	36.280
16	26.888	29.324	32.003	34.950	35.950	41.753
17	29.840	32.750	35.953	39.545	43.501	47.883
18	32.999	36.450	40.301	44.599	49.393	54.750
19	36.379	40.446	46.019	50.159	55.939	62.440
20	39.995	44.762	51.160	56.275	63.203	71.053
21	43.865	49.423	56.764	63.002	71.265	80.700
22	48.006	54.457	61.873	70.403	80.214	91.500
23	52.436	59.893	68.532	78.543	90.145	103.60
24	57.177	65.765	75.790	87.497	101.17	117.16
25	62.249	72.106	82.701	97.347	113.42	152.33

Years	*13%*	*14%*	*15%*	*16%*	*17%*	*18%*
01	1.0000	1.0000	1.0000	1.0000	1.0000	1.0000
02	1.1300	1.1400	1.1500	1.1600	2.1700	2.1800
03	2.4069	2.4393	2.4723	2.5056	3.5388	3.5722
04	3.8500	3.9214	3.9933	4.0666	5.1406	5.2156
05	5.4800	5.6100	5.7423	5.8769	7.0147	7.1544
06	7.3231	7.5357	7.7540	7.9775	9.2071	9.4422
07	9.405	9.730	10.067	10.414	11.772	12.142
08	11.757	12.233	12.723	13.240	14.774	15.327
09	14.415	15.085	15.786	16.518	18.285	19.086
10	17.420	18.337	19.304	20.321	22.393	23.521
11	20.815	22.044	23.349	24.733	27.200	28.755
12	24.650	26.271	28.002	29.850	32.824	34.931
13	28.985	31.089	33.352	35.786	39.404	42.219
14	33.883	36.581	39.505	42.672	47.103	50.818
15	39.418	42.842	46.581	50.659	56.112	60.965
16	45.672	49.981	54.717	59.925	66.647	72.939
17	52.739	58.118	64.073	70.675	78.984	87.067
18	60.725	67.393	74.840	83.144	93.406	103.74
19	69.054	77.971	87.213	97.606	110.28	123.41
20	79.946	90.029	101.31	114.38	130.04	146.63

			Annual Compound Interest			
Years	*13%*	*14%*	*15%*	*16%*	*17%*	*18%*
21	91.469	103.77	117.81	133.84	153.20	174.02
22	104.49	119.44	136.63	156.41	180.17	206.34
23	119.21	137.30	158.28	182.60	211.80	244.49
24	135.83	157.66	183.17	212.98	248.81	289.49
25	154.62	180.87	211.79	248.21	292.11	342.61

Years	*19%*	*20%*	*21%*	*22%*	*23%*	*24%*
01	1.0000	1.0000	1.0000	1.0000	1.0000	1.0000
02	2.1900	2.2000	1.2100	1.2200	1.2300	1.2400
03	3.6063	3.6400	2.6743	2.7086	2.7430	2.7778
04	5.2896	5.3680	4.4457	4.5241	4.6039	4.6842
05	7.2968	7.4415	6.5690	6.7395	6.8926	7.0483
06	9.6832	9.9300	9.183	9.442	9.708	9.980
07	12.523	12.916	12.321	12.740	13.171	13.615
08	15.902	16.499	16.119	16.762	17.430	18.123
09	19.924	20.799	20.714	21.670	22.669	23.712
10	24.709	25.959	26.274	27.657	29.113	30.643
11	30.404	32.150	33.001	34.962	37.039	39.238
12	37.180	39.580	41.141	43.873	46.787	49.985
13	45.245	48.497	50.990	54.745	58.739	63.110
14	54.842	59.196	62.910	68.009	73.526	79.496
15	66.263	72.035	77.329	84.191	91.670	99.820
16	79.853	87.440	94.781	103.94	113.98	125.01
17	96.021	105.93	115.90	128.02	141.43	156.25
18	115.27	128.12	141.44	157.40	175.19	195.00
19	138.17	154.74	158.07	193.25	215.71	243.03
20	165.94	186.69	209.76	236.99	267.79	302.60
21	197.85	225.03	255.02	290.35	330.60	376.47
22	236.44	271.03	309.78	355.45	407.87	468.04
23	282.36	326.24	376.05	434.86	502.91	581.63
24	337.01	392.49	456.22	531.77	619.83	722.46
25	402.04	471.98	553.24	649.95	763.61	897.08

Appendix G
Area of Normal Distribution that is *X* Standard Deviations to the Left or Right of the Mean

Number of Standard Deviations	Area to the Left or Right	Number of Standard Deviations	Area to the Left or Right
0.00	0.5000	1.55	0.0606
0.05	0.4801	1.60	0.0548
0.10	0.4602	1.65	0.0495
0.15	0.4404	1.70	0.0446
0.20	0.4207	1.75	0.0401
0.25	0.4013	1.80	0.0359
0.30	0.3821	1.85	0.0322
0.35	0.3632	1.90	0.0287
0.40	0.3446	1.95	0.0256
0.45	0.3264	2.00	0.0228
0.50	0.3085	2.05	0.0202
0.55	0.2912	2.10	0.0179
0.60	0.2743	2.15	0.0158
0.65	0.2578	2.20	0.0139
0.70	0.2420	2.25	0.0122
0.75	0.2264	2.30	0.0107
0.80	0.2119	2.35	0.0094
0.85	0.1977	2.40	0.0082
0.90	0.1841	2.45	0.0071
0.95	0.1711	2.50	0.0062
1.00	0.1587	2.55	0.0054
1.05	0.1469	2.60	0.0047
1.10	0.1357	2.65	0.0040
1.15	0.1251	2.70	0.0035
1.20	0.1151	2.75	0.0030
1.25	0.1056	2.80	0.0026
1.30	0.0968	2.85	0.0022
1.35	0.0885	2.90	0.0019
1.40	0.0808	2.95	0.0016
1.45	0.0735	3.00	0.0013
1.50	0.0668		

Index

Index

Accelerated depreciation, 84
Acceptance error, 215
Accountability, 231
Adjusted basis. *See* tax basis
Aesthetics, 27
Alternative minimum tax, 93
Amortization payments, 127
Amortization table, 128-134
Analysis paralysis, 262
Annuity, 68; definition of, 124; present value of, 124, 134
Artificial accounting losses, 84

Balloon payment, 67-68
Basis. *See* tax basis
Break-even ratio, 108
Broker's rate of return, 112
Business Risk, 179

Capital budgeting, 11, 153
Capital, 3, 153-165; cost of, 153; marginal cost, 164; opportunity cost, 153, 165; scarcity, 3
Capital expenditures, 30, 80
Capital gains and losses, 73, 92-93; accounting for, 92; and alternative tax, 93; and financial leverage, 73; holding period, 92; long term, 92; recapture rules, 92; reporting, 93; rules, 92; short term, 93
Capital losses. *See* capital gains and losses
Capitalization rate, 109
Cash flow, 28, 32, 232; and accounting flow, 28; before taxes, 32; certainty equivalent, 194; classification, 232; definition, 7; forecasting, 43; net, 32; statement of, 33
Cash flow forecast, 43
Cash flows, serially independent, 221; perfectly correlated, 222; partially correlated, 223
Cash-on-cash return, 111
Cash throw-off, 32-104

Certainty equivalents, 194-220; factors, 220; method, 219
Class life system, 85
Coefficient of correlation, 222
Complements, 21
Component depreciation, 86
Compound interest, 120
Cost of debt, 153
Contract for deed, 75
Contract rent, 34
Corporations, 271
Correlation, 266
Cost/benefit ratio, 165
Cumulative probability, 256

Debt amortization, 66
Debt-coverage ratio, 65, 108
Debt service, 30-67; and financial leverage, 64; constant, 66; definition, 30; determination of, 67
Debt-service constant, 69, 128
Debt-to-equity ratio, 64
Decision models, 5-9; choice of, 5; cost-effective, 6; definition, 5; efficiency of, 5; simplicity, 6
Deed of trust, 75
Default, 75
Demand, 12-19; and market equilibrium, 18; and utility, 13; definition, 12; for space-time, 19; market, 14; volatility of, 14
Demand function, 12-20; definition, 12; interdependence, 20
Demand schedule. *See* demand function
Depreciation, 28, 70-95; allowable methods, 86; and cash flows, 28; and financial leverage, 70; and preference tax, 95; and useful life, 84; component method, 86; definition, 84; declining balance method, 88; entitlement, 84; expense, 83; straight line method, 86; sum-of-the-year's-digits method, 86
Discount points, 140

About the Author

Gaylon E. Greer is currently associate professor of finance in the College of Commerce and the Graduate School of Business Administration of DePaul University. A graduate of the University of Colorado (Ph.D., 1974), he is the author of *The Real Estate Investor and the Federal Income Tax* (Wiley-Interscience, 1978).

In addition to his academic achievements, Dr. Greer has been active as a real estate broker specializing in commercial and investment property. He has also been a consultant to a Colorado land development firm. He is a member of several professional organizations, including the American Real Estate and Urban Economics Association, the Financial Managers Association, and the American Finance Association.